Reconstructing Science and Theology in Postmodernity

Pannenberg, ethics and the human sciences

JACQUI A. STEWART
Centre for Science and Religion
Lecturer in Theology and Religious Studies
University of Leeds

Routledge
Taylor & Francis Group
LONDON AND NEW YORK

First published 2000 by Ashgate Publishing

Reissued 2018 by Routledge
2 Park Square, Milton Park, Abingdon, Oxon OX14 4RN
711 Third Avenue, New York, NY 10017, USA

Routledge is an imprint of the Taylor & Francis Group, an informa business

A Library of Congress record exists under LC control number: 00134435

ISBN 13: 978-1-138-73841-6 (hbk)
ISBN 13: 978-1-138-73839-3 (pbk)
ISBN 13: 978-1-315-18480-7 (ebk)

RECONSTRUCTING SCIENCE AND THEOLOGY IN POSTMODERNITY

Exposing the science theology dialogue to the complex issues of postmodernity, this book presents the first major critique of Pannenberg's use of science in his theology. Although Pannenberg's name is widely known to theologians in the English-speaking world, his theological writings have received little critical analysis to date. Stewart brings Wolfhart Pannenberg's work to a wider audience, summarising his theological views and entering into critical dialogue with his writings, exploring their strengths and weaknesses.

Setting Pannenberg's appropriation of the biological and human sciences against the background of Bauman's priority of the ethical in postmodernity, Gadamer's conversational mode of dialogic rationality, and Archer's analysis of knowledge in social theory, Stewart argues for a more thorough recognition of values and ethics in the construction of epistemologies in both science and theology. This book offers important insights for all those concerned with issues of science and religion, bringing the relation of science and theology into contact with the philosophy of hermeneutics and the ethical implications of current social theory.

Jacqui Stewart is a lecturer in the Department of Theology and Religious Studies, and co-director of the Centre for Science and Religion, University of Leeds, UK.

ASHGATE NEW CRITICAL THINKING IN THEOLOGY & BIBLICAL STUDIES

Ashgate New Critical Thinking in Theology & Biblical Studies presents an open-ended series of quality research drawn from an international field of scholarship. The series aims to bring monograph publishing back into focus for authors, the international library market, and student, academic and research readers. Headed by an international editorial advisory board of acclaimed scholars, this series presents cutting-edge research from established as well as exciting new authors in the field. With specialist focus, yet clear contextual presentation, books in the series aim to take theological and biblical research into new directions; opening the field to new critical debate within the traditions, into areas of related study, and into important topics for contemporary society.

Series Editorial Board:

Contents

Preface and Acknowledgements

There is ever increasing public interest in the relations between science and religion in general, and science and Christian theology in particular. The study of science and theology requires an exceptional interdisciplinary engagement. Theology, history of science, philosophy and sociology of science, and the sciences themselves are all involved in a web of interactions. I am grateful to Haddon Willmer for suggesting Pannenberg's work in this area as an appropriate subject for study from my academic background in both theology and science.

The upheaval caused by persistent critiques of modernity has affected philosophy, theology, the arts, literature and social theory. The natural sciences have seemingly been least affected, although their situation is rapidly changing. Dialogue between theology and science must be adjusted to take account of the problems of modernity. The work of Wolfhart Pannenberg provides at least a starting point for a postmodern account of science and theology. He has combined the hermeneutical epistemology of Gadamer with a detailed account of theology and science. Pannenberg has a prominent theological anthropology, and he is at pains to demonstrate the coherence of his account of created humanity with the sciences of biology, psychology and sociology.

In this book, I examine and critique Pannenberg's elaboration of hermeneutics, and I evaluate his use of the sciences against the background of postmodernity. I do not attempt a presentation on Pannenberg's theology in itself because there are already many excellent books on this. Neither do I deal with controversial issues such as the extent of his debt to Hegel. This study is confined to a critical assessment of Pannenberg's engagement with the biological and human sciences.

Chapter One introduces Pannenberg's theological background and his anthropological presuppositions. Chapter Two presents a critique of his appropriation of Gadamer's hermeneutics for theology and science, and queries Pannenberg's account of science. Chapter Three gives a critical assessment of Pannenberg's use of biology, particularly ethology and evolutionary theory, in both a scientific and a political context. Pannenberg's approach to psychology and mind is evaluated in Chapter Four, with specific attention to the place he gives to Heidegger. Chapter Five offers an analysis of Pannenberg's account of society and culture, using the work of Margaret Archer as a tool. Conclusions about Pannenberg's concept of rationality and the unitary nature of his view of reality are supplemented by further philosophical, theological and sociological critique in Chapter Six.

If my overall conclusions are critical, it should nevertheless be remembered that Pannenberg's attempt and achievement is unique. No other theologian has taken on such a daunting task, and Pannenberg must be applauded for the depth of his scholarship in theology and philosophy, and for facing the questions of truth in postmodernity.

I thank the many colleagues who have commented on parts of the manuscript, including Nigel Biggar, Linda Hogan, Kim Knott, Ingrid Lawrie, Al McFadyen, Alistair Mason, Philip Mellor, Hugh Pyper and Haddon Willmer. I also thank Geoffrey Cantor, Dan Hardy, Esther Reed and Anthony Thiselton for discussions, encouragement and support. They are not responsible for any errors and omissions which may be found in this work; those are mine alone. I am very grateful to Sarah Lloyd at Ashgate for her interest and help. I particularly thank Susie Millard, without whose careful preparation this book would never have gone to press.

I also thank Jenson, Petena and Gavin for their patience, love and shared memories of Bod, who was a good scientist, and to whom this book is dedicated.

To Bod

For a boat has sailed into
the sea of unknowing;
you are on board.

(from *Triple Burden*,
by Norman MacCaig)

Chapter One

Introduction

Wolfhart Pannenberg has made a significant attempt to relate science to theology in the context of a hermeneutical epistemology. This book presents a critique of that enterprise by bringing it into conversation with relevant voices in postmodernity. The definition of what is modern and what is postmodern is problematic. Different authorities favour different perspectives; the view from the creative arts is not the same as the historian or philosopher's view.[1] The problems centre on the perceived failure of Enlightenment rationality to deliver its promised improvement in the human condition. Some authors feel that the Enlightenment project has failed – for example, Baudrillard – others that it continues in a changed form, for example, Bauman. There are some significant features which appear to be frequently associated with postmodernity, and might be diagnostic for it. They include a hostility to positivist criteria for knowledge, a concentration on semiotics and the philosophical problems of language, an abandonment of claims to overarching frameworks of knowledge or 'metanarratives' and a suspicion of hidden ideology in claims to knowledge. But there can be disagreement within a subject area. For example, in social theory, James Beckford (1992:19) includes disjunction, irony and playfulness, does not stress suspicion, and tends to relativisation, whereas Zygmunt Bauman (1993:10-15) sees the characteristic of postmodernity as the deconstruction of ideology and the revealing of the ethical as fundamental to human being.[2] Even a single author may not be definitively characterised; this is particularly true of Hans-Georg Gadamer,[3] whose work will play a significant part in this book. The difficulties and rewards of establishing the relation between

---

1 e.g. the art theory of Greenberg, the philosophies of Blanchot, Levinas, Baudrillard, Derrida, Foucault, Ricoeur, Habermas and Gadamer, the social theory of Bauman, the feminist theories of Irigaray and Kristeva and the theology of Barth have all been included under the umbrella of 'postmodern' at one time or another.

2 It may be noted that some authors equate the deconstructionism of writers such as Rorty, Derrida and Deleuze with 'postmodernism' and some further equate this with an absolute relativism. Pannenberg has been discussed in the context of such a classification (Shults, 1999). I do not make such assumptions in this study.

3 e.g. the comment of Weinsheimer that 'Gadamer's triunion of art, play and truth can be considered either reactionary or postmodern'. (1985:102)

religious discourses and those of postmodernism are revealed in work such as that of Anthony Thiselton or Roger Lundin.[4]

In the context of discussions about science and Christian theology[5] there seem to be two aspects of the modern/postmodern debate that are particularly relevant. The first is an epistemological question: how is the status of scientific knowledge to be secured, if the philosophical assumptions of the Enlightenment are no longer assumed to be inviolable? The second aspect is the problem of ideology and hidden values. Until recently, science was widely thought to be value free. The awful consequences of some science, such as nuclear physics, and the perceived potential of other science, such as genetically modified foods, has led to a widespread rethinking of the relation between social values and science.[6]

There are few established authors who can relate science and theology in a context that acknowledges these postmodern issues. The theologian Wolfhart Pannenberg is certainly one of them. His theology combines a concern for the rational evaluation of knowledge with a conception of meaning and value as anticipatory of the ultimate revelation of all truth at the *eschaton.* He has a highly developed epistemology in the tradition of continental hermeneutics, and is accepted as a significant contemporary systematic theologian. Pannenberg can be distinguished from other major theologians of the second half of the twentieth century by the intellectual seriousness with which he treats the natural and social sciences. This, together with his recognition of the importance of the historical and hermeneutic dimension in knowledge, makes his contribution to theology one whose significance is widely acknowledged. This book is in no sense intended to be an introduction to Pannenberg's overall theology, but is concerned with the specific issues raised by his use of the sciences. Only brief reference will be made, therefore, to general evaluations of his work.[7]

---

4 e.g. Thiselton, *Interpreting God and the Postmodern Self* (1995), Lundin, *The Culture of Interpretation* (1993), Lundin, Walhout & Thiselton, *The Promise of Hermeneutics* (1999). See also Berry & Wernick, *Shadow of the Spirit* (1992), Rose, *The Broken Middle* (1992), Heelas, P. (1998) and Caputo & Scanlon (1999).

5 I do not intend to imply that all theology is Christian, nor that this is the only religion of importance.

6 e.g. Ravetz (1971), Mackenzie & Wajcman (1985) and popular works such as that of Appleyard (1992).

7 Books in English on Pannenberg's work have been published by Galloway (1973), Tupper (1974), Braaten & Clayton (1988), Polk (1989), Grenz (1990) and Shults (1999). Additionally, there are a multitude of evaluations in both English and German journals. Those of Schwöbel (1996, 1997) are useful for the English reader, as they cover the literature of both languages.

Pannenberg's theology – an overview

Pannenberg belongs to the generation of German theologians that inherited the consequences of World War II, and this is important for characterising his theology. He studied under the philosophers Nicolai Hartmann and Karl Jaspers, and completed a doctoral dissertation in 1953 with the theologian Edmund Schlink. He is a contemporary of Jurgen Moltmann, and is responding to the same theological situation, but in a very different way. By the end of the war, the failure of German Protestant theology to meet the challenges posed by Nazism meant that theology had to make a new start. Pannenberg, like others, is part of that new enterprise. He wishes to retrieve and rehabilitate the theological past, and his entire theological enterprise is marked by the detailed excavation and reconstruction of traditional theological authorities. However, his concern with the question of truth can be understood in the context of a strong desire not to repeat the errors of the past. And his preoccupation with anthropology can be also be seen against this background. The passing of a state sponsored inhumanity leaves the theologian with the task of reconstructing a true vision of humanity.[8]

Pannenberg's development has been marked by a series of notable publications, each of which stresses some facet of his theology, but contains or implies its other features, so that he is remarkably consistent. In *Revelation as History* (1979)[9] and many of the essays in *Basic Questions in Theology* (1983a, 1983b) he presented his understanding of all knowledge, including theological knowledge, as essentially historical. His theology is founded on the perception of revelation itself as history, as presented in his book of that name. God is indirectly revealed in his concrete dealings with humans in history (history being understood in the hermeneutical sense). He characterises knowledge as understanding: the provision of a necessarily historical interpretation in a historical context. This is associated with a coherence, rather than a correspondence, view of truth, which is always seen against the horizon of the future, and is therefore incomplete. His understanding of history is very specific, being the summation of all events that will ultimately be revealed at the end of time, and which is yet proleptically revealed in Jesus Christ. The historicity of both the Jewish people and the event of Jesus Christ – his life, death and resurrection – are of paramount importance for Pannenberg. Hence his book *Jesus – God and Man* (1968) is a Christology 'from below', but his understanding of what it is to work 'from below' is informed by an orientation to the eschatological future being brought about by God. He argues that the irruption of God into human history in Jesus makes concrete a proleptic, anticipatory manifestation of the end of human history. This is perceivable and accessible to any ordinarily rational human, precisely because it is history as Pannenberg understands it. Pannenberg gives a

8 Thus H. Willmer, pp 25-44 in Hartley & Willmer (1990), but I think that this view of the content of such a re-visioned anthropology differs markedly from Pannenberg's.

9 I give the dates of publication of the English translations of these works. The date of the original German edition is given in the bibliography.

detailed account of this appropriation of the philosophy of hermeneutics, particularly that of Gadamer, in *Theology and the Philosophy of Science* (1976). Gadamer conceives understanding as a process open to the horizon of a future yet to come. The parallels between this and Pannenberg's concept of anticipation are evident. Pannenberg differs from Gadamer in that he wishes to retain an objective dimension to language, and he excludes action from his account of knowledge. In his attack on positivism, we can also see another aspect of Pannenberg's postmodern credentials. Given that Pannenberg sees knowledge as hermeneutically and historically mediated, the question of what constitutes the humanity making this history is obviously significant for him. He summarised philosophical, scientific and historical contributions to this question in *Anthropology in Theological Perspective* (1985). This was not an attempt to found theological anthropology on secular discourses; rather, it is a demonstration of the coherence of secular knowledge with a view of humanity which is primarily theologically given. It includes not only accounts of biology and the behavioural sciences, but also a serious dialogue with post-Heideggerian philosophy as it accounts for human identity. For Pannenberg, the ultimate significance of humanity is revealed in the resurrection of Jesus Christ as a destiny toward fellowship with God. The resurrection of Jesus is the forerunner, both present and to come, of the fulfilment of all creation with and in God. This he set out in *Jesus – God and Man*, and it lies behind the theological agenda of *Anthropology in Theological Perspective*.

Most recently, he has published a three volume *Systematic Theology* (1991, 1994, 1998) which presents the logical connections between the different major presentations of his theology. It also contains modifications and revisions of what has gone before, and demonstrates some development. Pannenberg has, of course, written a great deal more than the works I have listed, including a number of short essays on issues relating more to the physical sciences, (collected in *Towards a Theology of Nature* (1993)).[10] His work has usually been reviewed positively in the English speaking world; for example, the account by Grenz (1990) is fairly typical.

In both the philosophical and the theological foundations on which Pannenberg builds, there seem to me to be three key areas which may be problematic. The first is the role of reciprocity and mutual transformation, both in understanding and human relationality, which Pannenberg seems to neglect. The second is the relation between action and knowledge. Is Pannenberg epistemologically correct and morally right to exclude action from knowledge? The third is the role of human community in the accumulation of knowledge; has Pannenberg taken it into consideration sufficiently? There are a number of intersecting issues here. If reciprocal conversation is truly the mode of knowing, then the resulting transformation must imply different consequent action. Conversations take place in and may constitute communities, but how does the community affect the

10 An extensive bibliography of Pannenberg's work up to the late eighties can be found in Rohls & Wenz (1988). Shults (1999) gives more recent references.

conversation? Such problems form part of the debate about postmodernity, and Pannenberg's contribution to this debate must be assessed.

Pannenberg and the sciences

For Pannenberg, theology is the basis from which all other knowledge can be evaluated, and to which it must conform, in order to protect the Christian from error. He does not regard science as having any prior truth claim over theology. However, science and theology must certainly exist in relation for Pannenberg. He views all knowledge from the perspective of a world created by God in which all knowledge must be ultimately congruent, since it is all about the same act of creation. This is an easier position than some from which to enter the discussion about science and theology. For instance, Barth's acute awareness of human limitations in respect to reason has the consequence that he finds it very difficult to give a constructive place to science as a human activity. On the other hand, it may turn out, and I shall claim that it does, that Pannenberg is over optimistic about the achievements of human rationality in science.

Pannenberg deals with the biological and the human sciences in detail. He does not confine himself to the questions about the origins of the universe and astronomy, or determinism and fundamental physics, which are typical of the general science and theology literature in which physics predominates. He confronts the major issue of what the sciences tell us about humanity itself. This could have far reaching consequences for theology, and yet is often neglected in accounts of science and theology.

The context in contemporary theology

Twentieth century theology has developed in so many directions and responded to the crisis in modernity in so many ways, that a complete survey is impracticable. The major theologians, for example, Karl Barth, Rudolf Bultmann, Hans Küng, Eberhard Jungel, Jurgen Moltmann, Karl Rahner, Edward Schillebeeckx, and in the USA, George Lindbeck, David Tracy, Stanley Hauerwas and Schubert Ogden certainly show awareness of the difficulties of Enlightenment epistemology. The frequent engagement of theologians with the work of thinkers such as Husserl, Heidegger, Habermas, Ricoeur, Gadamer, Levinas, Wittgenstein and Derrida demonstrates the concern with these issues that is present in contemporary theology.[11] Pannenberg belongs to this community of thinkers. It is noticeable that apart from Pannenberg, there has been little direct discussion of science by mainstream theologians in the last seventy years. For instance, in a survey of contemporary theologians by David Ford (1997) only four out of forty have ever

11 e.g. Ford (1999), Webster (1998).

dealt with science specifically, and in the same survey he devotes one chapter to science and theology out of thirty five on other theological matters. One reason for this may have been the growing awareness that even the natural sciences could not maintain a positivist or modernist epistemology, and that their intellectual challenge to theology was less urgent as a result. In acknowledgement of the historically conditioned nature of knowledge, Hans Küng and David Tracy promoted a joint approach to this from Continental Europe and the USA. This resulted in the volume *Paradigm Change in Theology* (1989). Küng's introductory paper spoke of the changes in the understanding of knowledge and the philosophy of epistemology:

> Hence, in the past fifty years the discussion has moved from an abstract, positivistic logic and linguistic analysis through innumerable interim corrections to taking *history*, the *community of inquiry*, and the *human subject*, seriously again. (1989:7)

The various contributors discussed the possible directions theology itself could or should take in the light of this, and different approaches were suggested. All of these arose from within the varied context of the Christian tradition.[12] The critique of positivist epistemology in science offered by T.S. Kuhn was cited by many contributors. There was a contribution from the historian of science, Stephen Toulmin, explicitly warning theologians not to tie their chariots too closely to the philosophy of science horse, since it was also subject to historical change.[13] This symposium seems to have been the only recent time at which science has played an important role on the international theological agenda.

Regrettably, Pannenberg did not participate in this symposium, although his use of hermeneutics in relating science and theology is noted by a contributor.[14] Nevertheless, he holds a place unique in contemporary Western theology, by virtue of the sophistication and scope of his systematic theology and his sustained interest in the sciences.

Science and faith

Despite the limited input from theologians as such, there does exist a recognisable literature in science and religion. This seems to originate in the desire of scientists to give expression to religious faith – usually Christianity – as it relates to their science. Much of this may be related back to the first book published by Ian Barbour in the USA – *Issues in Science and Religion* (published in 1966). His continued writings and his later book *Religion in an Age of Science* (1986) have been central to the continuing interest in this area. The significant names include in

12 e.g. Tracy on the hermeneutics of Gadamer, Moltmann on the future, Schillebeeckx on hermeneutics and ideology (Küng & Tracy, 1989).

13 Toulmin, pp 233-241, in Küng & Tracy (1989).

14 Lamb, pp 64 and 94, in Küng & Tracy (1989).

the UK, Arthur Peacocke and John Polkinghorne; in the USA, Ralph Wendell Burhoe, Ian Barbour, Phil Hefner and Bob Russell. Additionally, there are also a number of Christian philosophers who are concerned with the relation between religion and science, such as Phil Clayton and Nancy Murphy in the USA. It is worthy of note that Nancy Murphy (1990) has responded to Pannenberg's work by envisaging it as a research project in the terms of Lakatos. This will be discussed in Chapter Six. In general, the understanding of science in the science and religion literature appears somewhat insulated from much of contemporary philosophy and sociology of science. There are allusions to Popper or the modification of Popper by Lakatos, sometimes to Polanyi. There appears to have been no serious engagement with the developments in philosophy of science apart from this. The difficulties and questions such as the problems of progress, the relation of explanation to events, confirmation and evidence, and the question of the historical conditioning of evaluative standards are not often considered.[15] The findings of sociology of science are also often overlooked,[16] and issues relating to the politics and social workings of science are rarely dealt with.

The view of Christian theology represented in the science and religion literature is variable. For example, Barbour and Peacocke are both influenced by process theology, while Polkinghorne presents a conservative account of mainstream Anglican theology. The discussion in Küng and Tracy seems to have had little effect at all on the direction of this field, which has been characterised by just such a dependence on certain kinds of philosophy of science, particularly the Popperian tradition, as Toulmin warned against.

Even very recent publications follow this pattern. A large number of books on science have appeared in the last ten years, having remarkably similar themes and sources.[17] An exception is a recent collection of essays edited by Niels Henrik Gregersen and J. Wentzel Van Huysteen, which sets out to address the challenge of relating theology and science in the present pluralist context.[18] Some cognisance of recent philosophy of science is made in this. However, the essays concentrate on epistemological issues which are defined from a formalist methodological standpoint, even if this is one the authors wish to reject. Postmodern epistemologies such as those of MacIntyre, Habermas, Gadamer, Derrida, Ricoeur, Levinas are not mentioned or brought into play. There is only a limited involvement of theology as such. The 'rethinking theology and science' of the title takes place far from the

15 Authors dealing with these problems include Kuhn, van Frassen, Laudan, Hacking and Toulmin; for overviews, see Olby et al. (1990), Curd & Cover (1998) and Losee (1993).

16 e.g. the work of De Solla Price, Merton, Ravetz, Latour, Mulkay. For an overview, see Ziman, J. (1987).

17 e.g. Polkinghorne (1998), Drees (1996), Peacocke (1993), McGrath (1998).

18 Gregersen & van Huysteen (eds), *Rethinking Theology and Science: Six Models for the Current Dialogue* (1998).

frontiers of current theology or philosophy. Regrettably, the conversation is still very conditioned by the world of the scientist believers and philosophers.[19]

It may be said that the problematic relation between practice and reflection on practice is just as true for Christian believers and theology as it is for practitioners of science and philosophy of science. In the science and religion literature there is a similarity between the positions about science and those about theology in that they both tend to hold on to modernity. Both theology proper and science studies have spent much effort in the latter half of the twentieth century responding to the critique of modernity. This does not seem to be so true of the scientists and philosophers writing from religious positions who contribute to the science and religion literature. Pannenberg's work must be of great significance for this area, since he is part of a theological tradition that has taken on the questions of postmodernism, and yet he has also maintained a dialogue with the sciences.

Pannenberg's theological agenda for anthropology and the human sciences

In order to proceed with the intention of this book, to examine and critique Pannenberg's use of the sciences in a postmodern context, it is necessary to set out some of his presuppositions. These particularly concern his understanding of what it means to be human in relation to God. Anthropology is a significant component in Pannenberg's enterprise, because in his ideas of both history and rationality, human activity plays a conditioning role. He uses the sciences (and philosophy) extensively to support his concept of the human, but his understanding is primarily theological. In the next few pages, I will sketch out the form of Pannenberg's theological understanding of human being. It will then be possible to show in the succeeding chapters how much this influences his choice and shaping of the science he uses.

Pannenberg reveals most of his theological agenda for anthropology fairly explicitly in *Anthropology in Theological Perspective* – in contrast to his tacit assumption that the reader is familiar with his views on epistemology, hermeneutics and history. Pannenberg concentrates on the theology of the 'image of God', and gives significant time to a discussion of sin. He does not stress other features of theological anthropology in the Christian tradition such as the implications of creation or embodiment. He does not follow the Christocentric models of anthropology of Barth and Bonhoeffer, or develop the themes of relationship and love. Instead, he concentrates on retrieving and reinterpreting the concepts associated with the Reformation revision of the 'image of God' theology. Pannenberg's overall view of theological anthropology is most comprehensively given in Chapters Eight and Nine of the second volume of his *Systematic Theology*

---

19 The one exception is the contribution from Murphy & Ellis, *On the Moral Nature of the Universe: Theology, Cosmology and Ethics* (1996), but even this employs essentially modernist epistemologies.

(1994). Here he brings together the various themes that have received more detailed treatment in different earlier works. Again, he uses an interpretation of the 'image of God' tradition as human destiny to fellowship with God. This destiny is proleptically realised in the resurrection of Jesus, and an account of this is given in *Jesus – God and Man* (1968). The image of God is to be understood dynamically, not in substantialist terms, and, he claims, it has biological, psychological, sociological and philosophical correlates, which he explicates in *Anthropology in Theological Perspective* (1985). Sin is of particular empirical importance as a concrete expression of human refusal of the destiny in fellowship offered by God.

The significant themes here are, firstly, the connection of the theology of the image of God with human destiny as fellowship with God. Secondly, the role of Jesus Christ as actualising that destiny by his death and resurrection. Thirdly, Pannenberg's stress on the dynamic nature of the image of God, and the tension between orientation to God and destiny in God that this implies. Fourthly, the location of the orientation to God, implied in the image of God, in human nature, and its description by methods appropriate to knowledge of nature. Fifthly, sin as a refusal of our ultimate destiny with God. Finally, the relation of humanity to the rest of creation. I will consider Pannenberg's theological agenda in terms of these six themes.

The Image of God as human destiny

The theological roots of Pannenberg's concept of the image of God as human destiny are most clearly visible in his account in the *Systematic Theology*. It is here a major theme in his treatment of humanity. He begins with the association of the image of God in Gen. 1:26-28 with dominion, and redefines this as stewardship. He reviews patristic opinion on the image of God, noting that Irenaeus included the body whereas Origen, Gregory of Nyssa and Augustine saw it as connected only to soul. Pannenberg is certain that the Old Testament concept of image can only be interpreted in the light of the quite different usage of image by Paul. Pannenberg is particularly concerned with the texts that call for the changing of the believer – Rom. 8:29, 1 Cor. 15:49, 2 Cor. 3:18 and he asserts:

> ... the idea of Jesus Christ as the image of God in which believers have a share through the Spirit (2 Cor. 3:18) has a general anthropological significance that the NT statements develop. (1994:208)

This seems to be the basis for Pannenberg's interpretation of image as destiny to fellowship with God. He deals with the history of theological attempts to connect these Pauline ideas with the idea of image in the Old Testament, as a crucial link between creation and redemption in the Christian tradition. Irenaeus argued for Christ as the original of whom Adam was the copy or image, and Pannenberg retrieves this claim (1994:208).

Pannenberg interprets the context of Gen. 1:26 and its associated stories as pointing to a destiny of relationship with God. He cites the Wisdom literature as supporting this, with a view of Adam's destiny as a participation in God's glory, which was lost with sin. Paul refers these ideas to the image of God in the risen Christ, as second Adam. This image is one in which believers may hope to participate, as their ultimate destiny to fellowship with God (1994:220).

This is a slightly different view of destiny; a destiny which is the ultimately intended location, so to speak. Pannenberg seems to be conflating two aspects or senses of destiny. One is the sense in which one might speak of the destiny of a gifted child who became a great pianist; the child becomes an adult with an experience not normally granted to other adults; destiny here has a sense of opportunity and vocation. But the co-operation of the child in practice and study is quite indispensable. On the other hand, one might speak of the destiny of the heir to the British throne. Here, the sense is one of inevitability. Short of predeceasing the reigning monarch, the heir has absolutely no option but to become the next monarch. Destiny in this sense is very close to fate. Christian theology has always spoken of human destiny as vocation or calling, but there is an ambiguity in Pannenberg's development of the concept.

The demonstration of human destiny in the resurrection of Jesus Christ

Most contemporary theological anthropologies give a significant place to the role of Jesus. Pannenberg deals with this most comprehensively in *Jesus – God and Man* (1968). For Pannenberg, the validity of Jesus' call rests on his vindication in resurrection (1968:191). In dealing with the humanity of Jesus, Pannenberg considers in particular his freedom, and this in terms of his authority. Jesus took people into fellowship on his own authority, not that of the law, and in doing this, says Pannenberg, 'Jesus made himself equal to God' (1968:191). At the same time, his resurrection demonstrates the future for all men (1968:192). Pannenberg makes the connection between the revelation of God in the Resurrection and the revealing of true humanity by reference to openness to God as the essential feature of humanity.[20] This double revelation is demonstrated in the life of Jesus, says Pannenberg, by the specific calling of Jesus to include all humanity in the summons into the Kingdom of God (1968:193) and in his life as man dedicated completely to God (1968:195).

20 'The close association of God's revelation through the anticipation of the *eschaton* and the revelation of man is finally established in the fact that the essence of man, like his salvation, the fulfillment of his destiny, consists in openness for God. Openness for God is the real meaning of the fundamental structure of being human, which is designated as openness to the world in contemporary anthropology, although this designation means an openness beyond the momentary horizon of the world. Man's question about his destiny expresses itself in this openness.' (1968:193)

The stress here seems to lie very heavily on God's action in respect of Jesus, rather than the action of Jesus in itself. There is no explicit discussion of the features of his humanity which are prominent in many Christologies. Pannenberg talks about the validity of the authority of Jesus, not the quality of his love. Similarly, human election and destiny seems a matter entirely of God's decree; there is no sense of engagement between God and humanity. His later position, as given in the *Systematic Theology*, does not differ significantly, and reinforces these earlier comments. He introduces historical and biological material to suggest the essential openness of humanity. However, he makes his theological foundation clear. Biology can do no more than hint; only a biblically and religiously based knowledge can reveal the purpose and direction of humanity.[21] He goes on to observe that if fellowship with God is the ultimate human destiny, then the Incarnation is the complete fulfilment of that, since no closer union of humanity and God could be envisaged. Hence Pannenberg argues that Paul's description of Jesus as the image of God does not have to be derived from belief in his deity, but can be founded on the resurrection as a sign of his fellowship with God as Son. Pannenberg's account of the significance of Jesus seems to me to reinforce the suspicion that Pannenberg views human destiny more as fate than as opportunity. He reinterprets fellowship ontologically, not in relational terms. Humans have to be obedient, and not oppose God's will (see the section on sin), but there is no sense of any creative contribution from humanity to the fellowship with God that is its destiny, and there is no sense of any reciprocity between God and humans. Jesus is almost a passive figure, who consents to this destiny of fellowship as something done to him by the Father.

The Image of God as developmental

Pannenberg's understanding of the 'image of God' theology is interesting in that he tries to develop its dynamic nature. In *Anthropology in Theological Perspective,* he recalls the static categories of what he calls 'traditional Christian dogmatics' and contrasts them with the ideas of the eighteenth century German thinker, J.G. Herder. This is a developmental approach. Herder regards humanity as having a vocation to self improvement, which is given by God. Humanity is not complete or perfected, but is in the process of becoming so under the guidance of Divine providence. Herder does not regard humans as having had any initial state of perfection, in contrast to the tradition of creation and fall. Pannenberg summarises the development of the doctrine of the image of God in terms of the historical division between the reformers, who saw the image as a description of the relation between God and humans, and the Latin scholastics, who saw it as something

21 'Only in the light of the incarnation of the eternal Son as a man, however, can we say that the relation of creatures to the Creator finds its supreme and final realization in humanity.' (1994:175)

substantive in humanity itself. Pannenberg traces the controversy down to the dispute between Barth and Brunner on the 'point of contact', before observing that Herder's idea of the image of God in humans as evolutionary is clearly not to be found in this part of the Christian tradition. However, Pannenberg refers to Marsilio Ficino and Pico della Mirandola, writers of the Italian Renaissance, who both see the incarnation 'as the fulfillment of the human religious destiny' (1985:50). According to Mirandola, the original fall is a state of deficiency from which humanity moves, in a dynamic mode, to the completion of humanity in Christ. Pannenberg's approach here is interesting both for its retrieval of the categories of improvement and assimilation associated with Irenaeus, and because it is one of the few places where Pannenberg refers to the content of Jesus' life.[22] Pannenberg clearly feels that by demonstrating their ancient antecedents in some of the by ways of Christian theology, he is justified in retrieving these ideas. He is also concerned to show that they are consonant with contemporary Christian theology. For instance, he argues that Barth and Herder are not completely mutually incompatible, that at least, image of God as direction or destiny is common to both. Pannenberg concedes that Barth was much more cautious than Herder in locating God's creative activity in the human (1985:60)!

Pannenberg's treatment of this area in the *Systematic Theology* is similar to his earlier expositions. He reviews the Old and New Testament usages, prefers an Irenaean approach, rejects the substantialist theologies of the pre-Reformation theologians and prefers later interpretations of the image of God as relational. He disposes of the arguments about original perfection, in order to maintain the theological grounding of his view of the image of God as not any kind of static possession, whether that be perfection or reason, but a dynamic orientation to a future with God (1994:217). However, his view of the outcome of that dynamic, human destiny as an assimilation to divine likeness, is here defended theologically, and the theological agenda that has always underwritten his excursions into other areas of knowledge is made explicit. Pannenberg is clear that it is a mistake to view the image of God in humans as something completed and finalised in the origination of humanity. On that basis it becomes difficult to account for the human hunger for God, and Pannenberg claims to see this problem in Aquinas. Pannenberg also sees problems arising from the eighteenth century question as to how 'realised' the human eschatological destiny actually was. Should the image of God be seen as a destiny in a future life (under the platonic influence of the doctrine of the immortality of the soul) or should it be a call to moral life in the present world? Kant and Fichte were particularly influential in promoting the latter view, which came to dominate in Protestant theology. Pannenberg claims that Althaus and Brunner had views of the image of God which were related to human

---

22 Pannenberg observes that Calvin and Luther do refer to the completion of humanity in Christ in this sense, although this is not mentioned in Melancthon, and the discussion of the image of God subsequently centred on the questions about the loss of the original state of perfection and the implications for its restoration (1985:51).

personhood as some completed quality – not a line Pannenberg wants to pursue. On the other hand, he retains his differences with Barth.[23] He argues that human destiny to fellowship with God is what gives moral self-determination its basis. If moral self-determination is seen as ontologically precedent, then ultimately moral norms cannot be justified, and Pannenberg observes that 'in the course of history the moral autonomy of reason was finally replaced by the caprice of individual self-determination' (1994:224) and he cites Sartre's existentialism as an example of such philosophical degeneration.

There are some problematic aspects to Pannenberg's developmental account of the image of God. Herder clearly viewed the moral perfection of humanity as being worked towards in human history. Does Pannenberg mean to say, for instance, that the image of God was clearer or more developed in the nineteenth than the tenth century? Or, on the other hand, if what is being spoken of is something effective in the life of the individual, a developing relationship with God, how does it differ from an internal clockwork mechanism, driving humans to their fate? There may be other problems with the 'externality' that Pannenberg imputes to Barth, but the latter does give an account that includes some potential reciprocity in the relation of the human and the divine, if only as Word and response. Pannenberg wants to continue the traditional Christian view of human destiny as opportunity and calling, which itself implies externality, while describing its working out in terms internal to humanity. The relationality which is such a prominent part of the Reformers' view of the image of God seems to be suppressed.[24]

The philosophical background to Pannenberg's view of the Image of God

The consequence of Pannenberg's insistence on the rational accessibility and universal coherence of all truth is that for every theological assertion about the world, he claims there will be supporting evidence from all other disciplines, including philosophy. The later chapters of this book will deal with the evidence Pannenberg calls from the sciences, but at this stage, it is important to note the large role played by philosophy in Pannenberg's development of the concept of the image of God.

The idea of human self-improvement is given particular impetus by the Enlightenment philosophers. As noted in the previous section, in *Anthropology in Theological Perspective*, Pannenberg explores the theological account of the image

23 While Barth also sought some kind of developmental account of the image of God, according to Pannenberg he did not locate the call to fellowship with God in human nature: rather, it comes from outside human being and is not intrinsic to it. Pannenberg's counter argument is that if creation in God's image implies that our destiny is to honour God, then creation must have included some natural inclination toward this (1994:227).

24 For a radically different approach to Pannenberg's, one might compare the explanation of the image of God in Douglas Hall's *Imaging God* (1986).

of God given by Herder. Unlike some other thinkers, Herder recognised limits to the process of self improvement. Pannenberg sees that Herder's view of humans, as unlike animals in being not solely the creatures of instinct and therefore plastic in behaviour, can be thought to contain the philosophical or rational implication of an external requirement for direction in the development of behaviour. For this to be moral, it requires the action of God (1985:53). Pannenberg sees this argument as particularly significant. Herder removes the image of God from being a moral disposition and locates it in the concrete relations of humans in the world, thus moving against supernaturalism. At the same time, he does not elevate human abilities to the divine, but actually finds a new way of expressing human dependence on God. Pannenberg observes that 'Herder's ideas thus have surprising relevance to the contemporary discussion of theological anthropology' (1985:54).

Pannenberg locates that contemporary discussion in the thinking of the twentieth century German school of philosophical anthropology, notably, the work of Plessner, Scheler and Gehlen. Pannenberg asserts that while Gehlen claims to be basing his account of humanity on the views of Herder, there is a significant difference between them. Pannenberg contrasts 'Gehlen's one sided recourse to action as the source of human self-realization' (1985:44) with Herder's supposition of 'reason and freedom as germ or source and disposition for the process of human self-improvement' (1985:44). In fact, Herder identified the 'disposition' for human self-improvement with the image of God in humanity. Pannenberg selects four key features of Herder's concept for further development; they are firstly, the parallel between the guidance given by instinct to animals, and by the image of God to humans, in giving 'a direction to the life of the creature' (1985:45); secondly, the image of God gives a purpose to human activity, which is to become that which God intends, fully human; thirdly, becoming fully human is not achievable by the action of an isolated individual, but by education, the practice of the community; fourthly, this process of education involves an interaction between tradition and learning, on one hand, and reason and individual experience, on the other, and the action of divine providence is to be found in the collaboration of these two strands. Pannenberg argues that faith in divine providence is essential for the coherence of Herder's account, and shows its compatibility with his own theological agenda. Pannenberg integrates these views with those of the philosophical anthropologists. Both Plessner and Scheler agree that humans have a capacity for self transcendence. Pannenberg develops an analysis of the possible mechanism of self transcendence. Human beings are unique, says Pannenberg, because:

> They also have the ability to be present in a new way to what is other than themselves, that is, in such a manner that they are not absorbed into that other through being wholly at the mercy of the content of their perceptions. (1985:62)

This much is agreed by all the philosophical anthropologists. Pannenberg explores their disagreement about how this happens. According to Pannenberg, the process of being centred outside of the self can be explained either by Scheler's assertion of the experience of the objective reality of that which is 'outside', or by Plessner's account of an inner ability to distance the self from itself (1985:63). Pannenberg prefers Scheler's explanation because it starts outside of the subject. Pannenberg asserts that in preferring Scheler and Gehlen in this way, he is following an initial insight from Herder. He goes on to identify the limitation in Herder's thought which requires further justification in a modern context, as the absence of any external orientation in Herder's description of the biological nature of humans. For Herder, the human is a creature of reduced instinct compared with other animals[25] but the guiding destiny of the image of God comes supernaturally from outside the individual. Scheler and Plessner find it within the structure of human being (1985:66). Pannenberg takes this further by asserting that the act of perception of an object as object implies a relation to other objects and the self. Citing Merleau-Ponty, Pannenberg concludes that the consequence of this is the transcendence of every particular object which is at the same time a condition of perception (1985:67). Pannenberg has to assert that exocentricity implies an openness to all that is infinitely possible, or it cannot be truly open. Pannenberg deals with Plessner's argument that humans have the capacity also to distance themselves from the infinite, by pointing out that the concept of God can be objectified, and therefore distanced, but the actual relation implied by openness to the world cannot be so disposed of.[26] Here, I think that Pannenberg is giving a philosophical justification to Barth's claim that we cannot view reality apart from God. That is, God is not an object; we are in relation to God whether we recognise it or not. Pannenberg rejects this as a claim to a natural theology; 'All that I have been saying does not amount to a kind of anthropological proof of God's existence' (1985:73). But he does claim that this shows that the anthropological question – what is it to be human? – always implies a religious dimension. This is grounded in the human experience of orientation to an external world. In this context, he reinterprets Luther's famous saying that believers exist in faith 'outside themselves in Christ', in terms of the parallel between exocentricity and trust. He claims that openness to the world implies a 'basic trust' in the conditions of existence.[27] This argument has parallels in Rahner and Küng, who come from a tradition of explicit natural theology. Pannenberg further extends the implications of exocentricity by arguing that since awareness of self comes only because of awareness of the other, the

25 This ascription of reduced instinct to humans will recur at various points in Pannenberg's appropriation of biology and psychology.

26 He observes 'every human relation to finite objects implies a relation to the infinite and therefore has in the final analysis a religious foundation and ... from the transcending of all finite realities it always returns to the reality given in each instance'. (1985:70)

27 'But when we become aware of the fact that in every turning to an individual, determinate object we have reached beyond all that is determinate and therefore all that is limited and finite, we are in the presence of the religious thematic and therefore of the question about the *basic trust* that supports our life ... Human openness to the world, the capacity for objectivity in relation to the objects of our world, thus has an implicitly religious dimension of depth.' (1985:72)

question of human identity – who am I? – is logically linked with the expression of trust also implicit in exocentricity. Hence the questions about ultimate human destiny, death, immortality and God. Pannenberg attempts to connect these questions of identity with so-called 'near death experiences' (1985:73-74).[28]

Pannenberg's account of the relation of philosophy to theological anthropology does not change significantly over time; his arguments in his *Systematic Theology* are similar to those outlined above from *Anthropology in Theological Perspective*. However, he does add an initial consideration of the unity of the human under the title 'Personal Unity of Body and Soul'. He cites modern knowledge as establishing interrelations between body and mind that do not allow of the traditional body/soul distinction (1994:182). His solution, as usual, is to excavate the theological tradition and attempt to demonstrate that it contains a fundamental approach to the subject which does not conflict with contemporary non-theological sources. He asserts that a body/soul dualism was not intended by the earliest Christian anthropology, and he cites Athenagoras, Justin, Irenaeus and Aquinas as opposing Platonist views and postulating some kind of psychosomatic unity for the human. However, none of these positions gave an adequate account, in Pannenberg's view, of the biblical relation between body, soul and spirit. He proceeds to argue from the biblical tradition, from spirit as in Gen. 2:7, and from St Paul's use of spirit, that it was a mistake for theologies to identify the human spirit with the capacity for reason or intellect. In the biblical tradition, it means physical life, animate as opposed to inanimate. The human mind is an integral part of the living body. Because humans are created for a relation with God, Pannenberg says:

> We can attain to the totality of our own lives, notwithstanding its fragmentary form at each moment, only in the relation to our Creator. (1994:200)

The language of soul is appropriate to speaking about that relation to God to which all humans are oriented, even if they are unwilling to consider it or unaware of it. But this relation is properly philosophically expressed in the concept of 'exocentricity' which, as we have seen, Pannenberg has developed from Plessner, Scheler and Gehlen.

The price of establishing theological anthropology's compatibility with philosophy in this way is that Pannenberg does not start with humanity as revealed in Jesus Christ, but with the elements this kind of philosophy demands. Consequently, there is a risk that they retain a kind of priority, and that Pannenberg's various repudiations of natural theology lose their force. Further, the attitude to philosophy revealed by this is instrumental; philosophy loses its function

---

28 I think this imprudent in the light of their physiological origins, but it illustrates the omnivorous and rather indiscriminate character of his epistemological method. He does not seem to be aware of the neurological, physiological and pharmacological phenomena associated with the process of dying, or of the scientific criteria for evaluating them.

of question and critique, and instead, becomes more like a bank of ideas for the theologian to draw from at will. On the one hand, Pannenberg is consistently creative in his retrieval of the 'image of God' as a dynamic, developmental concept of calling or destiny. This is in keeping with the positive value he gives to the eschatological perspective and the dimension of futurity in Christianity. It is also preferable to the many interpretations of the 'image of God' as something substantive or static – to that extent, Pannenberg would agree with the critiques by Moltmann (1974) or Hall (1986). On the other hand, Pannenberg's view of exocentricity, as taken from Scheler, Plessner and Gehlen, has overtones of determinism. More specifically, Herder's idea of the replacement of animal instinct by divine direction parallels the reduction of instinct that Pannenberg seeks to demonstrate from biology, as I will show in Chapter Three. (But Pannenberg's agenda in this area may lead him into misappropriation of biology.)

It appears that Pannenberg's view of humanity's theological destiny is more of a fate than something reached by any co-operative interaction. The Christocentric anthropologies of Barth and Bonhoeffer offer a very different view; 'Word as address' and human being as responsive relationality suggest an interactive dimension lacking in Pannenberg. An examination of a recent theological anthropology, such as that of McFadyen (1990) shows the gulf between Pannenberg and those using more reciprocally relational models. It appears that Pannenberg is dealing with a Hobbesian view of humanity by conceding the potential negative power in humans, and then suggesting an almost obligatory diversion of it in a direction which is guaranteed (by God) to be positive. The aspect of creative relationship, the re-creation of the individual empowered by the call of Christ, as McFadyen expresses it, is not significant for Pannenberg's theological anthropology.

Sin and human destiny

This is a major component of Pannenberg's theological anthropology. His treatment of sin in *Anthropology in Theological Perspective* is extensive, and moves from the philosophical via the psychological to the moral. He deals with sin and the problem of identity, egoism and the self, human nature and freedom, the universality of sin, and the concept of wickedness. His theological basis is in a reconstruction of Augustine's account of sin as love perverted to the self as ultimate object. He understands sin as fundamentally the refusal of human identity as exocentrically oriented destiny to fellowship with God.

Pannenberg uses the context of human rule over nature to introduce the potential ambiguity in human behaviour; dominion as responsible duty compared with dominion as unscrupulous exploitation. Pannenberg claims that of the philosophical anthropologists, Gehlen and Portmann ignore the issue. Plessner attempts to deal with the problem by locating tension between exocentricity and centrality in the relation between the human subject and its body. Scheler also suggested a pull between the human spirit and the physiological body. But Pannenberg sees this as inadequate, because it does not account for the human experience of psychological brokenness. Pannenberg finds Plessner more helpful than Scheler, because he deals with the issue of self consciousness in this context. The focus is still on the human as a bodily being which is aware of its existence as bodily and yet capable of transcending this. Pannenberg's complaint against Plessner is that he sees only the problem of the ego over against the body. Pannenberg finds a better explanation in an extension of philosophical anthropology by Wyss, in which tension is located in consciousness itself, particularly in the awareness of the products of the self's activity as other, just as the rest of the environment is experienced as other. This alienation from the results of one's own activity is the primary source of non-identity according to Wyss. He relates it to the desire of the ego for positive or pleasurable experience. Pannenberg concludes that the issue of the ambiguity of human behaviour can be located in the basic structures of human existence, but it is not merely a consequence of self consciousness. He moves very fast in his argument, from approving Wyss in establishing the ego's striving for pleasure as the root of potential conflict with reality, to an argument (which will prove to be Augustinian) that locates sin in the assertion of the ego in itself over against the other (1985:85).

The argument is suitably qualified, but Pannenberg compares this unlimited claim of the ego with the 'radical evil' described by Kant, as being the way the human destiny of outward orientation is subverted by the ego, itself the means of recognising what is outward. Pannenberg thinks that Kant was limited in that he restricted his understanding of evil to philosophical/moral phenomena, whereas Pannenberg appears to be locating it in the structure of the human psyche. It is, of course, essential, from Pannenberg's view, to eliminate any potentially external source of sin, in the service of the rationalisation of theology and the elimination of what he calls 'supernaturalism'. But since the loss of a view of a structured relation of the world, humanity and God, accounts of sin must focus on the disruption in internal relations of the human self, and Pannenberg offers Kierkegaard as giving the most complete account of it. He traces the development in Kierkegaard's thought of the concept of spirit as constituting the relation between the finite and infinite, and thus, the self.[29]

Pannenberg argues that when humans relate to themselves as synthesis of finite and infinite, they also constitute themselves in their self consciousness. If they attempt to do this by grounding themselves, not in the infinite which is centred beyond themselves, but in their own self, then the situation is that described by Kierkegaard as despair. Pannenberg notes that Kierkegaard argued that such despair could be avoided by human freedom acting under faith. Pannenberg is not

29 'Thus human beings are constituted as a relation to the infinite, not by themselves but by something else, and they are related to this something else, namely "to that power which constituted the whole relation" and which originally Kierkegaard explicitly identified as the power of God.' (1985:98)

happy with this solution, since he regards faith as given by God alone and not an internal human resource. He notes the importance of Kierkegaard's arguments for the subsequent development of philosophy. He feels that the result has been the focusing of attention on the component of human action in constituting the self, with a consequent neglect of the problem of grounding the self externally. Pannenberg approves Kierkegaard's attempts to oppose Schleiermacher's Irenaean-type theodicy by arguing that the concept of dread is the source of the transition in humanity from innocence to guilt, but he does not think the attempt successful (1985:102). However, Pannenberg explicitly connects Kierkegaard's dread with Heidegger's idea of anxiety (*Sorge*) for the self. Pannenberg claims that Heidegger's description of anxiety as the basic theme of human existence is evidence for the Augustinian concept of sin (1985:103-104). Pannenberg's use of Heidegger here may be misleading, because of the asocial concept of the personal project in Heidegger, as something to be grasped by the self as authentic individual existence. Heidegger himself would not have agreed with Pannenberg's conclusion that *Sorge* is a consequence of sin (for example, see Steiner's comments (1978:94)). While he acknowledges the postmodern contribution to the questions of the human experience of non-identity, Pannenberg's conclusion on the subject of dread is faithful to his Augustinian orientation. Pannenberg's theological basis for his explanation of sin depends heavily on classical theology and psychology, but less on biblical tradition. It is oriented to sin as pride and inappropriate self assertion. Such an account could not easily be defended against critiques from either liberation theology or feminist theology, both of which point to the one-sidedness of traditional views of sin. It seems hard to see, for instance, how sin as 'failure to act while under oppression' could be assimilated to Pannenberg's account of sin. Further, the manner in which he ties sin to philosophically and psychologically defined aspects of humanity, in terms of ego, self and exocentric destiny, may be storing up theological problems of freedom and forgiveness later.

It is not appropriate here to detail Pannenberg's theological analysis of Augustine and later sources. It is sufficient to note that Pannenberg's overall account of sin is exceptionally detailed, and is clearly structured to rebut secular critiques. He concedes the story of Adam and Eve as a myth of origin opposed to biological description, and cites the theory of evolution as a significant reason for doing so (1985:57). He rejects theories of humans as innately evil, and wishes to retain concepts of freedom and responsibility. However, his location of sin in the essential structure of the human psyche, and his desire to avoid any explanation of original sin in community terms, leads to a sense of sin as compulsion. His treatment throughout is rationalist, individualist, and tending to an internally driven determinism.

Humanity in relation to the non-human

In *Anthropology in Theological Perspective*, Pannenberg concludes his rehabilitation of Herder's idea of the image of God with an unexpected general discussion of the role of Gen. 1:26 ff. and an aside on ecology. He cites von Rad and Barth as connecting the possession of the image of God with the command to rule over creation, and kingship in general. He redefines the concept of 'rule' in terms of the human ability to be aware of the other, which nature does not possess (1985:76). With such a definition of 'rule', he excludes a coercive and unlimited mastery over nature. He cites Cobb as an example of recent theological awareness of the biblical tradition in the ecological context, and rejects Lynn White's accusations against Christianity.

This section, ending on an aspect of theology of creation and ecological controversy, is not easily connected with the discussion of the theology of the image of God that has preceded it. The non-human creation has a role only as the milieu in which humans experience their destiny to ultimate fellowship with God. Pannenberg does not invoke classical theologies of creation at all in his discussion of what it is to be human.

He gives similar arguments in his *Systematic Theology*. In this work, Pannenberg concludes his discussion of the image of God in humanity with a recapitulation of his view of human nature as essentially exocentricity, openness to the world. We acknowledge our difference from God, and in doing this, honour him. We do this only 'where we are already lifted above ourselves by the Spirit of God and are thus enabled to accept out own finitude' (1994:230), and this in turn enables us to conform to the image of the Son as distinct from the Father, and to participate in their fellowship. This is the anticipatory fulfilment of the destiny of human fellowship with God. In his final paragraph, Pannenberg connects this with a 'new turn' in the role of humanity in respect of all creation; dominion means acceptance of our own finitude and limits, giving respect to other creatures in their own place. Again, this seems a slightly awkward endpoint, for it deals with themes that have not really appeared very strongly in any of the preceding discussion. There, again, the rest of the created world has a passive role, as the location for the working out of an already given human nature.

Pannenberg's attempt to engage with the ecological argument may be judged not entirely successful, especially if compared with contemporary examples such as Hall's *Imaging God* (1986). The significance I want to draw from it here is that his picture of humanity and the world is of a totally instrumental world, which does not interact with God, but is merely a passive tool. The natural world appears to have little value in itself for Pannenberg, and he does not give much significance to human relationships with it in his anthropology. But if humanity does not seriously encounter God in relating to the physical world, both human and non-human, how is it to interact with God? Pannenberg's answer is that the basic human character of exocentricity is an orientation to the physical world beyond the self, given by God. But he discusses this only univocally, as it were, from within. He does not analyse the relation of exocentricity from the perspective of the outside world or the 'other' person. By not raising such issues, Pannenberg runs the risk of appearing to suggest that humans are internally programmed to pursue a destiny that is quite other-worldly. Issues such as the redemption of the non-human, and the aspect of the New Testament Kingdom of God as here and now, the questions of realised eschatology, need to be expanded in Pannenberg's theological agenda for anthropology.

Humanity and the sciences

In the rest of this book, I will examine Pannenberg's use of science in his account of what makes the specifically human being, paying particular attention to potentially problematic areas. To do this, I need to engage across disciplines, evaluating biology, psychology and sociology by their own internal standards. I have already indicated that Pannenberg has his own unique approach to the issues of postmodernity. I shall need more specialist resources to discuss this further, and I will make use of three in particular. Since I shall claim that conversation, reciprocity and transformation are features of Gadamer's hermeneutics that Pannenberg suppresses, I will bring Gadamer's own accounts to bear on these discussions of knowledge about the human, and I will similarly apply his connection of knowledge with action. Philosophies of hermeneutics have long been associated with validation of the social sciences. They have been rigorously scrutinised by the social theorist, Zygmunt Bauman, who has also placed the question of the rightness of action, the ethical question, at the centre of postmodern discussions of knowledge. Consequently, I think that Bauman is an appropriate interlocutor for Pannenberg in dealing with the nature of science and the ways in which it might be used to describe of define humanity. Finally, Pannenberg tries to deal with sociology, I contend, on an individualist basis. He does not give serious attention to community. I will introduce the analysis of the cultural theorist Margaret Archer, because this provides a detailed account of the relation between individual and community in the sharing of knowledge[30.] I think it illuminates the lacunae in Pannenberg's account, and provides an important tool for developing a much richer explanation of the issues he addresses.

All three of these authors are fully aware of the problems of postmodernity, and in their different ways address this situation, facing the problems of developing meaningful epistemologies after the last century's critique of Enlightenment rationalism. They also all address the social dimension in science, again in very different ways.

With the assistance of these commentators particularly, but also with many others, I will evaluate Pannenberg's contribution in the next five chapters. Pannenberg has presented an extensive discussion of epistemology in theology, the

30 I am grateful to Dr Philip Mellor for introducing me to the work of Margaret Archer.

social and the natural sciences. In the second chapter of this book, I will present an analysis of his appropriation of the hermeneutics of Gadamer. But, I shall claim, Pannenberg also diverges very significantly from Gadamer. Pannenberg wants to rescue objectivity from the wreckage of modernity, at least in the content of language in statements. Furthermore, he wishes to exclude all notions of action from knowledge. In contrast, Gadamer stresses the reciprocal and conversational nature of understanding as a transformative dialogue between the interpreter and that which they seek to understand. He also claims that the consequence of such transformative understanding is what he terms application (*Anwendung*), which he relates to the practical or moral knowledge, the *phronesis* of Aristotle. For Gadamer, action is integrally bound up with truth. As well as examining this difference with Gadamer, I shall discuss Pannenberg's rejection of positivism and critical rationalism and his evaluation of Popper. I also discuss some of the problems raised by his concentration on the rational component of science, and his neglect of the social influences within science. However, his most detailed engagement with the natural sciences has taken place where they concentrate on humanity itself. Pannenberg regards biology, especially comparative zoology, as giving a basic or foundational characterisation of the specifically human. In Chapter Three, I give a critical analysis of his selection and manipulation of aspects of biology. I am particularly concerned with Pannenberg's appropriation of ideas associated with attempts to legitimate forms of racism, and his lack of awareness of their status in both biological and political terms.

A major feature of Pannenberg's theological claim for humanity is the universality of religious awareness. He claims support for this from psychology, and in Chapter Four I present a discussion of the validity and extent of his use of psychology. This concentrates on the individual, and I discuss Pannenberg's omission of psychologies dealing with relationship. Pannenberg does not refer extensively to social theory except in *Anthropology in Theological Perspective*. However, the arguments presented there reveal his underlying epistemological and theological preoccupations. Chapter Five presents an evaluation of Pannenberg's approach to sociology in relation to his other concerns. I show that Pannenberg's attempt to explain society in terms of the rationality of individuals leads to inconsistencies in his presentation of social theory. It also limits his understanding of science as a social process with internal criteria of judgement by communities of expertise. Finally, in Chapter Six I summarise my characterisation of Pannenberg's handling of science and theology in terms of his preference for unity and coherence, his high view of objectivity, his non-interactional understanding of conversation, his aversion to including any element of action in his epistemology, his distance from the scientific community and his tendency to determinism. In spite of the monumental achievements of his theology, I conclude that his treatment of science and theology is seriously flawed by the lack of an internal critical or moral component in his rationalist view of knowledge. Although he engages with the issues raised by postmodernism, he may be judged a modernist at heart.

Chapter Two

Knowledge in Science and Theology

In his first major contribution to theology, *Revelation as History*, published in German in 1961, Pannenberg exposes concerns that have continued to motivate his theology ever since. In the introduction, he expresses anxiety that the concentration on theology as revealed by the generation of theologians preceding him has obscured the real epistemological issues surrounding the concept of revelation. He cites Paul Althaus, who, in 1941, criticised Barth for 'inflating' the concept (1961:3). Pannenberg wishes to protect talk of God from the charge of subjectivism. He accepts Barth's definition of revelation as the self disclosure of God, but he takes issue with Barth on the means by which it is achieved.

Pannenberg argues that such a definition does not imply the use of supernaturalist or non-rational means in that self disclosure.[1] The thrust of the exegetical chapters of the book, contributed by Rendtorff and Wilckens, is that the biblical tradition does not know anything of a direct, supernatural giving of knowledge of God, but that it records the acts by which God discloses himself. This is an indirect process; God is known by what he does in human history. Pannenberg then takes up this theme in a series of propositions of systematic theology; proposition three contains the kernel of Pannenberg's epistemology. He states:

> In distinction from special manifestations of the deity, the historical revelation is open to anyone who has eyes to see. It has a universal character. (1961:135)

He is resolutely opposed to any hint of supernaturalism, but he repudiates natural theology; he understands knowledge as something given, in some sense extraneous to the individual, as will become apparent later. Pannenberg is clear that theology cannot be irrational; he asserts that it can neither appeal to authority nor to religious experience in any attempt to justify itself.[2] He rejects Kantian forms of thinking that require *a priori*, already known or supernaturally given principles. Instead, he draws on hermeneutical philosophy, in favour of reason as a creative insight, always historically dependent on what has gone before, and always open to the future, pointing to a new insight (1983b:61). Pannenberg also rejects existentialist

---

1 See Pannenberg (1961:20, footnote 14).

2 e.g. his comments in the essay 'Faith and Reason' (1983b:53).

accounts of revelation which, he argues, reduce it to a subjective experience internal to the believer.

Pannenberg is not attempting a trivialised or triumphalist apologetics; his concern for the truth about God is fundamentally located in his concern for the truth about Jesus and the implications this has for the believer. In the introduction to his major contribution to Christology, *Jesus – God and Man*, he makes this clear (1968:19). Here his concern is clearly not primarily apologetic in the usual sense; he wishes to ensure that the believer has ground in reason for the truth claims that are made. Pannenberg's motivation is more governed by the believer who needs to be protected from the moral consequences of error, than by any need to condemn the unbeliever for the falsity of their position. He gives a similar reason in the introduction to his major work on theological anthropology, *Anthropology in Theological Perspective* (1985:15). The validity of epistemology as such has a high place in Pannenberg's scheme of things. From the beginning, Pannenberg talks about what we know, not what we do.

In his pursuit of this grounding of truth in reason, the truth of Christian faith and theology is always connected by Pannenberg with other branches of human knowledge as claims to truth, including the natural sciences. In another early essay, 'What is Truth?', he notes the necessity of including the reality of modern science in the Christian account of truth (1983b:1). Similarly, he observes the potential redundancy of religion in the face of science in an essay first published in 1964, 'The question of God' (1983b:201). He goes on to argue for the importance of the congruence of rationality across intellectual disciplines. Theology should not, indeed, it cannot, retreat from the question of the universality of the truth of the Christian message. He continues to make these points throughout his published work.[3] Further, he argues for the deficiency of any knowledge obtained without acknowledgement of the presence and action of God in the world. Hence theology has to show other disciplines the areas that are missing. This theme is given more detailed treatment in his account of theological anthropology, where he deals with the problem of a human science that has, he claims, incorporated atheist assumptions into parts of its basic framework. In his most recent work, the three volumes of the *Systematic Theology*, Pannenberg has brought these themes together in a coherent theological presentation. In dealing with the question of the truth of Christian theology in volume one, he says:

> All the details in dogmatics, being related to God's action, also relate to the world as a whole. This may be seen especially in Christology ... Related, too, is the including of non theological knowledge of humanity, the world and history, and especially of what the statements of philosophy that deal with the question of reality have to say about these themes, in the dogmatic presentation of humanity, the world and history in the

3 e.g. see the essays collected in *Towards a Theology of Nature* (1993:16,74) and in *Christianity in a Secularised World* (1988:52).

> light of the Christ revelation. Here again it is a matter of the universal coherence and therefore the truth of Christian doctrine. (1991:49)

Throughout these comments, Pannenberg assumes science to be both true and good. Apart from criticising atheist assumptions within some science, he does not take issue with it on any other ground.

It should be noted that Pannenberg does not lay the blame for the rise of secularism at the door of the natural sciences. He has a sophisticated historical argument, first laid out in the first chapter of *Ethics* (1981), and repeated later in *Christianity in a Secularised World* (1988) that the divisions within the churches and the wars of religion led to the substitution of political unity based in the state for the religious unity that had previously been thought to be the prerequisite for social order (1988:13). Pannenberg is perfectly aware of the advantages this separation of church and state bring (1988:37) as well as the problems, and he does not argue for any renewal of church control over the state. However, he does regard secularism and the assumption of atheist methodologies in the sciences as problematic, and may have been influenced by Karl Heim in this respect. He certainly approves of Heim's attempt to connect theology and science as commendable 'pioneering' (1993:75). Pannenberg is asserting the inevitability of a relationship between science and theology. His position does not in itself imply that theology has to 'baptise' particular scientific theories; but the effect of his apologetic is to require the coherence of certain parts of science with theology, at the expense, I shall argue, of preserving theology's proper critical distance from those particular scientific paradigms.

The background to Pannenberg's appropriation of Gadamer

Pannenberg first acquired general notice for his emphasis on the reasonableness of knowledge and how it related to theology with publication of *Revelation as History*. He then elaborated on his view of history in some key essays collected together in English as volume one of *Basic Questions in Theology* (1983a). The second essay, 'Redemptive Event and History', sets out his position and agenda clearly:

> All theological questions and answers are meaningful only within the framework of the history which God has with humanity and through humanity with his whole creation – the history moving toward a future still hidden from the world but already revealed in Jesus Christ. (1983a:15)

Theology is meaningful only in the context of history, because God is revealed only indirectly through concrete events in the world (see also 1983a:211). Historical knowledge is provisional, because only part of what is to happen has happened, and total truth will only be apprehensible at the end of God's history with the world.

However, in Jesus Christ there is an anticipatory revelation of what will be totally knowable only at the end.

Pannenberg regards Barth as having retreated from the concreteness of historically revealed knowledge of God in one direction, by suggesting a special kind of salvation history which is distinct from and above human history, and Pannenberg describes existentialist theology as retreating in another direction by removing knowledge of God from any constraint or basis in human history as such. In the early essay, 'Redemptive Event and History', he claims a similar source for both such movements, in that they both saw critical-historical analysis as scientific, so leaving no space for the action of God (1983a: 16). Clearly, if history is seen as the recounting of events which speak for themselves, then it would be hard to see how it could be the bearer of knowledge and truth as Pannenberg claims. He is clear that such knowledge is not possible, and thinks that Collingwood and the Anglo Saxon school of historical theory stray too far in this direction. Further, he argues that some post-enlightenment accounts of history, centring frameworks of meaning on human action, lead to a loss of basis for any certain knowledge, and consequently to historical relativism. Pannenberg sees a more robust alternative in hermeneutics, particularly the hermeneutics of Gadamer, as an account of knowledge which is appropriate to his view of the extensiveness and openness of history.

Pannenberg's epistemology involves a development of the hermeneutic philosophy of Gadamer, and includes as especially significant Gadamer's observations on the provisionality of the present in the light of the future. If the truth about the world will finally be known after it has all happened, so to speak, at the eschaton, then the historical truths about Jesus and the scientific truths about the world will be parts of the same whole, and, for Pannenberg, they will be congruent. There can be no ultimate separation of the physical world from the world of religious experience since they come to the same final fulfilment.

It is appropriate to mention some particular aspects of Gadamer's work at this point. The philosophy of knowledge has been subject to a great sea change in this century. After Heidegger's demonstration of the impossibility of objective knowledge in the Enlightenment sense, Gadamer recast the possibilities for epistemology in terms of interpretation and understanding, the philosophy of hermeneutics. But there is a profound ethical question behind this rethinking of epistemology. Robert Sullivan, in his book *Political Hermeneutics*, (1989) has traced the development of Gadamer's thought. The text for which Gadamer is now famous, *Truth and Method*, was not published in its original German until 1960. But Gadamer's work began in the 1920s, with his doctoral dissertation on the concept of desire in Plato's dialogues and his *habilitation* on Plato's ethics, which was published in 1931. Up until the Second World War, Gadamer worked on aspects of the ethics and politics of Plato and related issues. Only after the war, at the beginning of the fifties, did he begin to elaborate the work that was to become *Truth and Method*.

Sullivan suggests that it is important to consider these early studies in some detail in order to gain a full understanding of Gadamer's later work. The significant theme in the early work is not the problem of objectivity, but rather, the relation of ethics and politics. Gadamer saw the political dimension in Plato, and used a framework based on Aristotle's derivation of politics from ethics to comment on Plato's ethics. He interpreted not only explicitly political writings but also writings on education and literature in this way. Sullivan gives the example of Plato's exiling of the poets, defended by Gadamer as necessary on ethical grounds because their poetic discourse has distracted Athenian society from dealing with basic practical problems in the community (1989:8). Political reform is needed, and language must be reconstructed to make it appropriate to the concrete difficulties of the community. Sullivan also points out the difference between Gadamer's understanding of politics in his early work and that implied in the concept of the modern state. Political thinking of the classical period that Gadamer was developing is about the *polis*, the communal extension of ethical individuals. Truth is its ultimate goal, reached by language and conversation. By contrast, the modern state is about the rational management of social conditions and consequently, of human behaviour. It is not primarily about ethics or truth, and must assume some systematised concepts about human beings. Sullivan suggests that Gadamer was already offering a challenge to modernism long before *Truth and Method* was published (1989:10). This characterisation of the early Gadamer as concerned with the necessity of appropriate language for ethical social interaction is carried over into his later work. His promotion of conversation as essential to rationality becomes explicit, as does his opposition to modernist, foundational accounts of rationality. His insistence of the necessity of 'application' (*Anwendung*) in *Truth and Method* is foreshadowed by the understanding of *phronesis* in the Aristotelian connection between ethics and politics that informs his early approaches to Plato.

Gadamer himself, writing in his late eighties, confirms Sullivan's interpretation, asserting that the question of the good of human existence is the fundamental question for all philosophy, underlying his characterisation of the task of philosophy 'to follow the path of knowledge and think beyond what science has to say' by means of understanding language, which 'has its authentic life only in conversation ... living discussion ... '.[4] The primary force in the development of Gadamer's hermeneutics as it found expression in *Truth and Method* is his opposition to positivism, which was particularly strongly associated with the sciences. For Gadamer, the outstanding characteristic of scientific knowledge is that systematising, rational logic is used to acquire it, and he terms this 'method'. He contrasts this with the knowledge that comes by understanding or interpretation, and argues that only the latter actually gives truth, i.e., full knowledge which is experiential, transformative and ethical. On the other hand, he is not concerned

4 H.G. Gadamer, pp18-19, 'Gadamer on Gadamer' in Silverman (1991).

about the different forms method may take in the different sciences.[5] In *Truth and Method*, Gadamer does imply that only the natural sciences operate completely by method, and that the human sciences are subtly different. Gadamer's hermeneutics have been criticised, notably by Habermas, for allowing an innate conservatism and ideological domination by tradition. Warnke (1987) gives a detailed analysis and critique of this debate, and concludes that Gadamer does not need to be subject to such an interpretation, although his expression of his ideas has lent itself to it. She sees Gadamer's most significant contemporary importance as his promotion of dialogical conversation as a model for knowing (1987:4). Warnke observes that conflict and separation are indispensable components of the conversation that is Gadamer's model for the process of understanding. Further, she points out that the authority of tradition is always under review, and the lack of a universal position from which to evaluate it does not imply that no evaluation can ever take place (1987:137-138).

With these aspects of Gadamer's work illuminated, I turn to an examination of Pannenberg's version of Gadamerian hermeneutics.

Pannenberg's own account of hermeneutics as epistemology

In his early comments on Gadamer, Pannenberg is apparently very impressed by his approach. He gives some detailed comments in the essay 'Hermeneutics and Universal History'.[6] He agrees with Gadamer's analysis of earlier discussions of understanding by Schleiermacher and Dilthey. He approves of Gadamer's perception of the necessity for a distinction between the position of the (present) interpreter and the (past) event (1983a:118). He acknowledges the significance of openness as part of experience, and the importance of experience as confirming the provisionality of knowledge. He regards this assertion of the provisional, time-conditioned nature of knowledge as that which separates Gadamer from Hegel and makes 'any simple repetition of Hegel's system impossible' (1983a:122) – in other words, it is the point of separation of postmodern philosophy from the modernist project of the Enlightenment. Above all, Pannenberg sees Gadamer as bringing the essential rapprochement between history and philosophy that is required for Pannenberg's own enterprise.

Pannenberg's view of knowledge receives more extensive and explicit defence in *Theology & the Philosophy of Science*, which was originally published in 1973. In this book, Pannenberg again makes clear his debt to Gadamer and his development of Gadamer's position. He presents an account of the development of hermeneutic, and of critical developments in philosophy. He notes the problems

5 See, for instance, Weinsheimer (1985:1-35).

6 This was first published in 1963 and collected in the essays published in Volume One of *Basic Questions in Theology* (1983a).

raised by Heidegger, which make trans-subjective truth problematic. Pannenberg cites Gadamer as having overcome this, without resorting to the discredited objectification associated with method in natural science. Again, Pannenberg cites Gadamer's approach to the 'fusion of horizons' as essential, including as it does a recognition of the separation between the context of an utterance and that of its interpreter (1976:164). The tradition in which the interpreter stands is neither an objectification nor identical with his or her experience; the tradition has a claim, a priority over our understanding which is what establishes the distinct identity of the strange utterance. The link with the future is still in the anticipation of meaning given by situation in a particular tradition (1976:165).

But, even at an early stage, Pannenberg also disagrees with Gadamer. In his defence of hermeneutics, Pannenberg has to take account of many critiques from different directions. Arguments such as those raised by critical rationalism (by which is meant the philosophy of Albert and Popper)[7] do not affect my thesis, since the responses of both Gadamer and Pannenberg would be pretty similar. However, other arguments reveal both Pannenberg's general motivation and specific differences between him and Gadamer. For instance, he deals with the criticisms made by linguistic analysis by presenting them as a corrective to Heidegger's devaluing of the statement, in keeping with his general desire to retain content and objectivity in language (1976:183). More serious are the criticisms of dialectic philosophy, notably by Apel and Habermas. Both Apel and Habermas use the tradition of philosophical hermeneutics, and engage with Gadamer, but both have specific concerns about the protection of the process of interpretation from corruption by ideology. Pannenberg is critical of them both, and prefers to make use of Gadamer's approaches.

Pannenberg's disagreements with Gadamer and associated relevant arguments will be considered in the following sections.

Objectivity and the statement

Pannenberg thinks Gadamer's analogy of conversation is taken too far, because interpretation has a unidirectional character for Pannenberg. He is concerned that the interpreter must neither be absorbed into a text, nor herself absorb it, but that a distinction between the two must be maintained by the interpreter (1983a:117). This is connected with a further, significant disagreement. Pannenberg does not like Gadamer's holistic view of language. For Pannenberg, it is not only possible but necessary to separate statements or assertions from their linguistic contexts or horizons of meaning, because the differentness of the assertion is what defines the horizon of meaning against which it is set (1983a:126). Consequently, extracting

7 For continental definitions of Critical Rationalism, see Bubner (1981) and Schillebeeckx, *Christ* (1980:899).

and enlarging assertions is an essential part of the interpretative process for Pannenberg:

> ... to the extent that interpretation really intends to understand the author, *everything* must be turned into assertion; everything that was involved in the formation of a text ... must be made explicit. (1983a:127)

But, I would argue, the horizon which gives context to the text is unlimited, and therefore it is difficult to see how it may be made totally explicit. The nuances given by what is not said in a text are also hard to capture in assertion and Pannenberg does not deal adequately with this.

In *Theology and the Philosophy of Science*, Pannenberg asserts the need for 'objectivity' in understanding more strongly than in previous work, stressing the difference between the horizon of that to be interpreted from that of the interpreter, and requiring that the 'thing to be interpreted must be distinguishable from the subjectivity of the interpreter' (1976:167). He locates this separation of interpretation and interpreter in the use of representational language, and criticises Gadamer for not allowing this sufficient importance (1976:169). This is a development of his earlier criticism of Gadamer's devaluing of assertion and statement. In the same direction, arguing in favour of 'system' in the terminology of Habermas, and downplaying experience or 'lifeworld', Pannenberg also explicitly objects to the role of creative experience in Gadamer's view of understanding. This is in the immediate context of Pannenberg's repudiation of the existentialist theology of Bultmann and others as subjectivist. Bultmann's mistake, in Pannenberg's eyes, is that he has lost the content of interpretation, not that he commends interpretation as an epistemology. Pannenberg also criticises Fuchs and Ebeling, both of whom have followed the existentialism of Bultmann. He sees them as reducing theology to ethical prescription, and concentrating on the law/gospel dichotomy of the Reformation, making theology independent of history, and thus removing the foundation of all theology which is the Incarnation. Pannenberg wishes to expunge any aspects of Gadamer's approach that are in common with such existentialism. He intends to retain the givenness and necessity of the historical context for interpretation, without any hint of subjectivism.

Thiselton (1992) notes some of these differences between Gadamer and Pannenberg. He argues that in Gadamer there is a 'deep ambivalence' resulting from the openness of his view of knowledge, which was exploited by Rorty to support the suggested impossibility of universal or metacritical truth. Pannenberg, says Thiselton, has pursued a view that is the antithesis of Rorty's, and 'unlike Gadamer, Pannenberg assigns a more fundamental status to testable propositions or assertions' (1992:335). Thiselton notes the indeterminism in Gadamer and, from the point of a textual analyst, its unsatisfactory nature.[8] The issue of objectivity is one to which I will return; the question is whether Pannenberg's characterisation of Gadamer is correct, and whether Pannenberg's attempt to supply what is perceived to be wanting in Gadamer is successful.

Tradition and authority

Habermas has made widely noted objections to the apparently defining, and therefore potentially distorting, role given to tradition by Gadamer.[9] Pannenberg acknowledges the intentions of Habermas in seeking to remove ideological distortion from hermeneutics but accuses him of wanting to construct a social theory 'combining the approach of hermeneutic with the insights of Marx and Freud' (1976:188-189). Pannenberg allows that hermeneutic and the dialectic of Marx are both about relating the part to the whole, but he locates the difference between them in what he sees as the totalising effect of dialectic. This does not allow the provisionality which is always present in hermeneutical interpretation (1976:189). This is the basis of the criticism that dialectic itself is ideological; the totality must be defined or grasped beyond the limits of human experience. But in raising logical questions about the foundation of dialectic, Pannenberg is not answering the question that is being raised about the role of effective history or tradition in Gadamer's hermeneutic. Does it not lead to a political conservatism, and an authoritarianism of the past? Certainly for Gadamer, the authority of tradition, while real, is in no sense irrational obedience, and Thiselton comments that:

> Gadamer's key concept of 'effective history' (Wirkungsgeschichte) calls attention to the operative force of tradition over those who belong to it. ... *Authority, seen in its proper sense, has nothing to do with the abdication of reason.* Respect for authority rests on an entirely *rational* judgement that one is 'aware of one's own limitations', and has reason to accept 'that others have better understanding'. (1992:327)

---

8 'This is the very aspect which Habermas, Apel and Pannenberg believe to be Gadamer's weakest and most vulnerable aspect ... Gadamer asserts, to borrow Weinsheimer's words, that "the work exists *nowhere but in its representations* ... There can be *no determinate criterion* of correct interpretation" ' (1992:394) and further, he says 'The question raised in post-Gadamerian hermeneutics by Apel, Pannenberg and Habermas, was whether ... *hermeneutical* understanding must operate without recourse to some metacritical dimension, or whether Gadamer's "conversation" must simply "proceed" in whatever direction it proceeds'. (1992:440)

9 See Warnke above; also the discussion in Bleicher (1980:152-158).

This will be further discussed in my concluding chapter, since I am alleging that Pannenberg himself is tending to an unjustifiable authoritarianism. I will there take up the question of whether his dependence on Gadamer makes this inevitable.

Action

Pannenberg reviews the debate between Gadamer and Habermas on the status of meaning, in the context of the concern of Habermas to connect hermeneutics with social reality. Pannenberg claims that Habermas wants to subordinate meaning to action. Hence Pannenberg argues that meaning is displaced from the centre in Habermas' perspective, and hermeneutics is restricted to subjectively intended meaning. Habermas himself identifies the need for a wider interpretation, 'depth hermeneutic', based on psychoanalytic theory. Pannenberg cites Gadamer as defending his own definition of hermeneutics as much wider than Habermas has allowed, and as it is based on communication rather than action, not suffering from the same problems of truth. Pannenberg pursues the question of the concern with action over against understanding in Habermas. He finds it in Habermas' defence against the suggestion of inherent circularity in hermeneutics; where Heidegger saw the hermeneutical circle as really circular, limiting the possibility of objective historical knowledge, Habermas linked the process of experiencing meaning in language to non-verbal experience, action. Pannenberg is unhappy with this, arguing that it lays Habermas open to Albert's charge of illogicality (1976:200). Pannenberg's solution to the potential circularity of hermeneutics is to point to the provisionality, the hypothetical nature of anticipation or pre-understanding, which is logically confirmed or rejected by subsequent experience. He emphasises, against Habermas, his view that perception of meaning is prior to and underlies action, although he claims that his understanding of meaning is not passive, but is seen against the horizon of the eschatological future (1976:203-204).

Pannenberg's emphasis is all along on the philosophical correctness, the rationality, of his position. He does not actually engage with the issues motivating Habermas, the problem of the corruption of meaning into ideology which supports the domination of one human group by another. At least in dealing with the arguments he appears to be almost apolitical, and he does not mention the significance of application (*Anwendung*) for Gadamer. However, it is worth noting that Gadamer seems to have had a concern for right action from the earliest development of his thought. As mentioned earlier, Sullivan (1989) discusses latent political concern in the concept of *phronesis* in the early work of Gadamer. Moral knowledge, or practical wisdom, is certainly a prominent idea in *Truth and Method*, and clearly influences the development of Gadamer's concept of application. It would not be right, therefore, to conclude that Gadamer and Pannenberg actually hold the same position in this area, and I shall argue in my concluding chapter that they demonstrably do not.

Truth

Pannenberg does limit the hermeneutic possibility, in that although all perceptions of meaning imply some totality of meaning, this cannot be taken as a philosophical grounding of the value of all meaning that there is (1976:217-218). Pannenberg is going to appeal to history and incarnation as the basis for responding to that problem. But hermeneutics has one very positive aspect for the theologian, and that is the questioning of experience it implies (1976:219). Self criticism becomes part of the process of understanding. Here Pannenberg looks at the same problem as Habermas, but from the opposite end. He is equally sceptical about pure correspondence and pure consensus theories of truth, arguing that correspondence cannot be established without some reference to others, but they must be 'competent' others; judgement of facts is not a matter of convention but requires skill. Pannenberg is quite clear that his theory of truth is going to be primarily a coherence theory (1976:220). He claims that the difference between natural sciences and philosophy is not in the presence or absence of empirical testing, but in the restriction of issues to be included in the search for coherence and truth. Natural science limits the possible subjects of enquiry. Philosophy is unrestricted (1976:221).

It is also significant that for Pannenberg, philosophy must advance by complete revision of what has gone before. Here he converges with Thomas Kuhn; he refers back to a previous discussion of paradigms, and asserts of philosophy that it proceeds always by total revision (1976:222). It should be noted that Pannenberg regards the process of falsification in itself as part of the restrictive method of natural science; when he talks about philosophical hypotheses, what he has in mind is more like Kuhn's paradigms:

> Philosophical analysis of meaning, in its treatment of the phenomena it has to analyse and in the results of its analyses, proceeds by hypothesis just as much as the particular sciences ... (it) can operate only by systematically describing the totality of meaning which guides its reflection, although a systematic account of this sort is no more than an anticipation of the implicit and only partly defined totality of the meaning of all experience, to which it is related and in which it possesses its truth. (1976:224)

These comments by Pannenberg in *Theology and the Philosophy of Science* are reinforced by the account of truth that he gives in his *Systematic Theology*. In these theoretical justifications, he opts for a picture of truth as the historically built up coherence of reliable knowledge evaluated by skilled judges. However, this is not how he has always been understood, particularly in the USA. For instance, the evaluation of Pannenberg by Grenz and Olson in *20th Century Theology* (1992) suggests a rationality closer to the Enlightenment, and he is praised for rescuing theology from post Enlightenment subjectivism and relativism. More importantly for my thesis, I shall argue that in his use of the various sciences, Pannenberg does not actually behave in conformity to his own methodology.

Pannenberg's defence of the epistemology of the 'human sciences'

Pannenberg regards the emergence of separate accounts of philosophy of knowledge in the natural and the human sciences as a significant problem for the elaboration of the universal epistemology which he seeks. In *Theology and the Philosophy of Science* he gives a developmental account and defence of his espousal of an explanation of truth and knowledge applicable to both natural and 'human' sciences. It is significant for my arguments with Pannenberg that even at this stage, he regards the division of the natural and human sciences as basically unproblematic. For Pannenberg, for instance, sociology is a human science, and psychology is a natural science. He simply ignores the ambivalent position occupied by the social sciences, which may be found in either the arts or the sciences in most English-speaking countries. He appears to see the classification of the sciences as being based on unambiguous principles of rationality and method, ignoring the analyses of history and sociology of science which would challenge this.[10] I will discuss this in terms of its effects on the philosophy of science later in this chapter.

Pannenberg sees the problems of the epistemological validation of the human sciences in terms of the conflict between a positivist epistemology based on the physical sciences and the interpretative tradition associated with the emergence of social theory in the humanities (1976:72). Consequently, he sees the epistemology of the social sciences as inextricably linked with the philosophy of hermeneutics, and he sets out to defend and validate the latter in the context of the former. On the one hand he responds to positivist suggestions that human sciences are not objective enough, and on the other, to versions of hermeneutics that incorporate human action and so risk subjectivism in his opinion. There are two particular issues relating to the specifically human sciences in Pannenberg's account that should be discussed before I deal with his overall critique of philosophy of science as such. They are the role of human action and the problem of objectivity.

Human action and the human sciences

Pannenberg considers that the contributions to hermeneutics by Dilthey were significant for the incipient split between human and natural science. In Dilthey's work, the validity of the interpretation of experience in the human sciences was made initially to depend on Dilthey's view of general psychology. When he moved beyond this empirical foundation, he was left with the assumption that the act of reflecting on experience gives rise to an understanding of reality which can be shared with others. Pannenberg concludes that this is a move to a philosophical

10 e.g. Kuhn (1962), Ravetz (1973), Latour & Woolgar (1979). For a comprehensive review of the field, see Olby et al. (1990).

assumption which was then overlooked for ideological reasons.[11] After Dilthey, says Pannenberg, the new views on the human sciences, concentrating on the analysis of subjective experience, diverted attention from the philosophical concern for truth. Pannenberg gives this as one reason for the emergence of action-based accounts of the human sciences, such as Weber's (1976:80).

Pannenberg's critique of Weber's approach leaves room for the hermeneutical; for Pannenberg, sociology is never to be an account of external conduct, but an understanding of what people do. Pannenberg argues that Weber came to focus on the attitude of individuals to values, rather than the origins of the values in themselves, as the primary component of an explanatory process in sociology (1976:83). He extended this to a method whereby an account of subjectively intended meaningful behaviour is used as an ideal type against which to compare the actual behaviour of individuals. Pannenberg claims that in Weber, the use of value in intended meaning becomes increasingly associated with departure from the ideal type, so that finally an opposition between value and being is proposed in which concern with values can be represented as irrational (1976:86).

Pannenberg appears to be more favourably disposed to Talcott Parsons, as being opposed to the behaviourist/determinist element in sociological explanation, and insisting on the primacy of the intention of the actor in giving meaning to the act. Parsons assumes that cultural values are prior to reciprocal expectations of behaviour in a group, not constituted by them. Pannenberg takes up the critique by Habermas, that Parsons ignores the reciprocal relation between social institutions and the cultural values that give rise to or regulate them. Habermas argues that value formation is part of social action, and that it involves distinguishing ideological and utopian components from the intentional/rational. Pannenberg summarises his position as:

> In this analysis utopian and ideological contents appear as 'instinctual energies' which are 'not integrated' into the purposive rationality of the self regulating society and 'have no hope of satisfaction in its role systems' ... The stability of the social system would then depend on the degree to which utopias can be put into practice and ideologies neutralised. (1976:89)

Pannenberg picks on the concept of 'instinctual energies', suggesting that its use requires the fitting of societies to pre-existent criteria. He argues that this ignores the historical conditioning of such concepts; they cannot be independent of the

11 Pannenberg says 'Without this "metaphysical" assumption on Dilthey's part, the claim of his analysis of hermeneutical experience to "objectivity", after his abandonment of the attempt to base it on psychology, was left without support. Since Dilthey, under the influence of Comte and Mill, regarded all metaphysics as an expression of a period of human intellectual development that had been left behind, these implications were neither noticed, nor, therefore, confronted with his analysis of historical experience.' (1976:79)

socio-cultural system. He asserts that there are cultural values which are not dependent on a given society, in that societies can reject their values, and yet those values find expression in other societies (1976:90). This is preliminary to an attack by Pannenberg on the prioritising of interest over content in Habermas' account of enquiry and knowledge. Pannenberg argues that there is no logical difference between Habermas' elevation of knowledge-constitutive interest to the transcendental and Nietzsche's naturalism, citing Habermas' own arguments against Nietzsche. His anxiety is that Habermas, in describing knowledge seeking as interest-driven, has eliminated the possibility of rationally grounding value in society. Habermas gives importance to 'discourse' as a reciprocal process of communicative action in which interest does not dominate, but Pannenberg is not satisfied with this. Pannenberg argues that if values and meaning always imply action, then the awareness of meaning itself has to be explained; he says it cannot simply emerge in discourse.

Further, Pannenberg also mounts another argument against Habermas, attacking his characterisation of communication. This is not possible, according to Pannenberg, without some inter-subjective recognition of rules or criteria, which themselves must have some logical foundation. Indeed, he argues, the recognition of the other as an 'I' with whom to communicate implies a 'going beyond the self to the universal' (1976:97). Pannenberg is not arguing with the claim that the experience of meaning requires intersubjectivity. However, he wants to assert that meaning in itself is not a product of language or communication, but a necessary condition for it; even if the means of communication is itself constitutive for elaborating different kinds of meanings. All of these arguments are expansions of the tendency (already noted in my previous section) for Pannenberg to react against the inclusion of anything not strictly rational in a validation of knowledge. Any theory adverting to the role of human action is severely criticised by Pannenberg. In rejecting the role of communication in establishing understanding and meaning in Habermas, he may be at risk of undercutting its place in Gadamer as well.

Objectivity and the human sciences

Pannenberg attacks various critics on the positivist side, such as Kempski, Topitsch and Albert, who have tried, in varying degrees, to deny validity to the human sciences. He also refutes attempts to separate natural and human sciences on the basis that the former are concerned with explanation and the latter with understanding, and shows that both are intimately involved in the acquisition of any kind of knowledge. Although Albert's position is close to that of Popper, and Pannenberg has his own serious differences from Popper, it is typical of Pannenberg that he is quite prepared to use Albert's arguments, for an essential component of content to knowledge, against Habermas. As usual, Pannenberg's primary concern is to reject the arguments of Habermas and for that purpose, he gathers material from all sides.

Whereas Habermas copes with the postmodern problem by locating truth in free communication in the community, it is already clear that Pannenberg wants a more metaphysically secure place for it. Pannenberg relates the problem of the apparent non-objectivity of meaning to the incomplete nature of history; events never cease happening in relation to other events, thereby altering the relations between the parts and the whole. He objects to the concept of communicative action in Habermas on the grounds that it includes ideological presuppositions in this context, in that it must contain concealed anticipation of meaning, and that such concealment is in itself an ideology (1976:101).

Having thus turned Habermas on his head, Pannenberg also argues that universal perspectives are not always ideologies, even if they have the function of supporting social structures, which Pannenberg admits may be repressive (1976:101). Pannenberg's reason for this is that while such a system permits open questioning and the expression of alternative values, it is not claiming the exclusive truth of an ideology. He concedes the point that practical constraints and the function of domination which he seems to see as inherent in social institutions may limit the degree to which open evaluation of a system can take place, but he appears to argue that existing institutions offer as much openness as is possible under present conditions. The role of open questioning is important for establishing value as well as critiquing its application. Pannenberg concludes that the comparison of a world-view and experienced reality allows a deeper analysis than one restricted only to the actions and intentions of others, and that it is the possibility of critique of value contained in this that is the 'criterion of the difference between repression and emancipation' (1976:102). And, in Pannenberg's opinion, the world-views in human history that have functioned in this way are the religions. He concludes that the concept of meaning, although foundational for social sciences, cannot be properly elucidated with reference to them alone.

Again, this treatment of alternative hermeneutic positions reflects Pannenberg's anxiety to have rationally justified, secure metaphysical ground from which to operate. But in fact, it is this very ground which has been undermined by Gadamer. *Truth and Method* is an argument for the holistic and contextual nature of understanding, and its irreduceability to techniques of rationality. In his desire for a secure metacritique, Pannenberg seems almost to be self-contradictory. His replacement of the ideological dependence, by Habermas, on ideal communication conditions with the critique of value supposedly contained in the world views of religions is quite arbitrary. Further, such a world view could surely be considered as the sum of the intentions and actions of others, so that Pannenberg has not adequately explained why it would provide a 'deeper' analysis than provided by the approach of Habermas.

Pannenberg's view of knowledge in the human sciences is fundamentally historical – hermeneutic. But it includes his high valuation of objectivity, and almost wilfully ignores the problems of interest and power which are significant for this field. His account is impoverished compared to that of Zygmunt Bauman in *Hermeneutics and the Social Sciences* (1978) for example. Of the many authors who discuss the salient features of postmodernity, Bauman seems particularly appropriate to a discussion of both science and theology. His work spans an engagement with hermeneutics, major contributions to social theory, a critique of science and a restatement of value in the face of postmodernity. Bauman has argued in a series of works that the defining legacy of postmodernity is the primacy of the ethical dimension. He raises this in the context of the methods of the social sciences and in the context of science and technology as institutions. It is clear that the question of value is central to science and technology as integral parts of modern culture; it can no longer be evicted or suppressed.

Bauman has given serious consideration to the status of the social sciences as sciences in themselves. He describes the effects of the rise of hermeneutical theory on social science, in his survey covering Marx, Weber, Mannheim, Husserl, Heidegger and Schutz (1978). He points out that the nineteenth century development of hermeneutics as the study of meaning raised methodological difficulties about the study of human subjectivity which 'threatened to undermine the very foundation of social science' (1978:10). The new social sciences emerged in the train of the natural sciences, and concepts of intentionality were foreign to the latter. But hermeneutics made the intentionality of the author central to the creation of text, and it became apparent that any claim to understanding of a human act would have to account for the actor's intentions. Bauman argues that Comte and Durkheim largely evaded this problematic area, but the German influences on social theory were more affected by the philosophical implications of hermeneutics. In different ways, Marx, Weber and Mannheim sought to cope with the sociological dimension of history. Husserl and Heidegger advanced the philosophical analysis of the problem of the social- and time-conditioned nature of knowledge. Parsons and Schutz moved the process of understanding the social in opposite directions.

Bauman lays open the persistent problem of setting the objectivity sought by the natural sciences against the inevitable evaluation involved in understanding human agency. He acknowledges the importance of Heidegger in establishing the temporal aspect of human identity, but he is very critical of the neglect of the social in Heidegger's account. Heidegger may be right to say that my identity is constituted by my own grasp of my historical situatedness, but the Other is crucial in this, whereas Heidegger barely discusses interhuman relationships at all. Bauman is clear that the 'unremedial paucity of its ethics' is the key to the failure of Heidegger's philosophy as a satisfactory foundation for social theory (1978:169).

In *Modernity and the Holocaust* (1989) Bauman argues that the genocides of the Second World War that culminated in the Holocaust were not the aberrations of madmen in a rogue state, but on the contrary, made possible and desired by the combination of the technological rationality and the bureaucracy of the modern state.[12] The possibility of the Holocaust demonstrates the bankruptcy of the

12 He lists among the significant factors 'the role of scientific rhetoric in the legitimization of social engineering ambitions' and says that 'the Holocaust was a characteristically

Enlightenment project; what kind of truth can be guaranteed by ways of thinking that create states capable of this? And while science provides the mechanisms for the wholesale destruction of humanity by itself, it also is part of the discourse which legitimates that destruction. Bauman shows that modern bureaucracy is typified by systemisation, leading to division of labour, and the substitution of technical for moral responsibility(1989:98). Technological means are allowed to displace the question of the moral ends to which they are put (1989:116). This critique of the use of the rationality to evacuate the moral dimension from public discourse is given more extensive expression in *Postmodern Ethics* (1993).

In the context of the present discussion of hermeneutics and the human sciences, Bauman is able to see Weber in constructive engagement with hermeneutics, and indeed, struggling for the very objectivity that Pannenberg so values (1978:72). On this view Weber intended to rescue the social sciences from the inheritance of German idealism and the relativism of the kinds of hermeneutics associated with it (1978:87). This was surely an enterprise aiming at the same goal as Pannenberg's. However, Pannenberg's account of Weber is one sided, and suppresses this dimension. Similarly, Bauman points out that Talcott Parsons' use of phenomenology led to the innovative recognition that human action must be understood in the tripartite context of person, culture and social system. But at the same time, it was a supremely rationalist enterprise, which failed the test of applicability to the real world (1978:146). Bauman's critique of Parsons may be similarly relevant to Pannenberg, who is also concentrating on a rational world of rational actors, and this may influence Pannenberg's preference for Parsons over Weber.

The nature of truth and knowledge in natural science

Having examined Pannenberg's views on the specific status of the human and social sciences, I may turn to his response to philosophy of science as such, which has usually taken the natural sciences as the model for what constitutes science. Pannenberg's views on philosophy of science are extensions of his general view of what constitutes proper knowledge. Again, Pannenberg is primarily concerned with the problem of truth; science cannot present complete truth in his view. In an early essay on science and theology, he says:

> To be sure, the reality of God is not incompatible with some form of abstract knowledge concerning the regularities of natural processes, a knowledge that abstracts from the concreteness of physical reality and therefore may also be able to abstract from the presence of God in his creation. But such abstract knowledge of regularities should not claim full and exclusive competence regarding the explanation of nature; if it does so,

modern phenomenon that cannot be understood out of the context of cultural tendencies and technical achievements of modernity'. (1989:xiii)

> the reality of God is denied by implication. The so called methodological atheism of modern science is far from pure innocence. It is a highly ambiguous phenomenon. (1993:16)

For the theologian, the truth about the world cannot be encompassed by any means that denies the world's origin in God. Pannenberg is going to be resolutely opposed to scientific triumphalism in epistemology. However, this passage does raise the question of how well Pannenberg understands the methodological reductionism that is common in natural science. He does not appear to distinguish between methodological and ontological reductionism,[13] and nowhere does he give an account of it. The problem is that on one hand, if a sufficient scientific explanation of the function of, say, mammalian striated muscle can be got from an examination of the component cells, then no further level of explanation will be invoked, and the function of the whole muscle is explained as the sum of its parts. In the case of the mammalian kidney, which cannot be fully explained as the sum of its parts as studied in isolation, the further context of the body fluids and circulation is required for satisfactory explanation. But neither of these theories assume or refute atheism, because they are concerned with present phenomena in mechanistic terms, not with origin or dependency. This issue will be raised again in discussion of Pannenberg's use of biology and psychology. Apart from such possible confusion, Pannenberg is clear that he agrees with Popper's attacks on positivism, differs extensively with Popper's critical rationalism and acknowledges the contribution of Kuhn.

Popper's attack on positivism

Pannenberg is aware that the rise of natural science in the twentieth century has raised serious questions about the concept of truth; the practical success of science has become associated with the philosophical predominance of forms of positivism. In *Theology and the Philosophy of Science,* he cites critiques of this, including that of Habermas (1976:67). Pannenberg goes on to cite Popper's criticism of logical positivism, in particular, his attack on the principle of verification and his rejection of the identification of meaningfulness with empirical testability. Pannenberg traces the move from the empiricist reduction of all valid knowledge to sense data, via the recognition that sense impression can be subjective, to logical positivism. He summarises the logical positivist position as depending on the establishment of connections between statements about the world and some observable, empirical aspect of that same world (1976:30). He concedes that if this connection between demonstrable states of affairs and language statements is philosophically necessary for meaning, as the Vienna Circle claimed, then talk about God comes into the category of meaningless metaphysical speculation. Pannenberg does not regard any

13 See, for instance, Hull (1974).

escape from this into privileged religious experience as possible. He argues that the proper defence for theology is the critique of the assumptions of logical positivism, such as those famously advanced by Popper.

Pannenberg agrees with Popper's initial objections to practical verification as a criterion of truth, based on classic objections to inductive argument. Merely because an event happens repeatedly in an experimental situation, there is nevertheless no logically compelling philosophical reason as to why it should do so. A scientific law corresponds to a potentially infinite series of events in nature, which cannot possibly all be observed. Popper recognised the 'theory-laden' nature of scientific laws but rejected all claims to any kind of *a priori* authority. He sought to find a criterion of truth which would distinguish between scientific and metaphysical propositions, and proposed the principle of falsification. While any number of substantiations of a theory cannot make it logically true, one practical example of its failure establishes it as false by deductive reasoning. Pannenberg notes that Popper sees a role for metaphysical or untestable thought in the formulation of hypotheses about the world that can then be tested by attempted falsification. Throughout this discussion of Popper, it is clear that Pannenberg's primary motivation is the defence of the possibility of theology as metacritique; it is not primarily an appreciation of the philosophical problems that make positivism untenable even from an atheist perspective.

Pannenberg's disagreements with Popper

Pannenberg is unhappy about what he sees as a lack of clarity in Popper's account of the status of metaphysical theory. Popper's acknowledgement of the philosophical component of theory requires him to set criteria for false philosophical theories, which are those that do not rationally connect with any specific problem and suggest solutions for it. However, on these principles, true philosophical theories become assimilated to scientific theories, since they are testable. Pannenberg says that Popper is evading the issue of the truth of metaphysical theories by this approach (1976:39). Pannenberg is of course very anxious to retain not only the meaning, but criteria for the truth, of metaphysical statements. He discusses Popper's understanding of the truth of scientific statements, as being descriptions of the state of affairs in the one, real, world, and asserts that this is fundamentally a correspondence theory of truth (1976:41). Here, Pannenberg seems to be agreeing to a straightforward correspondence theory of truth as applicable to science. In a footnote, he rejects an argument for a consensus theory of truth which he ascribes to Habermas, but allows for the necessity of consensus in establishing truth, to such an extent that he says:

> The two factors of correspondence to objects and consensus each require the other, and neither can ultimately be subordinated to the other. To set up a correspondence theory and a consensus theory of truth as alternatives is therefore self defeating. Just as

> consensus about truth and factual correspondence can only be anticipated in any case, the unity between the two can also be achieved only in anticipation. (1976:41, footnote 62)

It is clear here, as it is elsewhere,[14] that Pannenberg does not subscribe to a correspondence theory of truth, but to some form of coherence theory.

Pannenberg does acknowledge the provisionality of truth in Popper's thought. He is critical of Popper's suggestion that truth acts as a regulative principle, pointing out that statements do not occur at the end of a process, but instead, are made in anticipation of an unknown future (1976:42). It is interesting that Pannenberg here uses Popper to support the introduction of anticipation, a concept originating in Gadamer that emerges with great significance for all of Pannenberg's thinking. Pannenberg points to a similar problem about provisionality in the early statements of Habermas on ideal dialogue as a criterion for truth. He raises a classic problem about truth as the ultimate state of affairs in the context of the provisionality of hypotheses. The difficulty is that the representation of what is to be known must be separable from what it actually proves to be; Pannenberg sees this as a 'new form of the old "metaphysical" distinction between substance and accidents' (1976:43). He argues that the consequence of this is that metaphysics is actually necessary for the grounding of the hypothesis formation and testing that is characteristic of science. Thus Pannenberg has used Popper's defence of science to establish the validity and necessity of metaphysical concepts inside and outside of science!

He also refutes some critiques of theology that claim to have been offered on a Popperian basis, starting with W. Bartley's book, *Retreat to Commitment* (1964). This outlines the argument found earlier in Popper, against both idealism and empiricism as forms of irrationality. Bartley simply argues that modern Protestant theology, in its appeal to revelation, is similarly irrational. According to Pannenberg, Bartley wishes to supersede idealism and empiricism in general thought as well as in science, and he thinks that Popper's hypothesis testing can be extended to a 'universal programme of pan-critical rationalism'. This has been elaborated on by others, particularly Albert, the continental critical rationalist philosopher. Albert expands the argument to make the claim that hermeneutical methods, centring on understanding (as are common in theology) are radically opposed to (Popperian) critical methods. Besides this argument against forms of 'revelation', Pannenberg also notes Albert's accusation that theology has, as it were, moved the goal posts; that the concept of God has been so redefined as to make it immune to critiques about objectivity. If the idea of God is restricted to 'moral and rhetorical functions', then the question of falsifiability is not an issue, and Pannenberg points out that this amounts to a qualification of a rejected hypothesis on the Popperian model.

---

14 See his discussion in the *Systematic Theology* (1991:21 & ff, 48 & ff).

Pannenberg asks whether, on Popper's assumptions, it is in fact legitimate to attempt to judge theology by the standards laid down for the assessment of science, and queries whether Popper's account of science is satisfactory. Is falsification an adequate principle in science, and if so, can it be reasonably transferred to theology? Pannenberg cites Carnap's objection to falsification as such; that it requires observation statements to have an epistemological status which is not derivable from first principles. Pannenberg cites Popper as saying that to be falsifiable, the basic statements about a hypothesis must be 'testable, inter-subjectively, by observation' (1976:51). Pannenberg argues that such tests result in further basic statements, open to further testing, and so on. He cites Popper's statement that agreement between individuals is required for the ultimate acceptance of what is basic, (Popper, 1959:106) and agrees with Carnap that this makes falsification less than logically compelling. Pannenberg also considers C.F. von Weizsäcker's criticisms of Popper. These centre on the unfalsifiability of the general propositions necessary for the formulation of any basic statement (e.g. any observation of colour implies a general theory of colour). Weizsäcker wants to argue from a Kantian position that certain kinds of verification could be compelling. Pannenberg does not accept this, but he argues that the importance of Weizsäcker's argument is that it strengthens the case for the theory-laden nature of propositions (1976:55). And he cites Thomas Kuhn in support of this.

Pannenberg's conclusion is that Popper has failed in his attempt to provide a philosophical means of discriminating between scientific and metaphysical statements:

> Not only does the language required for the formulation of basic propositions root natural science in the psychology of the individual investigator, but the logic of its statements fixes it firmly in general attitudes which are ultimately philosophical or religious in character. This statement does not exclude the possibility that these statements may be open to correction by experience; indeed it should be stressed that this openness must be a property of philosophical and religious views as long as they remain living and have not solidified into dogma. (1976:55)

It is clear that Pannenberg has extensive and unbridgeable differences with critical rationalism in general and Popper in particular. Recent claims that Pannenberg's epistemology can be classed as a version of the modification of Popper by Lakatos[15] have not taken into account Pannenberg's rootedness in the hermeneutic tradition, and some considerable transatlantic misunderstanding seems to have taken place. This will be further discussed in the last chapter.

15 Most clearly stated in Murphy (1990).

The historical and social in science

Pannenberg agrees with Kuhn's association of systems of hypotheses as paradigms, but does not regard Kuhn as having succeeded in undermining Popper at the philosophical level (1976:57). Pannenberg objects to Kuhn as trying to throw the baby out with the bath water; if Kuhn's objection to falsification on the lines of Carnap is true, he has described science in a way that makes it indistinguishable from other disciplines. Pannenberg says that it is significant that whilst falsification in itself remains possible, a hypothesis can be definitively rejected if observations contradicting it are made. This argument (1976:58) would certainly seem to place Pannenberg in disagreement with Lakatos and the concept of auxiliary modifications. Pannenberg notes Popper's desire to give a general philosophical account of knowledge, and his wish to include history as knowledge of specific events. He summarises Popper as arguing that in explaining individual events, some general laws must be invoked, which may be primarily sociological, but which nevertheless allow history to be seen as applied and generalising, so that it can be scientific (1976:59). This, says Pannenberg, was reflected in work by Hempel, which gave rise to some debate about the proper methodology of historical disciplines.

The division is between those who wish to follow a Popperian line, and those who wish to stress the uniqueness of historical event, such as the British historian, Oakeshott. Pannenberg presents the argument that:

> ... the inclusion of an event under a general law already presupposes a general description of the event, and this description in turn depends on a prior 'historical explanation' of the event as part of a narrative structure. But unlike a narrative sequence, a general law cannot connect the beginning of an event with its end, but only with the general class of events to which it belongs. Now this limitation applies not only to these of strictly general natural laws in the explanation of historical processes, but also to sociological or specifically historical types or structure of limited generality. (1976:61)

Pannenberg concludes that because of this, deductive explanations, and hence the test of falsifiability, are inappropriate for the historical sciences. He devotes a considerable amount of space to considering Popper's position on unique, historical events, and the problem of contingency. (It is interesting that this later becomes highly significant for Pannenberg's theology of creation.)[16] What Pannenberg is really after is forcing the conclusion from Popper that a hermeneutical approach to truth criteria is the ultimately justifiable one. He does this with the aid of Kuhn, arguing that the history of science itself shows less a process of falsification and more a process of interpretative collation of functional theories (1976:66). Pannenberg argues that the characteristic feature of the natural sciences, and all those he refers to as 'generalising sciences', is the requirement that the hypotheses

16 See also Pannenberg (1976:65, footnote 122).

invoked in explanations are in principle open to falsification, although he has clearly conceded that explanation in natural science does not always involve strict Popperian falsification. However, he argues that the intellectual basis for this approach is actually grounded in hermeneutic philosophy, and he therefore concludes that real knowledge, even of history, can also be obtained in situations where strict falsification is inappropriate (1976:67). The history he is referring to here is the empirical account of past events, not the wider interpretation of their meaning. He argues that philosophical statements seek to speak of reality as a whole, and again, the partial nature of our exposure to reality is stressed, since we are always open to the as yet unknown future (1976:68).

In the case of philosophical statements, the criteria for their 'testability' include coherence, effectiveness, and simplicity. Pannenberg wants to distinguish philosophical knowledge from natural science and history understood empirically, by its reference to total reality as opposed to the defined parts of reality explained by these other kinds of knowledge. He draws the distinction possible in German between on one hand, *Historie* as 'limited to the investigation of past events and processes' (1976:69) and on the other hand, *Geschichte*, which gives context and meaning beyond the immediate present (1976:69). In other words, *Geschichte* is real history, the relating of events to total reality, and it has an inescapable philosophical aspect. The criteria for its truth are then the same as those for philosophy, and we see Pannenberg's hermeneutical agenda from *Revelation as History* emerging.

In this account, Kuhn is cited, but a significant part of his contribution is effectively ignored. Kuhn's argument is that the rationality of science is historically conditioned; what passes for scientific method at one period is unacceptable at another. The implication of this is that social grouping plays a part in the choice of method and content that contributes to the paradigm at any one time. Pannenberg's suppression of this is understandable in the light of his desire to establish the objectivity of general statements, and his aversion to giving any priority to action as he opposes it to knowledge. But it leads again to a partial and uneven account of philosophy of science. Pannenberg does not engage with the controversies in contemporary philosophy of science about how truth and knowledge are affected by social and contingent factors. Logical positivism, claiming the total rationality and independence of scientific truth, and the absolute relativism of Bloor and the 'strong programme' (for example, see Mulkay, 1979), represent the opposite poles of the argument. But the majority of philosophy of science is somewhere in between.[17] The question is not whether social factors form part of the process of gaining scientific knowledge, but to what extent and how they do so.

An example of a recent creative approach to the problem, in the context of the relation of science and religion, is provided by Mikael Stenmark (1995). He reviews firstly, philosophies of science of the formal kind, such as empiricism and

17 For an overview of current arguments, see Curd & Cover (1998).

Popper's critical rationalism, which require universal logical rules to be applied. Secondly, he examines what he calls social evidentialist or practice oriented philosophies, which require informed judgement of evidence by the individual and in addition, submission of the opinion to an appropriate community of expertise. Gadamer, Habermas and MacIntyre fall into this class. Kuhn's philosophy of science is of this kind; he is not a relativist or deconstructionalist and Stenmark makes this clear (1995:124). He argues that Kuhn's rejection of a universal, formal, rule-based rationality does not imply a descent into subjective relativism; there is another way, which is the recognition of the role of experience and judgement in the selection and evaluation of material. Stenmark cites support for the role of the expert community and concludes that informed judgement, evaluating different sets of rules or material, is the real characteristic of science (1995:127). Stenmark therefore suggests what he sees as a third approach to philosophy of science, which he styles a philosophy of presumption, in which belief is assumed true unless there is some reasonable ground for rejecting it, and in which the community again plays a role in supplying and supporting belief. Stenmark provides an assessment of the ways in which these three modes of rationality affect both science and religion. He concludes that his presumptionism is the most satisfactory. Stenmark does not give a detailed account of the mechanisms by which knowledge accumulates on the practice oriented, community judgement model, and there is a similar lack of explanation in Kuhn. Later in this thesis, I will deal with a theoretical model which does make predictions about the interactions between knowledge and community, but the point I wish to make here is that Pannenberg does the subject less than justice by ignoring the issue.

Further, it is noticeable that Pannenberg does not discuss the views of Gadamer himself on science. Gadamer regards the sciences as secondary forms of knowledge, subsequent to the process of understanding and generalised in an objectifying way. He includes it under the umbrella of hermeneutic, and shares something of Pannenberg's views on Popper and Kuhn:

> It was a coherent sharpening of the logic of confirmation when Karl Popper raised falsifiability instead of verifiability to the status of a logical condition of scientific propositions. Actually the real process of research is not confined to this self-certification *e contrario* ... it does not seem to me at all contradictory to the logic of enquiry when Thomas Kuhn elaborated the significance of the paradigm for the progress of research. His theory of revolution in science rightly criticizes the false linear stylization supposedly connected with the progress of research. (1996:164)

However, Gadamer is aware of, and quite pessimistic about, the social dimension of science. He criticises science for promoting unacceptable coercive power over both nature and humanity and objects to the increasing automation and bureaucratisation of life under science (1996:3,15).

The application of hermeneutics itself to the philosophy of science has not been widespread in the Anglo Saxon world, but it is a significant Continental tradition.[18] Kurt Hubner, in his *Critique of Scientific Reason* (1983), has given an account of the problems of philosophy of science which I think illustrates the weakness of both positivist and Popperian approaches. Hubner is fundamentally sympathetic to hermeneutics, although he does not name Gadamer specifically. He demonstrates the inadequacy of ahistorical, rule based philosophies of science such as those of Carnap and Popper, and describes what he calls a 'universal historistic theory of the empirical sciences', requiring interpretative, historical methods of understanding.

Gadamer's views on the social dimensions of science converge on the position of Bauman. This is worth noting since, as mentioned earlier, Bauman has contributed to the critique of Heidegger's concept of hermeneutic on the grounds that it lacks any ethical component to understanding. Gadamer's linking of *phronesis* to understanding is an important correction in the development of hermeneutics. Heidegger also made criticisms of science, but they do not have the same social-ethical basis as those of Gadamer and Bauman. Bauman argues that the very objectivity of science, divorcing rationality from value and therefore reason from ethics, contributes to the problem; he says of the involvement of science in the Holocaust:

> The deadly potential of the most revered principles and accomplishments of modern science has been exposed. The emancipation of reason from emotions, of rationality from normative pressures, of effectiveness from ethics have been the battle cries of science since its inception. (1989:108)

And he feels that the situation is made worse by the distancing of means and ends that takes place in bureaucracy (1989:98). Bauman argues that the Holocaust was not the result of the activities of a minority of madmen, but that of an entire society united in a rationally justified and technologically empowered enterprise of isolating and murdering its Jewish population (1989:189). Jacques Ellul, whose theology follows Barth, has similar suspicions of technology and has written so extensively on this as to be frequently cited by sociologists of science.[19] Pannenberg never refers to the questions raised by these authors; he seems to be concerned only with the dimension of science that he can characterise in terms of rationalist epistemology.

---

18 A detailed debate on the implications of Gadamer's work for philosophy of science can be found in the exchange between Patrick Heelan and Joseph Kockelmans in Silverman (1991), where Kockelmans rejects the Rorty-like account offered by Heelan.

19 His major ideas are presented in *The Presence of the Kingdom* (recent English edition 1989), *The Technological Society* (1964).

I have raised questions about Pannenberg's desire for objectivity and rationality in epistemology. Having also noted his aversion to the inclusion of human action in theories of the formation of knowledge, in the next chapter I turn to his use of a major natural science, biology.

Chapter Three

Pannenberg and Biology

In the preceding chapter I have shown how Pannenberg modifies Gadamer's hermeneutical epistemology, stressing the status and knowledge content of statements in both science and theology. In this and the next two chapters, I shall examine Pannenberg's actual use of three areas of science. I shall evaluate it primarily by the internal standards of those sciences themselves, and secondarily in theological terms.

Humans can be considered in terms of their homologies with other animals, as individuals or in terms of their group interactions. Pannenberg takes all three approaches, and uses biology and genetics, psychology and the social sciences to illuminate his theological account of humanity. In this chapter, I shall consider Pannenberg's use of biology and genetics. As I noted in the first chapter of this study, Pannenberg refers back to the German speaking school of philosophical anthropology, developed by Scheler, Plessner and Gehlen, when he deals with human nature. In support of this approach, and contrasting it with the early behaviourist school of psychology, Pannenberg cites ethologists, particularly Konrad Lorenz and Eibl-Eibesfeldt, as supplying biological accounts of behaviour which can be appropriately applied to human beings. He also cites the work of Jacob von Uexküll in discussing the relation of the animal to its environment. Because of Pannenberg's fundamental dependence on these ideas, it is important to examine them in detail as science, and in their historical context. This turns out to have implications of Pannenberg's use of them.

Pannenberg gives his most detailed account of biology in *Anthropology in Theological Perspective*, in the first chapter. The biology he cites is also repeatedly adverted to as he develops other sections on the psychology of human development, the development of culture and language and the social nature of human beings. In view of the controversial nature of some of the material Pannenberg uses, I will deal in detail with his primary presentation of biological issues in connection with the concept of exocentricity, and discuss their use in other contexts separately.

Ethology, the theory that human behaviour is explainable in terms of instincts and drives, is a branch of biology that was fashionable in the early to middle part of the century, and was associated with groups in comparative zoology. It never gained more than peripheral importance in the English speaking world. Pannenberg justifies his choice of ethology as an appropriate explanatory system for human biology by reference to his perception of the philosophical background to biology.

He argues that behaviourism, which he appears to view as the only alternative to ethology, is influenced by British empiricism. This would, of course, be subject to Pannenberg's general objections to positivism. He perceives ethology, however, to be part of the Kantian tradition, in which all experience is claimed to be structured by pre-existing patterns. Pannenberg cites Lorenz's explanation of the role of the body in providing the structural function Kant anticipated, in the form of 'innate behavioural patterns' caused by innate drives.[1] This is noteworthy in that, as we have already seen, Pannenberg's epistemological attachment to hermeneutics owes little to Kant. He does not appear to be consistent at this point, and he does not evaluate the historical context of Lorenz, which might be important for a hermeneutical approach.

The behaviourism to which Pannenberg objects was an early school of psychology, which sought to study human behaviour entirely in terms of external phenomena, without reference to any subjective descriptions. Pannenberg is very critical of the classic behaviourists (1985:29). He cites the well known objections to classic behaviourism as a total explanation of human and animal activity. Such objections include behaviourism's inability to explain flexible behaviour (stimulus does not always produce the same response) and purposive integration of a range of behaviours (the subject as self-conducting). Pannenberg is not very concerned about the former, and much more concerned about preserving the concept of the human as self-conscious subject.

A number of issues arise here. Firstly, Pannenberg does not mention any other approaches to the study of human behaviour. In particular, learning and cognitive theory has been essential in the development of psychology as a science, in addition to areas such as gestalt psychology, physiological psychology, psychodynamics and social psychology. It is generally acknowledged in biology today that neither ethology, nor classic behaviourism gave adequate explanations of human learning, or of the flexibility of human behaviour. Ethology is effectively a very marginalised area of interest, and is rarely taught in any undergraduate course in biology in the UK today, for instance. Pannenberg's choice of it would be controversial if he were a biologist, and his omission of such enormous areas of modern psychology is really astonishing.[2] Similarly, even experimental psychology has advanced far beyond the confines of the early behaviourists, and it seems quite unreasonable to treat the subject as though it had not proceeded beyond the 1940s.

The second issue is that Pannenberg objects to the reductionism implicit in classic behaviourism. However, just as he does not distinguish between methodological and ontological reductionism in his discussions of philosophy of

1 Pannenberg notes that when Konrad Lorenz, the leading contemporary German student of behaviour, wrote a summary of his conception of behavioural research he entitled it 'The Innate Forms of Possible Experience'. (1985:31)

2 For example, the *Pelican History of Psychology* (ed. R. Thompson, 1968) lists eight schools of behavioural science in addition to behaviourism in the inter-war period.

science, so he does not make the distinction in his evaluation of experimental science (1985:29). All the biological sciences frequently resort to a temporary and admitted bracketing out of ontological considerations when faced with the construction of an explanatory system, as mentioned in the previous chapter. Psychology as a science is no exception, and Pannenberg should be much more precise in distinguishing between, on the one hand, specific philosophical claims made by particular individuals, and on the other, the general necessity of some methodological reductionism as part of all science.

The third significant issue raised by Pannenberg's choice of work in biology is that the work of both Konrad Lorenz and Jacob von Uexküll is controversial in an additional way. Both were active in Germany during the Third Reich, and both were sympathetic to the political racism current in that period. Both published biological works purporting to support, from an allegedly scientific position, the claim that the Aryan race was biologically definable and that serious negative effects would result from miscegenation with other, allegedly inferior races, including Gypsies and Jews. In the postwar period, as this material came to light, there was not only criticism of it on scientific grounds, but also extensive and polemical discussion about its political implications. Biologists today would make a most careful examination of any work by Lorenz that they wished to cite. Pannenberg does not mention these issues or problems, and in fact, as I will discuss further, he uses material originating in one of the most notorious and indefensible of the papers by Lorenz. The absence of any comment by Pannenberg on its context is most surprising.

In order to examine the use that Pannenberg makes of Lorenz and ethology, it will be necessary firstly to discuss its problems and status as biology.

Problems with the ethology of Lorenz and his school

Ethology invokes the existence of behavioural patterns due to a range of instinctive drives, which are said to permit the organism to respond to different environmental situations. The evidence for such patterns and drives comes from observations of animals, particularly birds. The observations were made under the same conditions of methodological reductionism as in other schools of psychology, which is to say, such concepts as intention were not invoked, but behaviour was described in external and 'objective' terms. The patterns of behaviour and drives are described as innate and the ethologists imply by this that they are genetically determined. Furthermore, it is assumed that presumptively homologous behavioural patterns in different species are caused by similar gene complexes. An unorthodox view of evolution is assumed, in that existing non-human species are seen as representing evolutionarily ancestral states, with humans as a 'high' point of evolution, and even within the human species, there are more or less 'advanced' genetic types. All of these features of ethology are vigorously disputed by other biologists. These four major areas of criticism, concerning the concept of drive, accuracy of observations of behaviour, the assumption of genetic determinism and the interpretation of evolution are summarised here.

The disputed existence of drives

Numerous physiologists have pointed out that there is little evidence for the existence of unstimulated behaviour or 'drives' as claimed by ethology.[3] Apart from hunger and eating, which can be argued to have a spontaneous onset when blood sugar drops, all other behaviours can be shown to be connected with external stimuli. Further, most behaviours are far more complex than allowed for by ethologists; for instance, there are biologically and physiologically separable kinds of aggression in animals which cannot therefore all spring from one drive. Many behaviours show change after altered response: i.e. they show learning, and this cannot be accounted for if drives are the primary determinant of behaviour.

Ethologists' observations of behaviour

There are repeated demonstrations in the biological literature that the experimental observations cited by ethologists are partial, or not substantiated by other data.[4] Several useful papers are collected together in Montague's book, *Man and Aggression*, (1973). For example, Helmuth criticises Lorenz for oversimplification of the evidence on comparative primate behaviour; not all studies show apes to be aggressive. Further, studies such as those of the Bushmen conflict; where Eibl-Eibesfeldt claimed to find aggressive behaviour, other authors did not. Eibl-Eibesfeldt also defined aggression imprecisely and included activities which other anthropologists do not recognise as aggression. Barnett (1967) disputes observations on density of bird distributions in relation to aggression; it has been suggested that this accounts for what is known as territoriality in birds. Montague (1973) also makes similar points about behaviour from fossil evidence of Australopithecus. A summary of a parallel critique by Crooke (1973) concentrates on aspects of territoriality. He makes the point that Lorenz rejects any possibility of learning different behaviour; there can be only sublimation or diversion of drives. His discussion is in the context of aggression, but the argument must apply to all behaviour if Lorenz is right about instinct and drives.

---

3 Lehrman (1953), Hinde (1974), Berkowitz (1969), Bandura (1977), Dewsbury (1978), M.S. Dawkins (1986).

4 Crooke (1970), Helmuth (1973), Barnett (1967), Gertz (1962).

The assumption of genetic determinism

This has been repeatedly criticised; a particularly famous paper by Lehrman (1953) provides an adequate summary. There have been repeated rejections of genetic determinism by major population and evolutionary geneticists.[5] Modern understandings of the nature of genes and DNA make it clear that the biochemical processes which lead to the construction of an organism must themselves involve interaction with the environment (as a source of chemical molecules if nothing else) throughout development. Gene action cannot take place without environmental action, and there is therefore actually no such thing as a purely 'genetically determined' character. The questions at stake in popular and political discussions of this kind are often actually about the degree of variability or plasticity of a character; we want to know if something can be easily changed.

Ethologists have often confused innate characteristics (i.e. those an organism has at birth), with characteristics which are allegedly 'genetically determined': by this is meant those that have little environmental plasticity. A simple example of an innate character that has little to do with the individual's genes would be the hearing damage caused by the *rubella* virus in utero. Children born after such an unfortunate infection have innate deafness, but this does not involve the genes and cannot be passed on to the next generation, and sadly it is not a 'plastic' character; it cannot be easily changed.

Montague's response to ethology summarises important points in relation to assumptions of genetic determinism by Lorenz. Montague (1973:11) restates the difficulty that extrapolation from animals to man is not in itself a necessarily valid procedure. Lorenz makes this extrapolation a feature of his method, and bases it on the assumption of genetic determination of animal behaviour. However, he never offers any evidence for this; for example, in *On Aggression* he says:

> Human behaviour ... is still subject to all the laws prevailing in all phylogenetically adapted instinctive behaviour. Of these laws we possess a fair amount of knowledge from studying the instincts of animals. (1966:237)

If this means that ducks have genes for paddling when put on water, and so we expect people to have them too, then we have a genetic hypothesis. Lorenz has never done any genetic studies, and the evidence is that genetic differences between species are considerable. Further, a pair of species that are thought to be relatively nearly related, for example, humans and guinea pigs, can still have surprising genetic differences leading to variations in biochemistry, physiology and anatomy which are not exhibited by other, more distantly related species. Even if we could

5 For example, Dobzhansky (1977), Thoday (1965), Lewontin et al. (1984).

show that ducks, or primates, did have a particular genetically determined behaviour, there is nothing about the mechanism of evolution which would allow us to predict whether or not humans would also have those genes. On the other hand, if Lorenz's 'laws of phylogenetically adapted instinctive behaviour' mean that ducks have nervous systems which respond to water by paddling, and people similarly have nervous systems, so we expect them to respond to water by paddling, then we have a hypothesis in comparative physiology, which fails very quickly because ducks also have a lot of differences from people, especially in their nervous systems. Lorenz, of course, has never used such an obviously unsuitable behaviour like paddling in his claims, but the structure of his arguments about aggression and other behaviour is exactly as I have outlined.

Helmuth (originally writing in German and therefore accessible to Pannenberg) restates the point that all behaviour is in the medium of the environment, and as this differs, so behaviours differ; they therefore cannot be 'genetically determined' in the naive sense. He suggests that in the context of Lorenz's claims about human aggression, the existence of Mennonites and similar groups disproves a simple theory of genetic determination of aggression as applied to humans. He favours learning (cultural reconditioning) as an alternative explanation of differing behaviours (Helmuth, 1973). He locates the significant difference between animals and humans in the symbolic use of language, following Cassirer. This permits the construction of 'alternative' worlds and new behaviours. Interestingly, this gives an account of what is specifically human without leaning on the inhibited instinct/openness to the world theories of philosophical anthropology.

Ethologists' explanations of evolution and race

Geneticists and others have repeatedly queried the understanding of evolution and race held by the ethologists.[6] The 'phylogenetic' assumptions of ethology assume that not only are characteristics genetically determined in a way that we know they cannot be, but that gene complexes presently causing given behaviours in existing animals have descended, unchanged, from a common ancestor to humans as well. Since the change of gene complexes is the essence of evolution, and given the enormous amount of genetic variation even within the human species it is extremely unlikely that such extensive genetic conservation could be the case. Some writers seem to suggest that existing animals represent ancestral forms themselves, which is even more unacceptable, since it requires the suspension of the evolutionary process in those cases. Further, human races are certainly not independent genetic entities; it is actually impossible to produce a satisfactory definition of a human race within population genetics. This is because the small number of visible

6 For example, Lehrman (1953), Dobzhansky (1977), Eisenberg (1972). A good discussion of racism in the history of genetics may be found in Kevles (1986).

differences between human races, and the superficial similarity of members of the same race, mask an enormous amount of invisible biochemically based genetic difference between all human beings. Members of the same race differ by around 30% of their genes on average, and there is relatively little additional difference between members of different races.[7] However, one of the least satisfactory aspects of the German ethologists is their ignorance of population genetics, and their association with theories of race that predate and are not compatible with genetics.

The association of Lorenz with racism

Many authors have raised this problem. Boulding (1973) points out the connection between Lorenz's writings and the racism of his period. Boulding makes clear that Lorenz's comparative method uses the assumption of genetic determination, and the assumption of linear descent of humans from present animals. As shown above, the former is unwarranted, and the latter shows a complete failure of understanding of the branching nature of evolutionary patterns, i.e. divergent as well as convergent evolution. Boulding is dismissive, referring to the views of Lorenz as 'scientific humbug'.[8] Eisenberg also offers a strong, negative critique of Lorenz; this is discussed further below. While authors vary in the degree of comment they make on the political dimension, there is general agreement among biologists that the explanatory powers of the Lorenz school's theory are very limited, and they promote some false conceptions of science that have very negative social consequences.

The implications of problems with ethology as science for Pannenberg's use of it

Pannenberg does not appear to be aware of any of these difficulties. This cannot be because of the dates of the material. There were many general critical papers in international genetics throughout the fifties, sixties and seventies; there is no doubt that these should have been available to Pannenberg. Why does he ignore the

7 Lewontin (1984), Futuyma (1986), Bird Stewart (1987).

8 He says: 'We have seen in the Nazi movement how appallingly dangerous a pseudo science can be in the legitimation of an absurd and evil system. I am not suggesting that either Lorenz or Ardrey is a racist theorist like Gobineau or Houston Chamberlain. However, one could imagine their superficially attractive neo-social-Darwinism applied to very ill uses indeed, and the fact that it is scientific humbug does not unfortunately detract from its attractiveness.' (1973:175)

problem? It may be that the hierarchical atmosphere in the German academic world delayed a proper dissemination of modern genetics in the postwar period, and that Pannenberg was ignorant of the technical problems with Lorenz's work. Pannenberg's own methodological approach, ascribing objectivity to the scientific statement, disposes him to this kind of difficulty more than others and leads to a conservative rather than a critical approach to perceived tradition. Pannenberg's rejection of specific philosophies of knowledge for different subjects may have led him to underestimate the role played by the scientific community in evaluating its own body of knowledge. But recognising the context of interpretation is central to any hermeneutical approach. Ironically, an analysis of modern genetics using the approach of Kuhn would certainly have identified the ethologists as holding to a paradigm that was controversial or marginal.

For whatever reason, Pannenberg sees no problem with Lorenz's views on innate behaviour and drive. He argues that Jacob von Uexküll had similar views. Pannenberg refers to von Uexküll's view that the environment of an organism is not to be considered in terms of its general surroundings (*Umgebung*) but in terms of the set of features that its innate drives and instincts permit it to react to (*Umwelt*). This was set out in early work of von Uexküll (1921). This means that the organism's capacity to react is limited to innate pathways, and by implication, that capacity for learning etc. is absent or limited by these pathways. Yet again, the theory as stated implies a genetic determinism of behaviour, and a misunderstanding of the nature of human evolution. It contains the seeds of biological determinism which emerged in some later work by von Uexküll. This is most painfully obvious in his *Staatsbiologie* (1933) which contains a biological defence of racist political theory.[9] Pannenberg does not discuss the implicit genetic determinism of this work, nor the problem of biological determinism in general, nor the political issues surrounding it. Yet he objects to behaviourist approaches to psychology on the grounds that they are ultimately reductionist, and nothing more reductionist can be found than genetically deterministic theories! He avoids the problem by asserting that human innate behavioural patterns are 'rudimentary' and so do not actually influence human behaviour very much. This is an amazing manipulation of what most ethologists claim, and they would repudiate Pannenberg's interpretation. But he offers as biological evidence for this an argument from Lorenz, which is of some interest. It concerns the apparent reduction in drives in domestic animals and the potential parallel in humans whose civilisation may be said to be a form of domestication. Pannenberg says:

> Konrad Lorenz, who observed ... a reduction of instinctual mechanisms in domesticated animals as a consequence of their domestication, sought to interpret the analogous situation in human behaviour as the result of a 'self-domestication'. (1985:34)

9 Müller-Hill (1988), notes that von Uexküll was the literary executor of H.S. Chamberlain, an important racial theorist of the immediate pre-Nazi period.

In this case, innate behavioural patterns will be weakened and made susceptible to modification by exposure to human culture. Pannenberg wants to use this as a further argument for the inhibition of innate behavioural patterns by socialisation and culture. But this is not quite what Lorenz intended.

Pannenberg does not cite the original paper, and does not mention the context of Lorenz's argument, which is that domestication and civilisation will cause 'degeneration' (Lorenz's term) of behaviour patterns because mutations in the putative determining genes will not be eliminated by natural selection (Lorenz 1940). This is offered as a reason for prohibiting marriages between human racial groups, and as a justification for the Nazi laws preventing marriage between Aryan Germans and others, which had been enacted at the time of Lorenz's paper. Surely Pannenberg must be aware of the inadequacy of this as biology? It certainly has been criticised by many biologists[10] and it seems a most inappropriate set of ideas in the context of Pannenberg's enterprise. A brief extract as translated by Eisenberg makes this clear:

> Our species specific sensitivity to the beauty and ugliness of members of our species is intimately connected with the symptoms of degeneration, caused by domestication, which threaten our race ... Usually a man of high value is disgusted with special intensity by slight symptoms of degeneracy in men of the other race ... The selection for toughness, heroism, social utility ... must be accomplished by some human institution if mankind, in default of selective factors, is not to be ruined by domestication-induced degeneracy. The racial idea as the basis of our state has already accomplished much in this respect. (Lorenz, 1940, cited in Eisenberg, 1972)

Eisenberg's response may be polemical but is typical of the reactions of many biologists.[11] He says:

> Lorenz found it possible to write, in 1940, that the effects of civilisation on human beings parallel those of domestication in animals (8). In domesticated animals, he argued, degenerative mutations result in the loss of species specific releaser mechanisms responding to innate schemata that govern mating patterns and that serve in nature to maintain the purity of the stock. Similar phenomena are said to be an inevitable by-product of civilisation unless the state is vigilant ... The wild extrapolations from domestication to civilisation, from ritualised animal courtship patterns to human behaviour, from species to races, are so gross and unscientific, the conclusions so redolent of concentration camps, that further commentary should be superfluous. (Eisenberg, 1972: 57)

---

10 Notably Lehrman (1953), Eisenberg (1972).

11 For a discussion of the history of Lorenz, see Muller-Hill (1988), Proctor (1988), Kalikow (1976, 1978, 1983).

These postwar biologists react extremely critically to the use made by Lorenz of his claim that human civilisation parallels the domestication of animals, and reduces innate behavioural schemata. Surely Pannenberg must be aware of the political implications and history of the argument he cites? His epistemological position would not be helped even if there were no such complications. His need to protect human freedom by emphasising the reduction or inhibition of instinct in humans as opposed to other animals runs counter to the basis of ethology. It is the case that Pannenberg's conclusion would be very heavily disputed by any of the Lorenz school, whose whole thesis is that innate behavioural patterns and drives do exist, are not rudimentary and do explain human behaviour.

Pannenberg's assimilation of biology to German philosophical anthropology – the misunderstanding of neoteny

Having thus interpreted and, it must be said, rearranged some concepts in ethology, Pannenberg builds on it to show how the ideas of Scheler, Plessner and Gehlen can be related to his modification of the theories of the ethologists. Scheler is regarded as having effectively originated 'philosophical anthropology' in his book, *Die Stellung des Menschen im Kosmos*, first published in 1928. The principles underlying this philosophical reflection on the nature of the human are said to be that, firstly, humans can only be interpreted in terms that encompass their bodily nature; secondly, the behaviour of humans must be understood as the expression of a subjective centre (as opposed to early behaviourism); thirdly and lastly, humans are qualitatively different from all other animals. According to Pannenberg, Scheler drew on Husserl's method and Von Uexküll's biology, and attempted to reunite body and spirit in anthropology, by correlating the spiritual dimension of human being with bodily factors (Pannenberg, 1985:35). He identified the human capacity for 'openness to the world' as particularly important in this respect. This is significant for Pannenberg, who wishes to avoid an appeal to the supernatural, and must therefore find a bodily basis for his anthropology. But it also meets his desire to avoid reductionism, because Scheler also sees bodily drives as reduced or inhibited, and this is what makes humans open to the world. For Scheler, human behaviour differs from other animals essentially in its plasticity; humans are not merely vehicles for innate behavioural patterns, but can modify their responses at will. This capacity to apparently inhibit instinctual responses is seen by Scheler as the reason for human 'openness to the world'. Scheler locates this capacity outside of the body; it is a function of the spirit, and Scheler asserts that this spirit acts externally to the biological process of evolution. Pannenberg claims that Scheler implies that spirit originates in a direct act of God (1985:36).

Additionally, Pannenberg uses the ideas of Plessner, who also contributed to the development of philosophical anthropology, but who avoided metaphysics. Plessner specified 'exocentricity' as the key feature of humanity. He saw human self-consciousness as arising from an ability to be oriented outside of the self, and regarded this as a developmental stage reached by humans, but not by other animals. He did not offer any account of how such a developmental step occurred. Pannenberg is critical of Plessner at this point, arguing that in fact his concept of exocentricity overlaps with Scheler's use of 'spirit' (1985:37). Pannenberg also thinks that Plessner does not properly specify the context of exocentricity in the sense of the relation between the inner human and the outside world.

To supply the apparent deficiencies in Scheler and Plessner, Pannenberg turns to the work of Gehlen, who offers a third, related approach to these problems. Gehlen wishes to avoid some of the issues which Pannenberg identifies as difficulties. Gehlen is committed to the position of human uniqueness, but does not wish to admit a metaphysical explanation for it. Like Scheler and Plessner, he sees humans as fundamentally undetermined, having a freedom to create their world by chosen interaction with their environment. Gehlen views humans as having 'reduced' or limited instincts compared to other animals.

He does so by finding a biological explanation for the apparent inhibition of instinctive behaviour that characterises human activity. He argues that humans are born with undeveloped instincts and incompletely formed innate behavioural patterns, so that they cannot respond spontaneously to the environment, but must become socialised to overcome this hiatus in response. His explanation of this is that humans are evolutionarily 'deficient beings'. He adduces Bolk's description of the phenomenon of neoteny, the observation that certain adult human organs have superficial similarities to foetal organs in other species. Gehlen interpreted this to indicate that humans have been 'inhibited in evolution'. He supposed that humans have organs that are actually in only a foetal state compared to other animals and therefore cannot be capable of fully formed physiologically instinctive responses. Humans are then born 'prematurely' before development has come even to its potentially limited conclusion. The human is consequently thought to be a 'tabula rasa', and requires socialisation, as perceptions of the environment do not release an adequate innate behavioural response. Instead, there is a hiatus between stimulus and what must be a socially learned response.

Pannenberg adduces these arguments in support of his modification of the ethologists' position; he supposes that human drives and instincts are not fully functional because of the 'prematurity' of the human infant. But Gehlen's use of Bolk depends on a naive misunderstanding of evolution; human organs cannot be presumed to be immature in comparison with other primates. They are certainly different, and are subject to different sets of evolutionary pressures. There is no biological support for Gehlen's suggestions, which are rooted in a biological hypothesis which has long been discarded.[12] The anatomical similarities between

12 See, for instance, Gould (1980: 63-75).

adult human organs and foetal animal organs are often superficial. The physiological functions of the human organs are far more extensive and complex than those of the animals. The physical resemblance may well represent some type of what is referred to as convergent evolution.

Convergent evolution is said to occur when different organisms develop superficially similar features, usually in response to selection pressures from similar environmental components, even though the organisms are in quite separate evolutionary lineages. A good example would be the tails of sharks and whales. Any large body being propelled through sea water has problems steering, and a movable device which alters water flow at the rear is capable of influencing the direction of the object. Hence ships have tillers and water creatures have various tails. Possession of a tail that will be effective in steering confers ability to survive; other things being equal, the more effective the tail, the greater the survival probability. Since sharks and whales are in the same environment, an efficient tail is likely to be superficially physically similar on either animal. In other words, they look the same, but the cellular changes in their development are different, and whales are not fish; they are mammals. The whale's tail does not mean that the whale is in any way retarded or at an ancestral fish evolutionary stage. Equally, the shark may be anatomically or physiologically simpler than the whale, but it is not any less evolved; sharks have been through as much evolution as whales.

Gehlen goes further, and conflates the idea of neoteny with the 'physiological prematurity' thesis of Portmann. This relates to the observation that compared to other primates, humans are born with less well developed brain tissue, more of the developmental process taking place after birth than in other animals. Again, Gehlen argues that this means that the infant human must be dependent on the social world to order the stimuli it receives and structure its behaviour, since the nervous system is not completely developed, and could not therefore supply appropriate instinctive responses. This is also an extremely inadequate argument in basic biology. Capacity to produce instinctive responses is not associated with the complex parts of brain structure which develop last, but with the parts of the nervous system which develop first. Even a foetus *in utero* will exhibit instinctive responses to light and touch. Further, although the newborn human will experience further development of the nervous system after birth, at birth its existing nervous system is already infinitely more complex and sophisticated than that of any other animal. Pannenberg cites this biology without showing any awareness of its deficiencies, or the alternative explanations that it might suggest. The obvious conclusion to be drawn from the extreme sophistication of the human nervous system is that there must be some human ability connected to the extra functions that the human nervous system exhibits, that other animals do not possess. The human capacity for flexible learning is the ability that does not appear in the discussions of the ethologists, and it would serve Gehlen much better as a basis for the independence humans show relative to animals.

It is notable that Pannenberg focuses on Gehlen's use of 'hiatus' between perception and impulse in describing this (1985:39). This situation, of hiatus, or free space between perception and innate behavioural response, could just as well be postulated between stimulus and response on a behaviourist model, and would lead to the same conclusions. Many, much more sophisticated, accounts of the plasticity of human behaviour exist.[13] Pannenberg's purpose could as well be achieved with other models, particularly in cognitive psychology. He does not need to espouse the ideas of drive and innate behaviour characteristic of the ethologists. He certainly does not need to take up incoherent accounts of zoology such as the misapplication of neoteny. His handling of this material displays a distance from the field of zoology, and an absence of awareness of context, which are startling in one so apparently committed to a hermeneutical path. This is the more so in that Pannenberg prefers Gehlen, and argues for his importance, while acknowledging that there have been critics of Gehlen (1985:40). The criticism he refers to includes that by Portmann, who as a biologist knows that his findings do not imply that humans are in any sense deficient, and who asserts the points I have made about the mistaken assumptions concerning neoteny made by Gehlen. Pannenberg appears to be simply undisturbed by this.

Pannenberg prefers Gehlen's anthropology to Scheler's, because he regards it as supported by biology. This is interesting in view of the methodological priority he gives to philosophy, and unfortunate in view of the critiques of that biology which I have cited. Above all, Pannenberg is seeking to buttress his view of humanity as innately or structurally 'exocentric'. Pannenberg relates Gehlen's view of the 'hiatus' between perception and reaction to Scheler's 'inhibition' of instinct, arguing that the difference between them lies only in the basis for the phenomenon. Scheler invoked an external spirit, whereas Gehlen does not need to, having apparently located the 'hiatus' in the biology of the human organism itself. This has further consequences for Gehlen's philosophy. Because of their lack of pregiven behaviour, humans have developed language and culture to provide a context for action. Pannenberg views this as the key to Gehlen's ideas; humans are seen as 'acting beings' (1989:39). Gehlen sees humans as acting to create, in language, a universe of models which then enables them to order and manage the complex stimuli of their environment. Where Scheler sees the activity that is characteristically human as depending on (external) spirit, Gehlen sees it as arising as a compensatory mechanism from basic human biology. But Pannenberg does not refer to the critique of Gehlen by Habermas, for instance, or other philosophers.[14] Pannenberg again demonstrates the

---

13 For instance, the cognitive psychiatric schools such those of Frankl (1987) or Rogers (1942), learning theory such as Hebb (1949) & Deutsch (1960), and so on.

14 It is worth including Bubner's assessment of Gehlen for comparison: 'Culture creates, according to Gehlen, a second world of artificial objectivity in the form of *institutions* ... The nature of man makes the artificial products of culture necessary ... The anthropological foundation of culture relativizes, as a further consequence, the

selectivity that he uses in detaching particular aspects of a body of work and applying them to his argument irrespective of the implications they may have held for the original author.

Drives and exocentricity – Eibl-Eibesfeldt and Plessner

However, Pannenberg does acknowledge Plessner's philosophical objection to Gehlen's view of an unlimited human 'openness to the world', partly because this involves an even stronger tying of anthropology to biology. Plessner's objection is that human experience of the world is itself partial and limited, and cannot therefore support the radically unqualified openness to the world postulated by Gehlen. For humanity, everything is not possible. Pannenberg cites the behavioural work of Eibl-Eibesfeldt as supporting Plessner in this. This is a further restatement of the claims of ethology. Eibl-Eibesfeldt asserted that humans do have definite innate behaviours, based on his observations of infants crying, smiling, sucking and similar behaviours. He claims that these innate behaviour patterns, while not setting limits to freedom, do determine the starting point for human activity. Again, Pannenberg does not refer to the scholarly evaluation of Eibl-Eibesfeldt's work, which is controversial, to say the least. The critique from biology I have already referred to. Social scientists are no happier. In a relevant symposium, Thomas Luckmann (of whom Pannenberg is aware since he uses Luckmann's work later) comments:

> ... I find Eibl-Eibesfeldt's exposition of the key concepts of ethology instructive, the summary of his far ranging empirical work on the universality of basic expressive movements and certain face to face rituals wholly admirable, and the programmatic statement of his views on what he calls cultural evolution and on the presumed selective pressures operating on cultural patterns, sufficiently wrong headed to provoke me into resolute opposition. I do not believe that anyone who has dealt systematically with the complexities of social organization and cultural process in history could accept such a view of 'cultural evolution'. The notions of selective pressure, reproductive success, group fitness and the like cannot be transferred, without danger of simplification as well as confusion, from one explanatory level to another. The social sciences have been blessed by misleadingly vague biological analogies before! (1979:58)

Pannenberg, however, is happy to accept Eibl-Eibesfeldt as providing further biological support for his own conception of human being. Pannenberg sees the

---

widespread over-valuation of history. However unremittingly history brings about changes, the essence of human beings changes little with it ... From this conservative position, Gehlen has produced penetrating diagnoses of modern civilization. He has carried on a *critique of culture* in opposition to the popular Rousseauist version ... His provocative slogan "Back to culture!" has been brilliantly opposed by Habermas in the name of progress and enlightenment.' (1981:211)

human as primarily activated by biological drives, which are modulated by an essentially human orientation to or dependence on the external world. This attitude of 'openness to the world' describes, not so much a given state, as a process of self creation and self realisation, which is not necessarily reducible to individual human action alone.

Ethology and self-consciousness

Biology is significant for Pannenberg as he develops his anthropology in other areas. He refers repeatedly to the work of the ethologists, and also to other aspects of biology. His dependence on ethology is initially and primarily in his explanation of human openness to the world, or exocentricity. However, he uses examples, usually from ethology, to support various observations on self-consciousness, sin, culture and language.

In his attempt, discussed previously in Chapter One, to harmonise the developmental view of humanity presented by Herder with modern philosophical anthropology, Pannenberg tries to reinforce the argument with biology. In particular, he argues for the need of religious context to explain the origin of self-consciousness. In this case, a non-reductionist biological account of the human is required. Pannenberg cites Eibl-Eibesfeldt as allowing for the modification of innate behaviours in response to cultural change (1985:61). Pannenberg must of course make room for the possibility of self-transcendence and cultural change among humans. But this is one of the weakest aspects of Eibl-Eibesfeldt's approach, provoking responses such as that previously quoted from Luckmann. Pannenberg also alludes to the space created by the inhibition of immediate instinctive responses as making room for what Konrad Lorenz calls 'fulguration' (1985:61). In doing this, humans can distance themselves from their own situation, unlike other animals. But the evidence for such distinctions between humans and animals is weak, and in the case of ethology, all such suggested modifications of drives emerge as responses to critique. They are not part of the basic picture.

Pannenberg's restatement of a picture of humanity as depending on the self-conscious inhibition of drive is given in the context of the question of self-consciousness in humans. What is the basis of human self-consciousness and how may it be described philosophically? Pannenberg is committed to a position in which a religious context is necessary to fully account for self-consciousness. He therefore cannot accept a reductionist account of human biology. However, he could as well use accounts of neurophysiology and cognitive psychology which describe humans as making choices based on learning. There is no need at all to assume theories of drive and inhibited instinct.

Ethology and sin

Similarly, Pannenberg is committed to the Christian tradition that as created, humanity is in itself good. In Pannenberg's account of sin, he asserts that the material, or biological, is not innately evil. It is noteworthy that Pannenberg cites Lorenz as providing supporting biology for this. He repeats Lorenz's famous comment that aggression is only 'so-called' evil. Lorenz claims that properly speaking, aggression is a desirable instinct that is required for the survival of the species; it is only when humans find themselves in the allegedly unnatural conditions of civilisation that they become 'domesticated' and the instinct leads to inappropriate behaviour. Pannenberg agrees with this, and traces the origins of the idea back to Freud's concept of the death wish (1985:143). Here Pannenberg presents Lorenz as correcting his mentor, Freud. In a footnote, he identifies the 'many others' who support Lorenz in 'the Freudian school' as Gehlen and Eibl-Eibesfeldt. Here Pannenberg presents two problems. The first is that he does not face the critique from other biologists showing that Lorenz's understanding of aggression as a single behaviour arising from instinct is untenable. Secondly he seems unaware that a view of humanity as morally neutral in itself is widely held, if not universal, among biologists. Freud's conclusions would be seen as philosophical by the present generation of behavioural scientists, and therefore simply as belonging to an area in which they claimed no expertise. However, Pannenberg does cite Montague, without referring at all to his extensive critique of Lorenz! He takes Montague to task for claiming that the Christian doctrine of original sin is an example of a doctrine of innate evil, but quite amazingly, does not refer to any of the evidence in Monatgue's book against the general theories of Lorenz, which I summarised earlier.

Curiously, it is in dealing with the problem of evil and sin that Pannenberg himself demonstrates that his argument can be as well supported by accounts of human biology that do not depend on the concept of drive or instinct. Pannenberg wishes to have an account of the psychological development of humans, and leans heavily on the psychoanalytic school which introduced serious thinking on the subject. However, that school tends to see aggression as connected with the frustration of the wishes of the ego. Pannenberg has some criticism of the frustration hypothesis, but concludes that it is significant in that it connects the issue of agression to the question of the development of personality (1985:149). In fact, the reasons for the emergence of work on frustration included many of the observations about aggression that make Lorenz's theory unsustainable, particularly those on flexible responses.

Pannenberg concludes his section on sin with reflections on human responsibility and self transcendence The issue is that if sin is not radical evil in itself, but a perversion of love itself from its proper object, God, to the self, then aggression has to be accounted for in these terms. Pannenberg's theological account of the image of God in humanity as a destiny of humans being called out of themselves to fellowship with God requires a compatible version of human psychology which allows humans to realise their identity with reference to what is beyond themselves. This conclusion, however, is completely at variance with the whole tenor of Lorenz's view of humanity, which is not of humans as developing and constructing themselves, but as carriers of pre-existing impulses which have to be ordered and restrained.

The only reference to a significant problem for ethology, the existence of cathexis and love, is made when Pannenberg is trying to provide biological support for the account of human development given by the psychoanalytic school. A crucial feature of this is the role of trust which is the initial and basic response of the infant human. Pannenberg claims the support of Eibl-Eibesfeldt's observation of behaviour patterns for this (1985:227). The reference is to a late work (1974), *Love and Hate*, which represents a considerable modification of the ethologists' position. Love was not recognised as a classic drive (because it is not observable in animals or humans as an appropriate innate behaviour pattern). Pannenberg does not refer to this inconsistency.

Ethology and culture

The random nature of Pannenberg's grasp of biology is further demonstrated by his use of bird behaviour in his development of the concept of culture. Here Pannenberg is looking for support for his contention that culture has its roots in play as representation and game. He begins by citing Lorenz on the investigative behaviour of young birds, which is claimed to show behavioural flexibility in curiosity, and thus to represent play. It is argued by Lorenz that such behaviour in young animals disappears as they mature, whereas humans retain the capacity as adults. Pannenberg sees this as another type of neoteny (1985:323). The reference is to a late work of Lorenz, *Behind the mirror: A search for a natural history of human knowledge* (1977). This is another totally inappropriate use of the concept of neoteny. There is no evidence whatsoever to suggest that adult human play behaviour is physiologically or psychologically describable as juvenile in contrast to other animals. Adult human neurophysiology is characteristically adult; the hormonal environment and biochemistry is adult. The behavioural analogies between adult humans and young animals are here stretched too far. Lorenz's argument is unaccepted in psychology and human sciences in general, but Pannenberg does not appear to know that.

There are less controversial uses of Lorenz's work; for instance, Pannenberg cites Lorenz on the role of inspiration in children's play (1985:325). This is less problematic, since it does not depend on inappropriate comparisons with animals. However, Pannenberg's overall biological foundation for his view of humanity is a frequent reiteration of the basic concepts characteristic of ethology. He repeats the incorrect conclusions made from comparisons between humans and other animals by ethologists. For instance, in his discussion of the dependence of culture on the emergence of language, Pannenberg argues that language and reason are characteristic of humans alone in the animal kingdom. He presents again his argument that human exocentricity is biologically determined, and concludes that culture must result from that since humans have a biological need for social order. He states:

> Language and reason are specific to the human being as a biological entity. But in the final analysis, the same can be said of culture ... since human drives with their nonspecialized openness to the world and their exceptional dependence on the security given by society need direction from a cultural order that transcends the world of nature. (1985:339)

This is a good example of Pannenberg's confusion about biology. Firstly, it is not true that only humans have reason; other primates show elementary reason. Secondly, it is not true that humans have 'drives'; as previously argued, human behaviour has been shown always to be physiologically responsive. Thirdly, humans have not always lived in complex societies, and survived perfectly well, as do animals, without 'cultural values', in the past. Therefore we have need of additional material to explain the development of culture over time. I do not think that Pannenberg is attempting to present a sociobiological argument for the appearance of culture. Sociobiology would claim, firstly, that there is genetic determination of all those elements required for the development of values in humans; secondly, that having culture is beneficial to the survival of those with a genetic disposition to it. Therefore culture has evolved by natural selection. But there is no foundation for the first supposition at all. The second supposition, that culture is inevitably beneficial for survival, is not proven – and some of the most cultured civilisations have perished – and the overall argument is not accepted in modern genetics. I think that Pannenberg's argument is different; he wants to show that the development of culture, while explainable in non-supernatural terms, is part of the collective movement of humans to their destiny with God, a kind of realised eschatology. But he has not been precise enough in his choice of biology to support this.

Evolution and language

As part of the same argument, Pannenberg considers in detail the fact that most animals have no language, but some primates have elementary signalling systems, and humans have fully developed language. He observes:

> The phylogenetic problem of the origins of language makes clear the extent to which the emergence of language from initial intelligent contacts with the environment leads us to the relation between language and religion. A discussion of this theme must start with

> the question of the peculiar nature of linguistic communication among human beings as compared with prelinguistic forms of communication in the animal world and especially among the primates. (1985:352)

But here again, he confuses the methods of comparative biology with phylogenetics. It cannot be assumed that the gradation in characteristics between presently observed life forms reflects increasing evolutionary complexity, and therefore genetic determination of the characters involved.

All observed life forms have undergone the same amount of evolution from common ancestors, but in different directions. For instance, the great apes will have lost some previously possessed genes which would otherwise have been held in common with present humans. They will also have accumulated different mutations not present in humans, and vice versa. Without an understanding of the specific genes, biochemistry and physiology of a character, a phylogenetic conclusion, that is, a conclusion about differentiation in gene pools between two groups, cannot be drawn. We know almost nothing about genetic variation as it affects human language. In fact, the conclusion Pannenberg wants to draw is not, I think, phylogenetic anyway. His point is that as primates can be taught language, although not naturally using it, to express some kind of thought, then it follows that thought is logically prior to language, and not vice versa. Here, as in other places, Pannenberg would have done better to avoid complicating his argument with incorrect biology.

Ethology and the family

Pannenberg fares no better when it comes to discussing the potential biological dimensions of the family as a human institution. Again, in attempting to provide some biological basis for the need for culture and socialisation, he modifies the ethologists' characterisation of human sexuality by suggesting that this involves the 'blending' of drives (1985:428). One of the more unsatisfactory features of the theory of drives is that it does not explain the different priority people can give to different behaviours at different times. If drives are to be 'blended' then they must do so according to some physiological order of priority, but human sexual behaviour is so plastic that this is clearly not the case. Pannenberg is obliged to combine in one paragraph the assertion of human adherence to 'preprogrammed' behaviour and the assertion that human behaviour is 'much less rigidly fixed' than in other animals, both made by Eibl-Eibesfeldt.[15] This really illustrates the difficulties Pannenberg gets into by first accepting an extremely determinist biology and then

---

15 1985:428, footnote 60.

having to modify it in order to allow for human integrity and responsibility. Pannenberg links this with the argument that because human sexual behaviour is not confined to a mating season, as in some animals, then the putative sex drive is ever present in all activity (1985:428). But many psychologists and all physiologists would disagree; Freud may have stressed the sexualisation of human life, but the biochemistry of eating, for instance, is different from that of sexual activity. That connections between the two can be made is obvious in a culture that has Haagen Daz ice cream, but the connections are not dictated by biology.

There is only one significant reference where Pannenberg seems to acknowledge a conflict between the ethologists' account of human behaviour and what might be accepted as part of the general canon of knowledge in that area. This concerns the issue of *gestalt* perception, and Pannenberg accepts that this cannot be explained in terms of innate behavioural patterns.[16] He cites Piaget's comments on this, and further attempts to deal with a conflict between Lorenz and Piaget on the question of imitative behaviour. Lorenz claimed that this is peculiar to humans; Piaget notes (as have many others) that it is also found in other primates. Pannenberg's solution is to suggest that Lorenz uses a narrower definition of what constitutes imitation than Piaget. Why is Pannenberg so sensitive here when he has ignored devastating critiques of Lorenz elsewhere? It may be that Piaget's observations on the development of human thought and language are too important for Pannenberg's general theme for there to be any unresolved dissonances, but the points made here do not represent significant portions of that argument. The explanation is not obvious.

Evolution and human origin

Given the stress laid on genetic determination by the ethologists, it is interesting to see how Pannenberg deals with the theory of evolution itself. He does so only in the context of the theological tradition of the fall of Adam. Pannenberg uncompromisingly declares that evolutionary biology gives a reliable historical account of the beginnings of humanity, that this is incompatible with the story of the fall of Adam, and that theologies based on that should be abandoned.[17] This is interesting, because he does not give such an epistemological priority to science anywhere else. It may well be because this is one of the few areas in biology to have an explicitly historical and concrete character.

---

16 1985:354, footnote 107.

17 'As a historical claim about the beginnings of human history, the idea that there was an original union of humankind with God which was lost through a fall into sin is incompatible with our currently available scientific knowledge about the historical beginnings of the race. This being the case, we should renounce artificial attempts to rescue traditional theological formulas; one such attempt is the idea of an origin that is supposedly nonhistorical.' (1985:57)

In conclusion, there are likely to be extensive problems for Pannenberg as a consequence of his use of ideas of drives and instinct. His underlying biological assumptions seem to supply the force in the concept of 'exocentricity'. Wherever Pannenberg uses this (and much of his argument depends on it, since his theological anthropology is basic to his view of society and politics) it is in the sense of an active orientation. Internal movement to the outward is implied, and 'unfinished' drives are the source of the dynamics. At the same time, drive-induced behaviour has a negative implication; it is 'animal', sexual or violent. This becomes interesting in the context of Pannenberg's theological concentration on the importance of sin in his anthropology, and his omission of the implications of creation for theological anthropology. Has he unwittingly given a negative cast to his theology by his adoption of particular (and objectionable) theories in biology? Or has he selected the biology because it fits in with his theological presuppositions? I will argue that as with the areas of science to be discussed in other chapters, the latter is the case. Pannenberg's epistemologically and theologically rationalist agenda drives him to a Procrustean methodology, in which theory is made to fit by pragmatic amputations. In doing this, he is oblivious to the social and political context of the scientific ideas selected, however unsuitable they may turn out to be.

Chapter Four

Science and the Person

In Chapter One, I showed that Pannenberg's basic approach to theological anthropology stresses the importance of his theological understanding of humanity as exocentric being, called to a destiny. On the one hand, I shall argue that his use of psychology is limited by this orientation, and to that extent, to be criticised. Thus he sees the intra-human relationship, the structure and function of human consciousness as a key area, which he wishes to defend from reductionist philosophies. He does not examine the contributions of psychology to the study of inter-human relationships, or the cognitive psychologies dealing with change and development. On the other hand, his epistemological agenda, as indicated in Chapter Two, requires the establishment of a hermeneutical-philosophical ground for concepts in psychology. It is especially important for him to deal with the problems raised by idealist conceptions of the self.[1] His approach to this is a serious attempt to deal with the philosophical issues behind the concept of human identity in postmodernity, and is unrivalled in contemporary theology. Not surprisingly, therefore, his theological engagement with psychology is very different from other contemporary approaches, whether Continental or Anglo-Saxon. Examples such as those of Moltmann (1974) or, for an English example, McFadyen (1990) show much less of an apologetic intent at the philosophical level, and much more of a creative interaction with the political and social, as well as an awareness of contemporary practical psychology. In contrast, Pannenberg devotes enormous effort to a very thorough philosophical grounding of the concepts of self, ego and self-consciousness, and does not deal with the psychology of human social relationships at all. His choice of psychological theory reflects this.

Pannenberg's most extensive account of his view on psychology is given in Chapters Four, Five and Six in *Anthropology in Theological Perspective* (1985). I shall discuss this in detail, because it contains explanations and connections between ideas not elaborated in his other writings, particularly in connection with his thought on the psychological sciences. In this work, Pannenberg strives to preserve a concept of essential humanity as something developed in each individual, but not possessed as a state or fixed structure. It is seen as dependent on the outside world of the individual, but is internally oriented to an external goal. He

1 For an account of the metaphysical background to his position, see the comments by Schwöbel (1997:187).

rejects positivist and materialist accounts of the human psyche, in order to protect the rationality and responsibility of the individual. Arguments that might make the self illusory, or the human a social puppet, are vigorously criticised. In pursuing this, he leans heavily on the psychoanalytic schools of psychology. His key themes are self, identity, self-transcendence, destiny, alienation, sin, guilt and death. Pannenberg does not rely much on theology of creation in his anthropology, and spends little time discussing the positive possibilities of humanity. From his theological standpoint, this may seem hardly necessary, since humanity is empowered by and included under the Lordship of God. However, it leads to a picture of humanity which is one sided by contemporary standards. The most obvious omission from his discussion of psychology is any of the literature on the positive human relationships. He does not discuss the psychological foundations of love, or community, although he occasionally refers to them as essential phenomena. Indeed, he is concerned to promote the importance of rationality as the foundation of human psychic structure, and the emotions are dealt with only insofar as they may be argued to contribute to that. Issues problematic for the promotion of the rational, such as forgiveness and reconciliation, are not mentioned.

However, in his comments on human consciousness in the more recent *Systematic Theology*, he gives further theological foundations for his concerns. He introduces an argument for the action of the Holy Spirit as the 'infinite ground of being' within which human awareness of self and other develops, and he argues that the human rational perception of the other involves a participation in the Trinitarian self distinction of the eternal Son from the Father. Thus he presents human reason as dependent on the Spirit for this self-differentiation.[2] In doing so, he illuminates his concern for the exclusion of action from accounts of human rationality (1994:202), which I discussed in Chapter Two.

Despite the theological coherence of these arguments, Pannenberg proves himself to be almost idiosyncratic in his approach to the psychological sciences. He displays no awareness of the ambiguity in status of different aspects of psychology, although the differences between experimental psychology and the study of mind have riven the subject since its inception. In the UK, for instance, this is still represented by the existence of psychology degree schemes in faculties of both science and humanities. Pannenberg's arguments are dependent on Freud and the psychoanalytic schools, but he never refers to any of the serious critiques that have been offered of these, which question their status as science.

2 Pannenberg (1994:196-201). This is one of the rare areas in Pannenberg's work where there seems to be some significant theological development over time. The detailed discussion of consciousness in the earlier *Anthropology in Theological Perspective* has much more logical force when seen in the light of these much later comments.

Subjectivity and the self – the origins of self-consciousness

In the *Systematic Theology*, Pannenberg introduces the importance of human consciousness in explicitly theological terms (in distinction to his approach in *Anthropology in Theological Perspective*, where the theological agenda is not overt).[3] He then gives a series of arguments that are derived from and set out in much greater detail in *Anthropology in Theological Perspective*, and I shall discuss them below.

His primary question is, do we know that we are not 'other' because we are self or do we know that we are self because we are not 'other'? Pannenberg sets out to argue for the latter, in terms of cultural history and psychological theory. He cites Democritus and early Greek tragedy as demonstrating the emergence in culture of moral conscience – the *synoida emauto* – and William James, followed by G.H. Mead, as proponents of the psychological theory of the social self. However, his argument depends on an awareness of 'otherness' as a 'universal basic structure of human behaviour' (1985:159) and this requires an explanation of the 'relation between my being present to the other and my being in myself' (1985:159). The explanation is apparently to be found in human awareness of the social realm. Pannenberg defends the necessity of taking self-consciousness into account in behavioural research with the conventional argument about humans as self directing, before adding a further reason from his philosophical account of exocentricity. Is the social world 'the place where their exocentric destiny is achieved?' (1985:160).

He refers to the relation of social theory and biology, briefly rejecting sociobiological reductionism, and citing Sahlins' (1977) objections, without any realisation that Lorenz, who he has used so much himself, is subject to the same critique. Pannenberg cites Gehlen in support of the view of humans as being distinctively culture creating – he says it is the 'question simply of an orientation to social relations which are always institutionalised in the form of a cultural world' (1985:162). He recalls Portmann's requirement for social interaction in human development and concludes that social modification of human biology presupposes culture as in some sense 'given' (1985:162). Pannenberg argues that humans cannot create their cultural context as individuals *ab initio*, so that the question of human identity in a social context is then the question of:

> … the determination of the ego itself by the community or, as the case may be, by the persons who serve as points of reference for individuals in their development. (1985:164)

3 He says 'The crucial role of the imagination ... in the activity of reason and understanding, helps to elucidate the dependence of reason on the working of the Spirit as the basis of our subjective freedom. ... it is necessary to attain some clarity on the relation of the Spirit to the general functions of the consciousness.' (1994:192)

In other words, I know that the 'other' is not 'me', but how much does the 'other' contribute to my 'I'? Pannenberg refers to Luckmann's view of the modern 'crisis in the relation of the individual to society', and highlights the privatisation of value in contemporary society (1985:165).[4] Pannenberg argues that this is not a completely modern phenomenon. He cites Judaism after the Exile and the Greek culture of Plato's time as both being moments when it became clear that individuals had value and identity over and against particular societies, and this resulted in the hopes of resurrection in post-Exilic Judaism and in the concept of the immortal soul in Greek thought. On the other hand, Pannenberg agrees that value-neutrality in the social sphere is a new development. He summarises the contribution of Locke and Hobbes as a 'secularisation of the Christian idea of human rights' and he regards the separation of an *a priori* freedom of the individual from responsibility and obligation to the community as the key to the new tension between the individual and society.

In order to explain this better, Pannenberg excavates the potential theological assumptions behind the theories of 'social contract' which originate in Hobbes. According to Hobbes, individuals sacrifice freedom to preserve security; according to Locke, the regulation of freedom is what preserves freedom. Locke includes calls for limitation on the exercise of power by authority whereas Hobbes does not. Pannenberg notes Reinhold Niebuhr's (1944) criticism of social contract theory; that reducing social relations to the contractual ignores other kinds of relations such as the familial (1985:174 footnote 40). He summarises the significance of Rousseau, viewing him as closer to Hobbes than Locke in his stressing of the demands of the community over against the individual, and summarises the social contract as the exchange of natural freedom for civic freedom (1985:174). Pannenberg compares this with Feuerbach's contribution to the development of Marxist theories of society, which he regards as completely subordinating the individual to society (1985:175), and with Kant. Pannenberg finds Kant preferable because he starts with an assumption of human sociableness, and he allows for human perversity. The antagonism between the two is, says Pannenberg, an integral feature of his conception of the human.[5] Kant expresses human destiny in terms of the awareness of morality that confronts humans, the moral 'ought'; Rousseau expresses it in terms of the emergence of society from chaos. Neither Kant nor Rousseau have a completely satisfactory position, because although the former keeps morality independent, he disconnects it from the concrete world, and the latter identifies it so closely with society that it loses independence.

Pannenberg claims that the twentieth-century development of 'dialogical personalism', in which he includes Buber, Rosenzweig and Ebner, provides the

4 Similar views were expressed in the seminal *Social Construction of Reality* by Berger & Luckmann (1966).

5 He says it involves a 'tension, unresolved in Kant, between the universality of the transcendental subject and the particularity of the existing ego'. (1985:178)

most significant approach to resolving the question of the relation between the individual and society. Pannenberg is here typically retrieving a strand in the intellectual tradition favoured by theology, but neglected by science, given the small role this group is said to play by historians of social psychology.[6]

The ideas of dialogical personalism concentrate on the analysis of one to one human relationships, in terms of the 'I-Thou' and 'I-It' categories familiar to theologians from the influence of Buber. Pannenberg cites a recent study of Buber by Theunissen, which describes a major limitation of Buber's approach, in that he is said to define the I-Thou relation only in terms of the I-It relation. Consequently, no positive content can be given to accounts of the claim of the Thou (1985:181). However, another of the group, Rosenzwieg, takes a different approach. He puts the idea of the I-Thou encounter in the context, not of the I-It relation, but of the temporal aspect of speech (between people) as opposed to the atemporality of thinking (about objects). Pannenberg, wishing to place all understanding against the horizon of the future, finds this inclusion of temporality most appropriate (1985:182). Unfortunately, says Pannenberg, most theologians have concentrated on using Buber to liberate themselves from the problems philosophy has been presenting in the area of objective reality, and so this insight from Rosenzweig has been missed.[7] This section of Pannenberg's argument with reference to temporality and the eschaton is interesting. But although Pannenberg makes reference to the future in this context of Buber et al., he does not appear to advert to it again in his discussion of the psychology of ego, self and identity, even though this involves looking at Heidegger's exposure of the temporality of the ego. And yet his thesis is that human identity is constituted by destiny to a future with God.[8]

Pannenberg's conclusion is that dialogical personalism is significant because it demonstrates philosophically the dependence of the ego on the other, as opposed to being a self positing, sovereign subject. But Pannenberg regrets that the opportunity for expressing this in social or political terms has not been exploited by theologians. He observes that personalism has general limitations in that it confines the interpersonal encounter to two subjects, and does not give any role to the

6 See for instance, Smith (1997), Hearnshaw (1989).

7 Pannenberg makes an exception for Barth, who he says does show signs of seeing that the human I is not constituted by the Thou, nor the inverse, but that the possibility of the relation between the two can 'point to God, that is, to the Trinitarian coexistence of Father and Son' (1985:183, footnote 73). Pannenberg goes on to complain that Barth does not go far enough; he does not locate the power of encounter and relationship in the being of God, which Pannenberg wishes to do.

8 Other authors of theological anthropologies have noted Pannenberg's inclusion of a future oriented dimension of intentions, promises and shared hope in his understanding of personal identity. For instance, McFadyen (1990:159) cites Pannenberg in support of such a contention. But he cannot draw on any psychological evidence from Pannenberg; his citation of Pannenberg is from the treatment of human being and history, at the end of *Anthropology in Theological Perspective* (1985:526).

'shared objective world' (1985:184). The inclusion of this is essential for his conception of human knowing, as noted in Chapter Two. By the time of writing the *Systematic Theology,* Pannenberg has further developed the importance of the differentiation of self from other against the background of the objective world, and gives a theological account of this, grounding it in the power of the Spirit. He says:

> The being with others as others mediated by perception awareness thus seems to include ... a field of consciousness in which the basic relation of I and the world takes on its contours. The feeling for life as an expression of the presence of spirit ... underlies, then, the formation of the field of consciousness ... the presence of the infinite ground of being, the Spirit, which declares itself in the feeling for life, transcends, however, the difference of subjects ... (1994:193)

Pannenberg is clear that psychology can be made to support the contention that consciousness of the self depends upon the distinction between self and world, self and other. This is crucial to his theological view of the divinely given unity of the infinite as the context for human self realisation. The possibility of perception of the world and the other depends on the creative act of God in the Spirit. Psychology can be shown to be consonant with that, but in no sense does it usurp or take priority over Pannenberg's primarily theological assertion.

I and me: The distinction between the ego and the self

Human consciousness of what is not self is linked to consciousness of 'I' as subject and 'self' as object. Pannenberg wishes to explain and validate this distinction in psychological and social theory in order to maintain the integrity and responsibility of the human subject against overt sociobiological or socially determinist arguments.

In *Anthropology in Theological Perspective*, Pannenberg describes Mead's contribution as providing the explanation for the distinction between the spontaneous ego, the 'I' and the reflective ego or self, 'me', which had been made earlier by William James. Pannenberg cites Mead's summary of the problem – 'How can an individual get outside of himself (experientially) in such a way as to become an object to himself?' (1985:185). Mead's answer is in terms of the individual's social experience. In order to see one's self from the standpoint of others, the skills of empathy are required; Pannenberg cites first Mead's requirement for human understanding of the gestures and movements of others, and the special place of vocal utterance in which the speaker is both heard by others and hears him or her self (1985:187). He goes on to point out that this is not the source of the human exocentricity postulated by the philosophical anthropologists, but claims it as a mechanism by which it can find expression, and which explains the origin of self-reflection, by which exocentricity comes to consciousness. The consequence of this is that the human self is dependent on the other for recognition of itself. One problem might be that as there are many 'others', so there are many relations giving rise to the awareness of self, and Mead argues that this is indeed the case. Unity is given to our concept of ourselves by the commonality of relations in the social group to which we belong, Mead's 'generalised other'. Pannenberg observes that for Mead, the 'I' is not socially constituted, but is the source of behaviour and the instigator of self reflection, although the 'I' is not accessible to direct experience, but appears in memory as representing the self. The unity of the 'I' and 'self' is not clearly delineated in Mead, according to Pannenberg, because such variable functions are ascribed to the 'I'. He claims that Mead's 'self', although a composite of reflections from others, has to be ordered by the ego, which in Mead appears to be independent (1985:189). He goes on to assert that it is in fact the ego that puts itself in the place of others to view itself as 'self', and that it therefore must be socially constituted in some sense, *contra* Mead. Further, such a social dependence is necessary, says Pannenberg, if there is to be a unity between self and ego, and he argues that Freudian theory provides the key to explaining such unity.

It may be noted that while Pannenberg makes clear his view that the self is socially conditioned, this is via a generalised 'other', not specific ones.[9] Pannenberg acknowledges a socially constituted self while assembling overall arguments which turn out to neglect social interactions, and abstract objectified components of shared meaning from social groupings.

Pannenberg chooses to develop his analysis of human identity and social development in terms of Freudian theory. He cites Paul Tillich as thinking that 'opposition to an excessive esteem of consciousness was the common denominator in psychoanalysis and Marxism' (1985:191). Here Pannenberg explicitly refers to some of the issues raised by postmodernism, but as I will argue later, he seems strikingly unable to apply them to his own analysis. He introduces the development of the concept of ego in Freud, pointing out its conflicting functions in repressing or controlling instinct on one hand, and on the other, of representing libido. Pannenberg notes that Freud's location of the 'ego ideal', in the internalisation of parental values, has a parallel in Mead's socially constructed self. He prefers the Freudian explanation of identification, because it specifies the individuals from whom identity is derived – parents – and because it explains why the impact of the other does not remain external or alien. Pannenberg identifies three aspects of the ego, two of which are developmental – the pleasure ego, which is represented by the infant's desire for nourishment (and self preservation) and the pleasure of being fed; the real ego which emerges from the child's overcoming jealousy of the father

9 It has been suggested (McFadyen, 1990:95, footnote 25) that Pannenberg roots consciousness of the self in awareness of the object world rather than the social world. The evidence for this is given from Pannenberg's later argument about the origin of culture and shared meaning (1985:407 & ff). In view of Pannenberg's lack of explicit discussion of social interactions, the ambiguity is understandable, and Pannenberg may almost be said to be objectifyinging the other in this generalisation.

by identifying with him, and the superego, which corresponds to the ideal ego, the internalised parental ideal. The instincts and emotions are represented by the id, and Pannenberg agrees with Freud that the control of the id by the ego is the 'lifework of the human person' (1985:195). This coheres with the assumptions behind the biology Pannenberg cites elsewhere, as discussed in Chapter Three. His view of humans as potentially unconstrained animals in need of the control of culture has curiously little of the positive, of love, of the constructive creativity of human relationships. Freudian theory lends itself to a portrayal of the human as internally driven. However, Pannenberg demands philosophical precision in his account of human identity, and therefore pursues the problem of the unity of these psychic components. He considers Erikson's version of ego synthesis, and concludes that it implies a pre-existent and effectively unchanging ego, which amounts to precisely the kind of unwarranted philosophical assumption he is not prepared to make. For Pannenberg, the key question is:

> But how can ego and self be identical, as the fact of self-consciousness shows them to be, if the self is constantly changing while the ego remains unalterably what it is? We are back once again with the problem of the unity of ego and self that was raised as a difficulty against G.H. Mead's views. (1985:198)

He observes that the problem is not the relation between the interior and the exterior of the person as in Mead, but between the process of development of the individual and the subject of that process, which is prior to it. If my self changes, then I must change too; there is a corresponding change in the ego. Pannenberg locates the difficulty in identification of the ego from the beginning as its own 'central organizing agency'. He asserts that the question of the relation between the ego and the self represents a 'religious thematic' underlying psychoanalysis and, indeed, all psychology (1985:200). The key issue for Pannenberg is the source of the identity they share: how can ego and self have a unity which preserves the integrity of the subject without grounding it in supernaturalist or idealist assumptions?

The identity of 'I' and 'me': The relation between ego and self

Pannenberg points out the distinction of ego and self as subject and object of self-consciousness which goes back to Fichte. He claims a present neglect of the problem, in that the unity is taken for granted at the same time as ego and self are spoken of in disparate and contradictory ways. Pannenberg thinks that modern psychology is particularly culpable (1985:201). Fichte himself modified his approach, because of the problem raised by the concept of the self-positing ego. Pannenberg puts the question – how can whatever is doing the knowing actually know itself? Can it remain the same thing once it does know itself (1985:203)? According to Pannenberg, this led Fichte to explore mystical religious philosophy in an attempt to find a solution. Thinkers who followed (Kant, Hegel, Feuerbach) did not fully appreciate the development in Fichte, and 'began to think of the objective mediation of self-consciousness on the basis of objective reality' (1985:205). In Pannenberg's view, this led to a new naturalism, and to a series of developments emphasising the importance of the body. The idea of the subject became extended in terms of the self, as in Mead and the psychoanalytic school.

Pannenberg regards Nietzsche as significant for establishing the body as the location of the self, and he notes the connection with Freud's ideas, (without citing Freud's known admiration for Nietzsche). He also sees a connection between Nietzsche and the ideas of William James, who rejected both supernaturalist ideas of spirit and materialist psychological reductionism. Pannenberg's account of the history of these concepts agrees generally with those of historians of psychology. For instance, Hearnshaw (1987) agrees with Pannenberg on the importance of the influence of philosophy on psychology.[10] But Hearnshaw also gives appropriate weight to other founding fathers of psychology, such as Wundt, the founder of descriptive psychology in Germany. He is hardly mentioned by Pannenberg, probably because of his empirical orientation and his separation of the physical and mental.

Pannenberg identifies linguistic analysis as significant in the further exploration of the relation between ego and self. He discusses the developments in the philosophy of mind initiated by Ryle and Wittgenstein, as important contributors to 'body-centred' ideas of mind. In his early work, Wittgenstein concentrated on the observable use of 'I' in language; he attempted to avoid pure behaviourism in that he saw speech as equivalent to expressive gesture, and could therefore claim that the speaker was in contact with that which they expressed (rather than creating it). Pannenberg cites Tugendhat as questioning the success of this evasion of reductionism – that I am in relation to my own pain does not itself solve the problem of how the verbal expression of such pain is to be epistemologically validated (1985:208). Shoemaker agrees with Wittgenstein in thinking that there can be no external means to validate such knowledge, although he does postulate an unvalidated 'normless ascription to self' of knowledge of past states. This is not satisfactory for Pannenberg, who reviews at length Tugendhat's attempts to solve the problem. Tugendhat accepts that a given human can be in error in describing their own state of mind. We must therefore have some norms or understandings which make this concept of error conceivable. According to Pannenberg, Tugendhat uses Heidegger's concept of *Dasein* in terms of the self as self for itself

10 But he gives a different reason. Hearnshaw says 'In the face of Nietzsche's demand for a "revaluation of all value" philosophers had to search for some certainty, and they did this along two divergent roads, firstly by way of logic and linguistic analysis, and secondly by a direct recourse to immediate experience. Their divergent prescriptions must be regarded as a root cause of the opposing "models of man" that prevail among contemporary psychologists.' (1987:229)

in the present, and appeals to the 'generalised other' of Mead for a social reference point by which the possibilities of action for the self can be evaluated. Pannenberg observes that Tugendhat is thus adding to Heidegger the community dimension that is notoriously lacking (note, for example, Bauman, 1978). However, Tugendhat uses Heidegger inappropriately, according to Pannenberg, because he eliminates the context of the future. This is of course essential to the reading of Heidegger and Gadamer that Pannenberg is committed to.

The context of the future is particularly significant because of the relation of meaning to identity. For Pannenberg, following Gadamer, complete identity comes from the future; the self is constituted by that which it will prove to have become, just as meaning is similarly future-dependent. Pannenberg also accuses Tugendhat of misunderstanding Freud, and failing to include the developmental (and therefore temporal) understanding of ego identity. Pannenberg concludes that Tugendhat has not managed to overcome the original idealist problem of defining identity (1985:212).

Pannenberg sees the solution to the problem in a rejection of idealist and transcendentalist ideas. They must be replaced, he says, by an understanding of the ego as generated or developed, rather than given. The basis for such an understanding can be found in Heidegger (1985:212). For Pannenberg, a proper philosophical defence of the person must now take into account this developmental understanding of ego and self. The 'I' cannot be the source of the basic unity between ego and self which leads to personal identity. The process of consciousness is a process of differentiation of what must be a prior unity. This is made clearer in the *Systematic Theology*. Pannenberg restates the awareness of self and the infinite, arguing that it is an implication of the distinction of self from not self.[11] He argues from this that the awareness of the inter relatedness of finite things against the background of the infinite, that he ascribes to consciousness, cannot be due to the ego (or any part of the structure of the human psyche) but must be due to the creator of all that is. He says:

> Not the I but the divine Spirit is the basis for the interrelatedness of that which is distinct in the consciousness, of the interrelatedness also of the I and the things of the world, especially similar living creatures. (1994:196)

He enlarges on this foundational presence of the religious dimension, citing Romans 1:20. This makes clear that the roots of Pannenberg's concern for the valid explanation of the unity of the ego and the self can be found in his philosophical assumptions about the divine as the ground of being, as indicated at the beginning

11 '... we can distinguish the infinite from the finite ... only on the condition that it is not just something other than the finite, in which case it would itself be finite, but that it also comprehends everything finite. This thought of the infinite One ... forms the mental space in which there can be distance from the other and definition of ... the space that is opened thereby for the consciousness.' (1994:195)

of this chapter. The developmental explanation of the ego and self requires further defence, which Pannenberg supplies, in the face of existentialist attacks on the subject-object distinction.

The dissolution of the subject

Pannenberg's reason for dealing with Tugendhat so extensively is that he believes the key to the problem of defining identity lies in Heidegger, but not at all in the way Tugendhat proposed. In *Anthropology in Theological Perspective*, Pannenberg identifies the significant feature of Heidegger's early contribution from *Being and Time* as the introduction of the dimension of the future. The ego not only relates itself to the self as past and present, but to the future. Pannenberg says:

> ...the Dasein, which according to Heidegger must be thought of in terms of its future being, is also described as that which relates itself to this future. (1985:212)

It is the ambiguity in this mode of expression, says Pannenberg, which caused Heidegger to use a different approach in later presentations of his thought, as he attempted to show that *Dasein* is constituted by *Sein*; that is, the supposed transcendental ego is based in the empirical ego. Pannenberg argues that Heidegger's treatment of this area demonstrates the importance of an apparently empirical science like psychology for philosophy; the practical difficulty in explaining the origin of the ego reveals profound philosophical implications (1985:213). The problem is that of making an absolute distinction between the human 'I' as subject and 'me' as object; it is not possible to do this after Heidegger because he showed that part of 'I' is given to 'myself', as it were, and in this process, the ego becomes object-like. But this is not a problem for Pannenberg, since he has carefully rejected arguments based on making the 'I' the sole basis for the legitimation of self awareness.

Pannenberg has also to deal with Sartre's development of the existentialist ego. Sartre started, according to Pannenberg, with Husserl's phenomenology of consciousness, and the intentionality or directedness of consciousness. For Sartre, the ego is a secondary effect of consciousness, and both 'I' and 'me' are products of reflection. This does not require a subject to do the reflecting, *contra* the idealist position, and 'the reflexive movement of consciousness antecedently excludes anything like identity with self'. (1985:214). But the reflective consciousness points beyond what is given to a constructed self, and it can deceive. The deceit consists in the 'bad faith' which conceals the fact that the self is a reflection, and presents it as independent in itself. Pannenberg thinks this is a particularly complete disposal of the idea of subject (1985:214), and therefore regards it as important to rebut. He argues that if as Sartre claims, self is the reification of our states and qualities, and ego the reification of our actions, abstracted from the totality that is the person, then the problem is that the person is not in fact complete, and it is a misrepresentation to claim the 'I' as an objective totality. But this is a consequence, says Pannenberg, of Sartre's attacking something like the idealist position of the permanent ego as underlying consciousness, whereas this has already been rebutted. Pannenberg goes on to advert to alternative conceptions of the ego as time-dependent, 'snapshots' of the person as the 'I' in the present moment. Pannenberg argues that from Hume to Russell and Ayer:

> The ego is primarily *given with* the experiences of the moment. The same holds for linguistic utterances, in which the word 'I' functions primarily as an indexical term. (1985:216)

Pannenberg says that this would undermine Sartre's objection to ego as objectified, since on this reading the ego has only momentary existence and is already past when reflected on; on the other hand, it would support Sartre's objection to a permanent and unchanging ego underlying consciousness.

Given the success of Sartre's dissolution of the idealist ego, Pannenberg asks if it is possible to do without a concept of a permanent ego, given the fact that humans actually behave as though 'I' has continuity and identity (1985:217). Pannenberg answers his question by demonstrating continuity in the process of establishing self-identity. Others are identified in bodily terms; memory may be involved in the identity of the self, but is not sufficient. Pannenberg asserts that the basic source of self-identity is given by the connections made between succeeding moments of consciousness. He cites Kant in support of this (1985:219), and widens this approach by borrowing from William James, in particular, the idea of the social self. James does not confine the self which is represented to isolated interiority, but includes the maternal body in early development and a wider socially supported world later. Pannenberg says:

> ...self is not, however, to be limited to the person's *own* body but at least includes in the 'symbiotic' stage of early childhood the bodily presence of the mother, and later on what James calls the 'social' and 'spiritual' self. *Familiarity with 'oneself' is therefore mediated through trust in a sheltering and supporting context in which I originally awaken to myself.* (1985:221)

Here Pannenberg's own italics emphasise the convergence between his view of human psychological development and his previous account of humans as unique animals with behaviours which create the environment to which their drives orient them. This view of James differs from Freudian ego psychology in that the self is prior; the ego does not 'posit' itself and is not the subject of development. Instead, the development and successive states of the self come to consciousness in the series of representations that are the ego. This takes place in a social context which is 'sheltering and supporting', and which will be developed further in his argument about basic trust. Pannenberg picks out key stages in this developmental formation of ego as the process of separation from the mother and development of object perception, with the use of language completing that process. He remarks that psychoanalytic theory should observe the early distinction between id and self, rather than id and ego, because self is the totality of the person on which the ego reflects. However, the ego can only reflect in the moment; its continuity and therefore consciousness of identity is only given by linkage to the self as it develops in time. Since the self is active, an agent, the individual is responsible by virtue of the continuity of the ego in relation to the self (1985:222). It is important for Pannenberg to establish this, in order to face down tendencies in modern philosophy or psychology which would deny accountability to the individual human.

Pannenberg completes his account of the relation between ego and self with a revision, not only of psychoanalytic theory, but also of Mead. A socially conditioned self was recognised by Mead, but he assumed some kind of idealist ego. If the ego is developmental, as described in the preceding section, then Mead's problem of opposition between ego and self disappears. Pannenberg sees the social conditioning of the human as affecting both ego and self (1985:223). He adverts very briefly to the constant adjustment necessary between the individual and social expectations of that individual, and concludes:

> Even when others do not grant the desired recognition, individuals can assert themselves by taking refuge in privacy (to the extent that this is allowed) or by asserting their spiritual selves against the social appraisal with which they cannot identify. Nonetheless, the acquisition of an acceptable measure of social recognition is indispensable as the basis of all life in society, from two party personal relationships to the institutional structure of society and relations between states. (1985:224)

It is interesting that here he suggests the assertion of the 'spiritual' self in the face of unacceptable social appraisal. He has given no time at all to any explanation of how such a self is developed. His whole enterprise has been devoted to showing the significance of the external world for the development of the self, but he has never discussed the necessity for discrimination or judgement in respect of that external world. In particular, his account of self-consciousness centres on it as primarily a form of knowing. What is important is that rational understanding gives rise to an awareness of both I and me in the context of the unlimited externality of the world. Pannenberg is certainly not dealing with the external world as the 'other'; the philosophies of Levinas and Ricoeur are not even hinted at.

While Pannenberg correctly draws attention to the temporal dimension of self-consciousness and human identity, there may be a problem with his use of Heidegger's analysis of self and ego. The sense of future in Heidegger originates in the awareness of death, whereas the orientation to future that Pannenberg wants as a theologian is eschatological, encompassing much more than death. But he seems to elide a sense of future, of what is not yet but is to come, with a sense of totality, the sum of past present and future. The differentiation of ego and self seems to arise, for Pannenberg, against a background of the infinite, rather than an exclusively temporal succession.

His account of the self and the ego in his *Systematic Theology* reveals further the limits and specificity of his understanding of the human psyche. He argues:

> ...in a rational distinction of each finite thing from every other ... the divine Logos is at work ... human intelligence in its perception of the otherness of the other participates in the self-distinction of the eternal Son from the Father by which he is not merely united to the Father but is also the principle of all creaturely existence in its individuality. (1994:196)

This makes overt his fundamental concern with establishing a Trinitarian structure of reality. Rationality, understanding and intelligence depend directly on the action of the Spirit (1994:197). Pannenberg equates human reason with knowing. It is awareness of 'I' and 'me', human knowing of self and other, and is mediated by the Spirit. But there is not the expanded sense of knowing that we find in Gadamer, of transformation and *phronesis*. There is no sense of the whole person, including emotion and action, being changed by knowledge. Indeed, Pannenberg specifically repeats his rejection of theories which see the human as primarily as agent or acting subjects (1994:202). Pannenberg's aversion to the concept of action will be discussed further in Chapter Six. I wish here to note that it depends on his interpretation of human self-identity as knowledge and as time-conditioned. Pannenberg claims that knowledge of the self is possible because the unity of ego and self which constitute human identity is part of the wider unity of all created diversity, which is held together by the power of the Holy Spirit. The time-conditioned ego can know the changing self only against the background of the infinite, which Pannenberg identifies as God. The continuity of the ego-self relation is directly empowered by God. In the next section, I will discuss Pannenberg's view of the development of this identity.

The development of ego and self in interaction with the world

Given the creative action of God in the context in which self-consciousness arises, what is the proper role for religion in the formation of self and ego? Pannenberg locates this in the necessity for the individual actively to accept both themselves and their social identity. Self-identification cannot be explained simply in terms of external social pressures (1985:225). He makes this a key difference between humans and other animals, and cites the psychoanalytic school in support of this. He suggests that in early human development, the bond with the mother is the basis for the experience of radical trust, which is extended to the whole of its social world as the child detaches from the parents and becomes independent. This radical trust corresponds to the external givenness of the self discussed in the previous section. Pannenberg moves easily from a philosophical account of how the ego can know the self to identifying the infinite in that account with the specific role of social interaction in extending an infant's capacity for trust beyond its parent figures

(1985:227). He is careful to defend his reading in Freudian terms against the accusation that what is being encouraged here is infantile regression or narcissism. He observes that basic trust allows individuals to survive negative experiences, and to give meaning to life. Religious formation is about fostering this and thereby developing courage in the face of life's complexities (1985:228). Pannenberg's characterisation of the effects of trust does not include any reference to extension of human relationships; the trust of Job certainly required him to stand firm, but did he do that out of a formative experience of 'basic trust' or because of complex learning in adulthood? Pannenberg's account could be read as an account of the self-confidence necessary for 'success' in our society. What would he say about those unfortunate enough to have been denied the experience of 'basic trust'? On the other hand, his inclusion of the negative side of reality is a welcome assertion in a feel-good culture which tends to avoid the reality of suffering. Pannenberg gives the mechanism for the development of such trust in terms of a Freudian style development of the ego in the context of the family. He argues that basic trust presupposes and is a response to an experience of love. He gives priority to the initial experience of maternal love. This is noteworthy in that it is one of the infrequent occasions when Pannenberg actually refers to love (1985:231). However, Pannenberg does not present any analysis or explanation of what is meant at the psychological and philosophical levels by love. This is in marked distinction to the intense and concentrated philosophical analysis he devotes to the structure of the person. Neither does he discuss the problems raised by the failure of love within or outside the family. Pannenberg argues that the unlimited nature of such basic trust gives it a religious dimension; the mother 'deputizes for and represents to her child the love of God that transcends her love and is directed to the child through her' (1985:231). He does not question the normative role that he ascribes to this; he may be read as supposing that any human who is unable to have this experience is destined to lack identity and be an abnormal, unhealthy personality. It may be that this is implicit in his argument; it could be restated in terms of a human lifelong task to find and develop a 'basic trust', and recognise its religious dimension. In that case, the argument would be made stronger, and misreading less likely, with reference to the literature in psychology on forgiveness, reconciliation, acceptance of self, healing and so on, and all the therapeutic approaches to this.

Pannenberg is certainly aware of the possibility of theological misunderstanding about the implications of 'basic trust' as he has described it. He notes that Küng has used the necessity of trust in human development and relations as an argument against atheism and nihilism. Pannenberg contends that Küng's basic trust is not given on the basis of any philosophical certainty, but is instead an existential decision. Pannenberg differs, arguing that it is part of a psychological development in humans that precedes the capacity to take such decisions. Hence Pannenberg is clear that it cannot be used to bolster claims for the reality of God, although he argues that it is evidence for the 'religious thematic', the inbuilt religious dimension, of the human being.

Pannenberg makes a further philosophical move in connecting the limitlessness of his understanding of basic trust with the sense of desired wholeness for the self.[12] He recalls his interpretation of the image of God in humanity, by presenting the argument that striving for wholeness can be an attempt to be like God and sinful, but that being called to participate in the human destiny of fellowship with God, which is the *Imago Dei*, gives the wholeness which is ultimately sought. This wholeness is manifested at any one time as personality; the 'person' designates the whole human, and transcends the discontinuities of personality over time (1985:235). Thus on one hand, Pannenberg seems to accommodate the philosophical consequences of postmodernity by acknowledging the time dependent and constructed nature of personality, rejecting idealist views of the self. On the other hand, he preserves a metaphysics of God, presenting it as the philosophical correlate of an exocentricity that he has defined biologically. I have already criticised this unsatisfactory marriage of biology and philosophy, and I shall argue that its conjunction with the philosophy of the self is likely to be problematic.

One consequence of the postmodern philosophical revision of understanding of person is that psychoanalytical ideas of the person as self-positing ego have to be revised. Personhood becomes the 'presence of the self in the ego' (1985:236). Temporality is a key feature in this, and Pannenberg invokes both Hartmann and Heidegger as reinforcing this insight, as well as harmonising it with Sartre's rather different view of the person. Whether in anticipation of death, (Heidegger) or in an attempt to transcend the incompleteness of the present (Sartre), Pannenberg maintains the judgement of philosophy to be that the 'person' is the manifestation at one present point in time of the implicit whole of that individual's life, including past, present and anticipated future (1985:240). The consequences of this for the psychoanalytic description of ego and self are that, as stated above, 'person' is the manifestation of self to the ego at the same time as the ego claims this particular self, in a time bound context which anticipates the future (1985:240).

Pannenberg connects this with a description of freedom as the potential to become oneself; for the ego to allow the presence of the self. He has accepted a role for social conditioning in the development of the self, but argues that the self is not completely socially determined. The orientation of the self beyond itself by a basic trust that is limitless indicates for Pannenberg that the self ultimately arises out of relation to God. In that case, individuals cannot be overwhelmed by one or other aspect of social mediation of this attitude of basic trust, and must retain an internal independence to any given manifestation of social relations (1985:241). It is difficult to see, using only the kind of psychology Pannenberg has chosen to support his concept of the development of the self, what psychological mechanism there might be for such freedom. Freudian theory depends on the postulation of

---

12 He notes and disagrees with Heidegger's view that this is accessible only in the context of the anticipation of death (1985:234).

internal psychological forces, analogous to the 'drives' of ethology. Internal freedom is difficult to allow for in Freud's terms. If Pannenberg had included more cognitive and learning theory, he would have been able to marshal more evidence from psychology in support of such a conclusion. Overall, the psychology and biology that Pannenberg has worked with is not at all conducive to his desired end point. Pannenberg's final conclusion from his consideration of the identity of the person in *Anthropology in Theological Perspective* is that the 'openness of persons to their divine destiny' is the basis of the essential dignity and inviolability of human beings, and that psychology and the philosophy of mind support this. While his treatment of philosophy of mind is interesting and constructive, the same cannot be said for his handling of psychology, and the authors he cites would surely disagree profoundly with his conclusions.

In his restatement of his views in the *Systematic Theology*, Pannenberg highlights the theological conclusions from his synthesis of psychology and philosophy. The unity of all that is created is reflected in the context of consciousness because of the ecstatic nature of consciousness. Consciousness 'stands outside' of itself, and enables a participation in the whole of life, rather than being a disconnected internal process. Thus, Pannenberg argues, self-consciousness implies participation of the creative activity of the Spirit itself. This participation:

> ...expands the soul by experience of the world, which the Spirit creatively permeates, and especially by the experience of human fellowship in face of the infinite ground of the world. Only in others do we meet a life that in its feeling for life is permeated in some way by the infinite ground of the world and the associated promise of the totality of life that is common to each and to all ... this dimension ... runs through all social relations, beginning with those of the family. Not least it gives personal depth to the encounter of the sexes. (1994:197)

Here he connects the action of the Holy Spirit with human interactions, which makes one wish he had spent more time discussing the latter. As it is, it is hard to see the detail of exactly how the creative permeation of the world by the Spirit is to intersect with human fellowship. But having introduced this theological context, Pannenberg repeats his assertion that human personality involves some kind of disclosure of the totality of the individual, even though it is limited in time, and relates this again to the action of the Holy Spirit in supporting humans to their destiny. He asserts the independence of personhood from actual self-consciousness.[13] This makes clear that at a theological level Pannenberg is not to be

13 He says 'Without the works of the divine Spirit in us there could be no personality in the deeper sense of the term. For personality has to do with the manifestation of the truth and totality of individual life in the moment of its existence. We are not persons simply because we have self-consciousness ... We do not cease to be persons when we no longer have this identity in the self-consciousness ... Personality is grounded in the destiny that transcends our empirical reality.' (1994:198)

misunderstood as identifying too closely with the schools of psychology he has used. This qualification of his view of human personality should pass the acid test for any theological anthropology, which is of being as true of the marginalised (e.g. the mentally retarded or the criminally insane) as of the main body of humanity. Pannenberg also refers to the limitations of psychology, which he sees in its inability to describe human freedom, particularly in the encounter with the other:

> We can understand this only on the premise that the ground of my own existence meets me in the person of the other. (1994:198)

Here, he comes closer to a description of real engagement between people than at any point in his earlier writings. This is one of the few passages in which he actually touches on the basis of inter-human relationships. It also contains the only reference to Levinas (he refers to *Totality and Infinity*) in his anthropological writings! This does, however, represent a real development, unusual in Pannenberg. His account of the self and the ego would be surely improved by further conversation with the philosophies of the other such as those of Levinas or Ricoeur, which are so notably missing from *Anthropology in Theological Perspective*. This would also require revision of his extreme rationalism, as I have already mentioned in the context of his treatment of Gadamer.

In the *Systematic Theology*, Pannenberg also gives the theological reasons for his stress on the role of time in conceptions of the person. We are not yet complete, but the personhood given to us anticipates the final truth to come. This anticipation is, says Pannenberg, 'mediated to us now through the Spirit by means of our feeling for life' (1994:200). Pannenberg here lays the foundation for the eschatological anticipation given in Christian revelation. He also points to the significance of feeling in his view of the human psyche; it functions as the means of knowing, and I will discuss this in the next section. But one of the most telling statements in all of Pannenberg's writings about the human person occurs at the conclusion of this account of the unity of the human person in the *Systematic Theology*. He says:

> In the person, then, the integration of individual moments of life results in an identity of authentic selfhood. In this process, the rational consciousness takes the lead, for by recollection and expectation it can hold the moments of life together in the present and reflect on their compatibility. (1994:201)

This hangs on 'rational ... recollection and expectation'. Rationality leaves out or excludes the hidden power of emotion, the faithfulness of love, the *gestalt* of art, poetry and music, the ethical dimensions of reality. Rationality alone can include explanations and defences of abuse. The high value Pannenberg gives to rationality is foundational for his conception of the human and the relation of the human to the divine, and I shall conclude that he puts too much faith in it, and leaves out the processes of love.

It may be helpful here to review this chapter's treatment of Pannenberg's account of the psychology of personhood and identity so far. The early passages in *Anthropology in Theological Perspective* expose Pannenberg's perspective; he looks upon an ideal world with happy families, wise government and a faithful church. Trust can be reposed in the system. He presents a very partial synthesis of biology and psychology that claims that such trusting is intrinsically necessary for human development. But any kind of writer on the question of human identity who starts from concrete situations gives a much more complex picture. Human families do not always provide nurturing communities of support. They can be violent and destructive. Social institutions are not always wisely and well run. They can be oppressive. And yet humans, although damaged by such experiences, can recover, and become functional adults. The processes Pannenberg describes are desirable, and facilitate human development, but they are not essential. An anthropology should be able to deal with this; for instance, McFadyen (1990) gives an account of human sociality as based on the experience of being loved in a range of possible relationships, rather than on the internal psychic structures underlying Pannenberg's 'exocentricity'. McFadyen can talk about the implications for the person when such love is not found. In contrast, Pannenberg relies on an idealised psychoanalytic pattern of mother/child interaction, and does not conceptualise the situations where this fails. Pannenberg omits many of the areas of psychology that deal with human relationships, including the cognitive psychologies which explain change and transformation in people. The consequence is that his account of the way in which psychology supports a theological view of humanity would be unacceptable to the scientific world he seeks to address. And this would be not because of any theological issue, but because his use of psychology is so idiosyncratic. Pannenberg seeks to place the psychology of the human person on what he regards as a safe philosophical foundation, which will not be susceptible to reductionist attack. In this, he is not alone. It is recognised as a general problem in psychology. However, Pannenberg confines himself to a rationalist analysis of Heidegger, and does not deal with any of the philosophies which have recognised that there is more to the human person than logic. The philosophers dealing with human interaction are ignored or dismissed. Pannenberg's first, minimal reference, to Levinas, for instance, does not appear until the second volume of the *Systematic Theology*.

How might this account be received from the perspective of psychology? It would be a mistake to assume that the subject is dominated by aggressive empiricism. For example, Hearnshaw, in *The Shaping of Modern Psychology* (1987) discusses the philosophical critiques of psychology. He observes the increasing concern with philosophy by psychologists, and gives reasons for it. He points out that rapid changes in scientific knowledge have been accompanied by a degree of philosophical innocence among psychologists. Further, 'revolutionary new movements in philosophy', by which he designates the critics of modernity, have had direct effects on the philosophy of mind (1987:227). Pannenberg certainly demonstrates the importance of the latter. Hearnshaw argues that early twentieth-century psychology clung to a philosophy of science appropriate to the pre-quantum age, and psychologists abandoned any philosophical training, so that they were prone to errors in concept and logic.[14] He points to the appearance of Ryle's *The Concept of Mind* and Wittgenstein's *Philosophical Investigations* as key criticisms of contemporary psychology of mind. Empiricism, reductionism and logical positivism were used to reinforce behaviourist psychology, leading to developments that emphasised method at the expense of content.

But Hearnshaw points out that other philosophical tendencies influenced a range of developments in psychology. These are some of the areas that Pannenberg does not mention. Hearnshaw argues that existentialism and phenomenology led, from Kierkegaard on, to a renewed interest in 'lived experience'. This has fed, via Husserl and Heidegger, into a range of different developments in practical psychology and psychiatry where content is more systematised than method.[15] Hearnshaw has, not surprisingly, a more eclectic picture of the philosophical tendencies in modern psychology than Pannenberg, and a much wider appreciation of the content of psychology.

Emotion, mood and the person

As previously indicated, Pannenberg regards the significant function of the emotions as providing the context in which the individual can know his or her self. They are the matrix in which self can become present to ego. However, this must depend on the familiarity of consciousness with itself (1985:243). Pannenberg is very aware of the negative side of such familiarity, as in shame, guilt and alienation. Much of his discussion of emotion and affect in *Anthropology in Theological Perspective* is spent on a detailed consideration of such negative aspects. He notes the varieties of distinction made between feeling as response to sense impression, on one hand, and emotion or mood as having some internal, dynamic component on the other.[16] He cites eighteenth century psychology as distinguishing between sensation, which is of an object, and feeling, which is of the impression made by the object. Pannenberg suggests that Kant was influenced by this, in putting feeling between the capacities of cognition and desire, and that Schleiermacher likewise saw the role of feeling as between that of knowing and that of willing. Both Tetens and Kant emphasise the connection between feelings of pleasure or displeasure and the desire of the self to be and become itself.

---

14 As evidence of this, he cites a critique by Peters of the concept of 'drive', coinciding with some of the arguments put forward earlier in this thesis.

15 e.g. Laing (1969), Rollo May (1960), Rogers (1942).

16 He displays an awareness of the divergence of Anglo-Saxon and Continental perspectives on these issues (1985:245) which is in contrast to his apparent isolation within the German paradigm when he deals with concepts of human physiological development, instinct and drive.

Pannenberg describes Schleiermacher as showing development in his view of feeling, in that although initially he separated knowing and feeling, and restricted feeling to the subjective result of 'the religious intuition of the infinite in the finite' (1985:247), later he located the 'immediate self-consciousness' which mediates between subject and object, in the area of feeling. Pannenberg asserts that here Schleiermacher follows an earlier thinker, Jacobi, in placing feeling as the ground of knowledge of both the world and one's own person. Pannenberg is of the opinion that Schleiermacher's insight is still valid, and is unreasonably neglected in contemporary psychology. The philosophical implication, says Pannenberg, is that feeling, as consciousness of the finite, can comprehend the totality of the finite as a possibility.[17] In other words, consciousness of the self and the world implies the possibility of the consciousness of God (1985:248). This is in no sense a proof of the existence of God, but for Pannenberg, it is something that must be accounted for in both theological and secular explanations of humanity and the world. He singles out Kreuger as having tried to acknowledge this issue in his discussion of feeling and emotion. It is possible to distinguish between immediate, momentary states of feeling, and general mood, to which they are referred, and which itself refers to the whole context of the individual. Pannenberg notes that while this may be accepted in general psychology, Schleiermacher's concept of self-consciousness includes more than this, because it includes the awareness not only of the ego and self, but also of the individual's familiarity with the world with which it is yet not identical (1985:250). The significant analysis here for Pannenberg is that given by Heidegger. *Dasein*, Being-in-the-world, is disclosed by mood, and is at the same time the experience of the disclosure (1985:250). Pannenberg does not mention the many critiques of Heidegger attacking the amorality of his elevation of the self.[18] Heidegger's self-consciousness objectifies or negates the other, and he cannot be thought of unproblematically as sympathetic to Pannenberg's project of uncovering a religious thematic in the phenomenon of self-consciousness.

Pannenberg sees the significance of Schleiermacher's understanding of feeling as his overt ascription of a universal religious dimension to it. This is particularly valuable to Pannenberg in his attempt to argue that a proper description of humanity cannot be given without a religious component. However, he has to take issue with Schleiermacher as he argues that familiarity with self precedes, and does not require a concept of self as such, whereas Schleiermacher, according to Pannenberg, fused the familiarity given by feeling with self-consciousness proper (1985:252). Pannenberg cites R.H. Lotze as giving a preferable account from two

17 The problem of Pannenberg's understanding of totality, the comprehension of the finite by the Infinite, the difference between God and the Infinite, and the role of Hegel's concepts in this, is quite beyond the remit of this study, but Schwöbel makes illuminating comments on this area in which he distinguishes Pannenberg's position from Hegel's (see Schwöbel, 1997:186 and 1996:508).

18 e.g. Ricoeur (1995), Adorno (1986), Bauman (1978), Levinas (1989).

perspectives in which self-consciousness, as the connection between thinking subject and object of thought, is located in feeling. Self-consciousness viewed as the unity of ego and self is a cognitive phenomenon. Pannenberg thinks Schleiermacher is right when he ascribes the religious dimension of feeling to receptivity or awareness.[19] But Pannenberg does not like the interpretation, which he imputes to Schleiermacher, of this receptivity of feeling as a kind of dependence, as actually opposed to freedom. He claims that Schleiermacher gives priority to consciousness of the world, and therefore dependence on it, over against consciousness of ego and self (1985:253). This is the wrong way round for Pannenberg, who thinks that consciousness of unity and differentiation within the psyche precedes awareness or experience of the world. He proffers his own scheme of maternal dependence, basic trust and subsequent detachment. He adverts to the tensions in the relation of the development of the individual and the 'religious thematic', and the relation of the affective life to this. At this point, Schleiermacher can be approved again, because he identifies the theological implications of such tensions in terms of sin (1985:254).

But whereas Schleiermacher sees these tensions resulting in the experience of the world as detracting from the emerging religious consciousness, Pannenberg prefers the approach of Kierkegaard, who focused on the emotions surrounding the self assertion of the individual.[20] Pannenberg cites Heidegger as providing the definitive working out of Kierkegaard's insight into the role of the mood of anxiety in the basic question of human identity. Anxiety is the most fundamental way in which the 'spirit can relate to itself' (1985:255). Pannenberg responds to the criticism that Heidegger overemphasised the negative side of humanity. He asserts that it is based on a misreading of Heidegger, who did not deny the prevalence of positive moods, but identified anxiety as the mood illuminating the relation of all other moods to the unity of the person and to freedom. Again, the problematic nature of Heidegger's deliberate exclusion of the ethical, and his great difference from Kierkegaard on this point, does not prevent Pannenberg from abstracting components of Heidegger's analysis.

This is strikingly demonstrated by Pannenberg's drawing of parallels between Heidegger's account of the ecstatic nature of mood and the Pauline account of the

---

19 This is in keeping with his desire to avoid contaminating the process of knowing with any form of action; theories of feeling which stress internal dynamics rather than passive sensation are avoided by Pannenberg.

20 He says 'It is on these that Kierkegaard, unlike Schleiermacher, focuses in his analyses of dread and despair, which may be regarded as paradigmatic for the phenomenological description of moods in our century. Furthermore, affects and passions, like moods, receive no attention from Schleiermacher in his theological interpretation of feeling, although affects and passions had traditionally had a central place in both theological and philosophical anthropology.' (1985:254)

effects of the Holy Spirit, particularly joy.[21] The sustaining of such equivalencies must be extremely dubious in the light of the critiques of Heidegger previously mentioned.

Pannenberg does note that not all positive mood can be identified with Christian joy (1985:256). This leads him to an assessment of joy in the light of antecedent Greek thought. The characteristic insight of Christianity is, for Pannenberg, the eschatological dimension; true joy can only be associated with the ultimate fulfilment of all things by God; pleasure is bound to the here and now and is therefore of this world. Further, Christianity affirms the validity of the affects, against the Stoic critique of them as destroying the harmony provided by reason. Pannenberg cites Augustine's defence of anger, sadness, fear and mercy as aids in the movement of humans to their destiny in God (1985:259) and he is careful to defend Augustine again from criticism based on his analysis of desire, sin and concupiscence. Pannenberg says that Augustine's judgement was not against pleasure, still less joy, but against the perversion of joy to egoism and pleasure whose object is not God. Having established the legitimacy of joy, Pannenberg asserts that Aristotle's view of the affects as necessary for human wholeness is still relevant, in that they both link the person to their present world, and yet point to a situation beyond that present for their satisfaction. He expands this to take into account Scheler's exocentric view of feeling as identification (1985:261). This is one of the few places where Pannenberg's analysis of mood has the other, rather than the self, as its object.

Pannenberg argues against David Hume's account of affect, which he saw as basically a reflection on ego or self. According to Hume, pride and humility are the fundamental moods or passions, reflecting positive or negative evaluation of the self, and love and hate are similarly basic in the context of others, because we relate to others as desirable for ourselves or not. Pannenberg says that this conflicts with the psychoanalytic account of ego development as socially conditioned, and it ignores the ecstatic nature of intense mood. Pannenberg could not possibly accept a view diametrically opposed to the exocentrically oriented, ecstatic and self transcending vision of humanity that emerges in continental thought. He notes the convergence of Hume with Sartre in that they both include this rift between the self and the 'other'; Sartre locates it in the kind of sexual desire that is an attempt to possess the other and thus eliminate difference by absorbing it in self. He dismisses both Hume and Sartre as one sided in the way that they deal only with the separated self. Jung's version of depth psychology, on the other hand, gets praise because it demonstrates the social conditioning of the self (1985:263). Pannenberg interprets

---

21 He actually says 'In the later Heidegger's statements about moods this phenomenon is connected with what in another terminology would be called the working of the *Spirit*, who elevates human beings above themselves. Thus for Paul, joy is an effect of the Holy Spirit (1 Thess. 1:6) and appears with righteousness and peace as a manifestation of the reign of God (Rom. 14:17).' (1985:256)

Jung's concept of the *anima/animus* as amounting to projections of parts of the self not present to the ego which nevertheless reflect the social context of the individual. He sees this as an improvement on Freud's theory because that limited the influence of the social context to the development of the superego in the context of the parental relationship only. Pannenberg does not accept, however, Jung's extrapolating from such functions of the unconscious to archetypes and the collective unconsciousness.

Pannenberg concludes his discussion of emotion, affect and mood in *Anthropology in Theological Perspective* by asserting the necessity for individuality:

> The perversion of passion may be described as a regression to the kind of identification that effaces individuality ... The seductive attraction of such regression is due to the fact that isolation and the chasm between ego and world do have to be overcome. But the result must not be achieved at the cost of eliminating the process of individual differentiation. Unity must be sought within differentiation itself. It is love that accomplishes this, for love bridges the chasm between ego and other by acknowledging its existence. (1985:265)

This passage is interesting, because it contains one of the infrequent references to the importance of love, again unaccompanied by any exposition or analysis. Love, according to this statement, is to overcome the chasm between the ego and the other that does indeed exist in Pannenberg's account of the human psyche. If he depended less on Freud and Heidegger, he might not have to appeal to love as such an inexplicable force.

Pannenberg's view of feeling and emotion is instrumental and rational; they provide the fundamental basis of human self awareness in a knowing that is separate from and prior to action. This view is reinforced in his later statements in the *Systematic Theology* (1994:192-193). On this subject, there is less of a development from the position of *Anthropology in Theological Perspective* than there is in his treatment of the ego and the self. In both earlier and later work, he confines the role of feeling and emotion to a mechanism for mediating the structure of the individual psyche. There is no analysis anywhere in Pannenberg of the necessity for empathy and sympathy in human relationships, either in one to one interactions or in group interrelations, no account of attachment and cathexis, or of interpersonal conflict either. His analysis of the role of emotion must be one of the weaker parts of his anthropology.

Alienation

Alienation is a key concept in modern debate about the human condition, and Pannenberg selects aspects of that debate to subsume into his theological framework. In *Anthropology in Theological Perspective*, Pannenberg concludes from his study of mood and emotion that positive emotion is associated with an exocentric orientation, whereas negative mood is associated with a turning inwards. He proceeds to draw a theological conclusion, citing Augustine, that humanity, as sinful, turns in upon itself. He equates this with the contemporary search for identity:

> The human beings who are trying to find their own identity are evidently sinners. Instead of dedicating themselves to service in the objective tasks of the human community and experiencing in this service the meaning of their own lives, their primary concern is with themselves. This by itself is a sign that they lack their authentic identity ... They may think they will attain to their identity by way of identity formation and self-realization ... when human beings who are concerned about themselves think that they come closest to their own identity through this kind of preoccupation with themselves, then they are really alienated from their true destiny and their true selves. (266:1985)

Here he expresses the debt to Augustine and Luther behind his approach to theological anthropology. Pannenberg believes that humans are called to a destiny with God, beyond themselves. If they do not accept that destiny, then the ills of fallen humanity, and present western society, ensue, as a result of individual irresponsibility before God.

His comment on self-realisation is noteworthy. Pannenberg never acknowledges the significance of cognitive psychology in the development of therapeutic practices. The approaches of authors such as Tillich (1952), Rollo May (1969), Frankl (1987) or Rogers (1942) have been conspicuously absent from his account of human psychic development and functioning. As I have previously observed, there has been no discussion of the mechanisms of relationships, love, transference and so on. Pannenberg is therefore unable to discuss the role cognitive therapies could play, even in religious formation, or of the proper place of counselling and self-help psychologies. He is therefore not in a position from which he can evaluate contemporary approaches to the problem of self-identity, and offer appropriate critiques.

While Pannenberg ignores material that does not fit into his narrative, he is willing to modify anything that may be made to support his view. Consequently, he can acknowledge the significance of Marx for the development of the concept of alienation. He alludes to opinions that locate the whole idea in Hegel, and proceeds to trace its roots from antiquity. He cites Aristotle as using alienation in the sense of exclusion from a community, and lists similar usages in the Old and New Testaments, where the community includes fellowship with God. The early church saw alienation from God as a result of sin, and Augustine regarded it as a consequence of concupiscence. Here Pannenberg sees it being used in relation to the self, and refers to the mystical tradition of a positive use, being alienated from self in order to make room for God, as well as the alienation from self and God that is sin.

Pannenberg views the significance of Hegel as making this self-alienation an essential process of psychic development and relating it to the Christian concept of the Incarnation. The spirit creates its world by a kenotic movement, and must re-appropriate the strange externality so produced. Hegel's God is similarly estranged from the world and reunites himself with it in Christ. Pannenberg is predictably critical of this, arguing that in the Christian tradition, God is not properly understood as separated from the world or himself (1985:271). The only separation that is compatible with Hegel's alienation, says Pannenberg, is the separation, by sin, of humans from their destiny of communion with God. Hegel's view of alienation is confused by his view of the self as subject and producer of its own world; on this basis, it is not possible to distinguish between self-divestiture and self-alienation. On Pannenberg's view of the self, they are different, and self alienation as sin is not so much turning to the world as turning from God. Pannenberg does note some similarities between Christian thought and the 'young Marx'; not only the preceding point but also Marx's criticism of the idea that relation to the world may be adequately summarised as a relation of possession. However, he is quick to draw a line between the fundamentals of the Christian and Marxist understandings of alienation. Marx sees humans as essentially active and fulfilled by their production; alienation comes when the individual is separated from the fruits of their activity. Behind this Pannenberg detects Fichte's view of the ego as positing itself. Pannenberg says this is fundamentally an individualistic and romantic view. Christianity sees humans as potentialities; called to a destiny that is not yet achieved. Hence alienation cannot be for Christians, as it is for Marx, the separation of the individual from their achievement. It must instead be a closure to possibility, to the future of their destiny with God. Pannenberg extends his critique to cover the understanding of 'reification', the 'fetishism of commodities', as another form of alienation, and its extension to the reification of social processes. Pannenberg does not believe that the theory built on Marx's insight is adequate to explain the sociological observations nowadays grouped under the term alienation. For a sociological explanation, he cites Peter Berger's approach as set out in *The Homeless Mind* (1973), describing the undermining of structures of meaning, such as religion, by the processes of modernity.

Before Pannenberg can proceed with his main agenda, which is the establishment of the theological nature of alienation as sin, he must deal with the criticism originating in Feuerbach that religion itself is an agency or expression of alienation. He makes the argument that merely because no perception of any kind can exist without some form of mental construction, it does not follow that perceptions cannot relate to some external reality. Pannenberg accepts that 'false reification' is a danger for many disciplines, including religion, and asserts that it is the consequences of this that raise questions of alienation, rather than the process of reification in itself (1985:278).

Pannenberg sees a development in Berger's thought in this direction. Alienation occurs when some part of the ego is not integrated into the person's self-perceived identity. Pannenberg wants to take this beyond what he regards as Berger's subjective position. He argues that there is a true meaning for the life of each individual, which is their destiny with God, and alienation is caused when the individual's perceptions of their identity does not take this into account. The role of religion is to illuminate this, but religion itself can be perverted from its proper goal in pointing to the reality of God, and then it will itself promote alienation (1985:279). Pannenberg claims that such failure to grasp the reality of God lies behind the existence of religious pluralism, and reflects a partial truth in the claim of Feuerbach about religious consciousness. However, he argues that Feuerbach and Marx were criticising a religious consciousness which had nothing to say about the present world, being entirely focused on another. Pannenberg contends that religious consciousness properly discloses meaning about the present world, which does not, *contra* Marx, simply become meaningful when properly organised.

Pannenberg's account of the true meaning of alienation starts with Tillich (1978). This is noteworthy because Tillich has been very influential on developments in psychology and religion, and yet Pannenberg refers to him very rarely. In the case of alienation, Tillich introduced the concept as coming from Hegel, and suggested it as helpful in describing the universality of original sin without the imputation of inheritance. He also stressed the empirical validation of alienation. Pannenberg notes that Tillich does not see alienation in social terms, but as a state of unbelief, hubris and concupiscence, universally characteristic of humanity. Pannenberg argues that these are not actually states, but acts, and that therefore they are not properly descriptive of alienation. He is looking for a prior disruption in the structure of the psyche, explaining the 'brokenness of human existence in relation to the self ... other human beings ... and God' (1985:283). Pannenberg believes that Tillich failed to make enough of the social component of alienation, and thus missed a significant opportunity of bringing all these themes together. Pannenberg sees alienation as arising from a feature of the human condition that precedes social structures, in agreement with Reinhold Niehbuhr (1985:285). The social dimension of alienation is important for Pannenberg not because of its concrete impact but because of its value in his theological argument. It is important for the description of the universality of sin, an inevitable symptom of that which is manifested concretely. Having established alienation as an empirical consequence of sin, Pannenberg concludes his treatment of it by discussing its manifestation in human consciousness. It is notable that he does not engage here or elsewhere in any discussion of the psychological or philosophical aspects of liberation, freedom or forgiveness from alienation and sin. I take the implication to be that Pannenberg see these as somehow not foundational for human being, not to be illuminated by psychology or philosophy, but secondary and derivative. Given the centrality of the Cross as salvation in Christian theology, this omission seems odd, to say the least.

In the *Systematic Theology*, Pannenberg's instrumental use of alienation is even clearer, because he uses it to introduce the whole section on anthropology, entitled 'The Dignity and Misery of Humanity'. The empirical fact of alienation is used to establish the need for the theological explanation of sin as opposition to humanity's proper destiny (1994:180). There is no sense at all that Pannenberg's theology is enlarged or developed by consideration of the contributions of psychology, sociology and history to the concept of alienation, and there is no development or change in his position over the years.

Sin and guilt

Pannenberg devotes a large proportion of his anthropology to the concepts of sin and guilt. His use of psychology in this follows his approach to alienation. That is, he selects, rather randomly, material which will support his theological proposals, and refutes such counter claims as he can by the same means. In *Anthropology in Theological Perspective,* Pannenberg presents the principal manifestation of alienation as that of guilt, but he argues that alienation is not identical with guilt, because guilt is experience of the specific, whereas alienation refers to the general condition. Pannenberg is ready to identify 'immature' and 'neurotic' guilt along Freudian lines, and to accept that these are inappropriate, but he is not going to allow the baby to be thrown out with the bath water. The existence of such phenomena cannot remove the necessity for a theological concept of responsibility for transgression (1985:287).This may present Pannenberg with some semantic problems in that the word guilt in contemporary public discourse is often now used to refer to that which was critiqued by Freud. Contemporary discussions in psychology would talk about acceptance of responsibility in the context which Pannenberg wants to keep and use the concept of guilt.

Pannenberg considers the origin of concepts of sin and guilt, emphasising the objective component, such as stain or defilement, that precedes the personalised and internalised aspects of sin that appear in religious traditions. He asserts that the history of religions shows the social necessity for making the link between act and consequence. Guilt is necessary in order to establish the concept of responsibility (1985:291). He agrees with Ricoeur's description of the development of guilt awareness from experience of divine punishment to an internalised 'diminution of the value of existence', but he wishes to retain an objective component to guilt against what he sees as Ricoeur's subjectivity. However, the subjective aspect of guilt linked to conscience is still significant for Pannenberg. He traces the emergence of self-consciousness and guilt in classical literary tradition, claiming that it first appears in Euripides. He observes that initially, conscience was connected with self-knowledge, and only later did it come to be associated predominantly with awareness of departure from moral norms (1985:298-300). He gives Kant and Hegel credit for reconnecting conscience to the idea of self-knowledge, and starting the development that resulted in Heidegger's treatment of the subject. Pannenberg asserts that Heidegger's account of conscience 'has become the most influential one in our day' (1985:301). Pannenberg delineates Heidegger's achievement as a philosophical grounding of an understanding of guilt as a failure to achieve true humanity, even if that understanding is limited by Heidegger's insistence on detaching guilt from any external or objective situation. It nevertheless establishes, according to Pannenberg, the necessary link between responsibility and human action. He argues that Heidegger's description of the call for *Dasein* to be authentically itself implies a foundational sense of obligation within the structure of the human person (1985:302). In Heidegger's account, this obligation is to the self alone. Pannenberg is critical of Heidegger for excluding reference to the community in understanding the obligation of the self.[22] But he seems to imply that a satisfactory account of the matter can be obtained by juxtaposing Heidegger with appropriate elements from Freudian theory:

> In the psychoanalytic theory of conscience, on the other hand, the human community is recognized as having, in itself, a central importance. This theory therefore presents itself precisely as supplying the lack in Heidegger's theory of conscience. It is another question whether psychoanalytic theory in turn does full justice to the complex phenomenon of conscience. (303:1985)

This is a typical pattern in Pannenberg which I find questionable. He seems rather like a magpie, picking up bits that will fit together in his theological nest, without examining whether they are truly fit for the purpose. The fundamental amorality of Heidegger arises precisely from the exclusion of the 'other' from the issue of responsibility. If responsibility is defined in terms only of I and myself, is it safe for Pannenberg to make the connection between Dasein and Heideggerian authenticity on one hand, and human destiny as the call to communion with God, on the other? How can such alien concepts be integrated with Freudian theory? Pannenberg outlines Freud's view of conscience as the individual's internalisation of external authority, which capacity has arisen during the course of human cultural development, as a concomitant necessity. He points out the irony that Piaget's work suggests that the Freudian superego does not in fact persist into adulthood, but is replaced by moral principles evolved in the experience of mutual consent with others and appropriated by the individual. Pannenberg cites various psychologists in this vein, and concludes that the basic principle remains, that conscience is mediated by a context of social relations (1985:306).

Pannenberg does not, unsurprisingly, refer to the critiques on moral development made of Freud, Piaget, and related authors, to the effect that they are excessively Eurocentric and male biased (for example, Gilligan, 1982). But, on the basis that the findings of psychology that he has cited are compatible with his

---

22 He says 'Heidegger's analysis fails to penetrate the depth of the nonidentity that makes itself known in the consciousness of guilt, for this nonidentity does not consist simply in the inauthenticity of being lost in the "they", but, as can be seen in Orestes' pangs of conscience, points to a rupture in the communal order by a rending of the ties uniting individuals to their fellow human beings ... He has also failed to see ... that the nonidentity experienced in conscience is overcome through expiation which is to be accomplished in the life of the injured community.' (1985:303)

position, Pannenberg presents a theological perspective on the requirements for the formation of conscience. The balance between the individual and the community must be maintained, and the function of conscience is not simply to present required norms, but to keep the individual in touch with the values of the shared world in such a way as to enable them to make their own judgements in concrete situations.

Pannenberg does not make allowance for the not infrequent problem of the shared world 'going off the rails'; the hermeneutic of suspicion is not strong in Pannenberg. Yet this major feature of the western world in the twentieth century has given rise to the wholesale suspicion of modernity. Pannenberg would simply ascribe the corruption of shared value to sin. Pannenberg is clear that the relation to God is mediated through the social context of the individual, and he takes issue with Ebeling, who superficially seems to develop an asocial account of conscience. Pannenberg suggests that Ebeling's description of conscience conceals an unmediated element:

> Because Ebeling does not thematize the world, in its relation to conscience, as a *social* world, the 'word', which is asserted to be the 'mode of encounter' between human beings and God, remains related to these human beings in an excessively extrinsic and supernaturally authoritative way, instead of being mediated through an understanding and appropriation of the world as a unified context of meaning. (1985:309)

But the acknowledged success of theologies of the Word, however unmediated they may be, in responding to distortion of the values of the shared world is not mentioned by Pannenberg. The 'appropriation of the world's meaning' and the consequent acknowledgement of the individual's relation to God is claimed by Pannenberg as the guarantee of the independence of conscience; is, indeed, what renders critique of social values and institutions possible. But he seems to have left little space for such independent development in his account of the socially conditioned emergence of the self, as described in the earlier sections of this chapter.

Pannenberg is keen to distinguish his view of conscience as awareness of God from Heidegger's use of the term in the context of preserving personal identity. Heidegger's choice in favour of the authentic self can lead only to despair, according to Pannenberg, since it must operate in isolation from the social world. But Pannenberg does not offer any account of exactly how, if Heidegger is right in his analysis of the responsibility of *Dasein* for itself, a Freudian account of the socially mediated development of the person and his or her conscience can avoid being inauthentic. Conversely, if the Freudian account he proffers is correct, how can Heidegger's account stand without being frankly wrong, since it suggests a psychic structure which is fundamentally independent of social relations.

Pannenberg wants to keep his psychological and philosophical cake and eat it at the same time, in order to meet his theological requirements. The appropriate response to awareness of non-identity must be one in which the social dimension is recognised, and therefore repentance and expiation are preferred – expiation because this is relevant to the social, objective dimension of guilt that Pannenberg has sought to preserve. Pannenberg concludes this discussion by inclusion of material from another context. He connects repentance and expiation with the eucharistic celebration:

> Here too the goal is the restoration of the community, the removal of alienation, the 'purification' of conscience from the judgement that condemns our work and keeps us imprisoned in nonidentity. Such as restoration can only be a communal event, since the deeds of individuals affect not only themselves in isolation but also the community (and precisely thereby 'themselves'). Individuals recover their identity through reintegration into the community; they recover a freedom which they neither possess nor can exercise for themselves in isolation, but which they possess only as recognized members of the shared world. (1985:312)

Here is another of the unexpected twists in Pannenberg's arguments. In a section devoted to personal identity and related issues, Pannenberg has not used any of the immense literature in psychology on human relationships, and yet he concludes with an assertion of the essential role of community. He has not discussed what is meant by community, how it is formed and maintained, the relationships between different kinds of community, still less the essential features of the church community and its experience of the Eucharist. And yet he concludes this section on sin, out of the blue, as it were, with a reference to the 'reintegration' of individuals into the ecclesial community. Is the absence of any account of the psychology of forgiveness and reconciliation a sign of the low theological priority Pannenberg gives it? Or is the psychology associated with such concepts unacceptable to him for other reasons, so that he chooses not to draw on it for the support of his theological anthropology?

A reading of the *Systematic Theology* does not help greatly. Pannenberg reinforces the account of sin he has given earlier, stressing its universality and the importance of individual responsibility. While Pannenberg claims to recognise the increasing loss of power of the individual in western society, he does not think structural sin important (1994:237). Again, he does not discuss the nature of forgiveness or reconciliation, but he does give them a place in his final conclusions. After a discussion of the connection between death and sin, Pannenberg then observes:

> A mark of God's intervention in the history of his creatures is that he has constantly limited the results of sin and evil so as to make the life of his creatures possible under the limiting conditions they face.
>
> We see here not only the outworking of God's patience with sinners but his continued creative activity in the government of the world, which again and again brings good out of evil. Traditional Christian dogmatics has paid far too little attention to this truth in its discussion of our fallen plight ... The measures that God the Creator has taken against the powers of sin and evil that have invaded his creation have been largely neglected ... the primary issue ought not to be that of human abilities but the continued

> creative activity of the good Creator and his providence ... by the continued creative activity of his Spirit, God constantly rescues his creatures from ... entanglement in self-centredness ... .(1994:274)

The more remarkable, then, that Pannenberg himself spends so much time on proving the reality of the origin and nature of sin by appealing to psychology, and so little time on gaining the same support for the reality of reconciliation and renewal.

Overall, in parallel with his treatment of biology, Pannenberg's approach to psychology is severely instrumental. He chooses such material as will support his vision of the human person as essentially self-aware, called to a destiny beyond the self and appointed to alienation and misery if that destiny is not embraced. He provides a creative and interesting account of the importance of Heidegger in offering a view of human personhood as constituted as a task in time, and there is a development in his theology of the Spirit which seems to flow from that. But he is not successful in dealing with the essentially asocial nature of Heidegger's anthropology. Those aspects of psychology which would conflict with Pannenberg's understanding of the human psyche, or modify his view of the human exocentric orientation to future fellowship with God, are often simply omitted. His view of emotion, affect and mood is limited again by his instrumental approach. In particular, psychology dealing with human relations is not allowed to disturb Pannenberg's individualistic perspective. The absence of whole fields of relevant cognitive and social psychology, dealing with love, cathexis, transference and so on is remarkable for a theologian. So is the absence of material on forgiveness and reconciliation. Further, his choice of material from psychology is exercised without reference to the scientific context in which it is located. The internal, scientific, critique of some Freudian claims is suppressed. This insensitivity to the judgements and evaluations of the scientific community itself seems to be a general feature of Pannenberg's use of science, and will come to light again in the next chapters.

Chapter Five

Social Science in Pannenberg's Perspective

I have claimed that Pannenberg's anthropology is built on individualist and rationalist foundations, and that he has invoked only partial aspects of biology and psychology in order to support this. If this is true, it might be expected that Pannenberg would experience some difficulties in accounting for the social and communal dimensions of human life, or at least, he would have to adopt a very reductionist approach to sociology. There are a number of positions within social theory from which Pannenberg might be criticised. From the many perspectives available in social theory, I shall use the work of Margaret Archer, because of its methodological transparency and relevance to science, to illustrate the unsatisfactory nature of Pannenberg's use of social science.

In Chapter One, I claimed that a postmodern reconstruction of the relation between science and theology must respond to the critiques of Enlightenment rationality, including its individualism, and it must account for the role of value and interest in the acquisition of knowledge. The explanation of shared knowledge and social action put forward by Margaret Archer addresses these issues in her analysis of social theory. Archer is in no sense a relativist; indeed, she includes an explicit critique of the 'strong programme' in philosophy of science, rejecting that claim.

It is relatively easy to show the importance of the ethical in the projects of both Bauman and Gadamer in relation to the question of knowledge in science and theology. It is a little more difficult to do so in the case of Archer, because the issues are dealt with more implicitly. Archer's main contribution is the complex study, *Culture and Agency*,[1] which is an analysis of the attempts in social theory to relate the individual to the social. Sociology has seen this relation mostly in terms of the relation of structure and agency; how is it that we are both free to act as individuals and yet constrained by social structures? Archer points out that the same problem exists in relation to thought, ideas, and knowledge. We are free to accept or reject concepts, but their cultural availability is limited, may be manipulated and must be negotiated through subject-object distinctions. Her analysis is directed to developing an account of how the social phenomenon of

---

1 M.S. Archer, *Culture and Agency: The Place of Culture in Social Theory* (2nd ed.), Cambridge University Press, Cambridge (1996).

culture, of shared ideas and traditions, is related to the agency of the individual. She wishes to reject explanations which would make culture a subsidiary component of agency, and vice versa. So culture is not to be seen as merely the ideology of a dominant group, to be changed at will by the next dominant group; neither is it a central value system so dominant that members of society are simply passive carriers of those values. Archer refers to these ways of conflating culture itself with aspects of the process that give rise to it as the 'Myth of Cultural Integration'.[2] This is characterised by an inability to accept inconsistencies or conflicts in the cultural system and a denial of cultural differentiation within societies. She demonstrates that such accounts are unable to explain either the maintenance of recognisable culture or the growth and development of culture. She finds versions of it in much social theory. She criticises Parsons and the Functionalists, Durkheim, Levi Strauss and the Structuralists, as 'downward conflationists'. That is, they effectively make cultural values the source of social differentiation. On the other hand, the neo-Marxists, are 'upward conflationists' in that they see cultural values as the result of social differentiation. Archer charges Giddens and Bauman with being 'central conflationists', in which every individual is regarded as always a fully functional participant in the social process. This avoids the extremes of the two positions mentioned above. However, Archer claims that it retains the notion of language as universal order which is part of downward conflation, as a prerequisite to any meaningful action, and from upward conflation, it retains the concept of culture as the product of the actions of individuals. She concludes that this position fares no better in explaining cultural stability and change. It will be interesting to see where Pannenberg is to be located according to Archer's analysis.

Archer presents an alternative approach. She suggests that culture can be seen as having a number of interacting components. The ideas, values and concepts available in a culture she terms the Cultural System. She is clear that cultures contain both conflicting and complementary sets of ideas and values simultaneously. It follows that not all individuals and groups within a culture hold all the same ideational components at once, and the relation between the different ideas and the different social groupings is termed 'Socio-Cultural' integration by Archer. The analogy is that of the Cultural System as a library of different books, which are borrowed by individuals or groups with socially different reader's tickets. The ideas in the books may be coherent or in conflict. At any one time, particular books or groups of books may become so widely read in some groups that they influence what other books are taken out by other groups, or even the type of books that become published. Some books may not be taken out at all, and this is independent of their content. Archer's methodological separation of the ideational Cultural System (the contents of the books in circulation) from the relation between the social and the ideational, Socio-Cultural integration (which groups read which

2 See Chapter One of Archer (1996).

books) allows examination of social influences on knowledge. The relationships between ideas at the level of the Cultural System are logical or rational in character, while the relationships between the Cultural System and Socio-Cultural integration are causal or historic, as are relationships between groups at the level of Socio-Cultural integration. Most significantly, Archer argues that relations at the Socio-Cultural integration level modify and create new relations in the Cultural System. These arguments provide the foundation of a social theory of knowledge, which does not adopt irrationalism or relativism. In the library metaphor, the contents of the books are discussed and critiqued and related to each other, and new books are written, in ways which involve some kind of reasonable evaluation. But the role played by social effects can be described in Archer's terms. She expresses this by descriptions of the degree of coherence of the Cultural System on one hand, and on the other, the tightness of Socio-Cultural integration. If there is a high degree of coherence of ideas, and a tight relation between particular social groups and the ideas they hold, there will be neither social conflict nor intellectual disagreement (Archer's Concomitant Complementarity). If there is only a limited intellectual coherence, but still strong Socio-Cultural integration, then there will be contradictions that are held back socially from developing into new ideas or theories (Archer's Constraining Contradictions). If the coherence of ideas is high but the tightness of Socio-Cultural integration is low, there will be unpredictable juxtapositions of coherent ideas which can be developed and extended (Contingent Complementarity). And finally, if coherence in the system of ideas is low, and the tightness of Socio-Cultural integration is also low, there will be competing groups of ideas held by competing social groups (Competitive Contradiction). In the library metaphor, different social groups choose what they will promote or expand in the library, and what they will ignore or suppress. The ease with which this happens is affected by the tightness or looseness of the social groups, and the degree of coherence and integration of the ideas. In particular, if there is Contingent Complementarity or Competitive Contradiction, then ideas change or develop; that is, new knowledge is gained.[3] Archer criticises Kuhn for not seriously considering the role of competition in normal science and assuming there can be only one paradigm. She also claims that he gives no proper status to contradictions; they have only a psychological effect as they accumulate. Archer effectively makes them part of the engine of normal science. Her objections to Bloor hang on her assertion that contradiction can be a universal logical principle and can be used as she does in a theory about the generation and relation of ideas, and her assertion that ideas can be successfully ascribed to social groups across space and time i.e. that 'translation' is possible.

Consequently, Archer's approach to the social dynamics of knowledge also gives predictions about the possibility and mechanisms for change in that

---

3 Expressed in Chapters 7 & 8 of *Culture and Agency*, and summarised on pp 226 and 270.

knowledge. On Archer's view, combinations of highly coherent ideas and tightly linked groups interacting with those ideas leads to protection and consolidation of culture. Her significance is that she gives an explanation with predictive power for the effects of social interactions on the accumulation of knowledge, without adopting a relativist stance. Archer's explanation fits the empirical study of many systems of meaning, in both the arts or the sciences, better than the alternatives. It is clear that social groupings do influence the outcome in competitions between theories or interpretations. 'Fashion' or socially influenced promotion or selective forgetfulness of material is recognisable even in natural science. This is not to say that rational criteria do not play a role; rational, critical evaluation is an indispensable part of such science. But at any one time, an individual or group can be actively concerned with only a small part of the scientific horizon, and a judgement or choice must be made as to what will be relegated to background information.

I would suggest that this represents the missing mechanism by which Kuhn's insight into the socially and historically conditioned nature of science can be explained. It also represents a mechanism for the elaboration and development of theological knowledge in the Christian community. I think it may have a more fundamental role in that by connecting culture and agency, Archer is providing a means by which the ethics of the individual contribute to the emergence of the *polis* in the Greek thought explored by Gadamer. Hence I am also imputing an ethical dimension to Archer's work. It seems to me that she explains how it is possible to give an account of truth which is related to action, which is conditioned by a community and which is rationally evaluated and not a mere matter of opinion. That would be something in a post-modern world!

In this chapter I apply Archer's analysis to Pannenberg's social theory. It turns out that he certainly does have a number of difficulties. The most obvious stem from his supposition, common in the history of the Continental tradition that Pannenberg belongs to, that culture is a monolith of ideas and beliefs sharing a fundamental unity. Allied with this is the problem facing all social theorists, including Pannenberg, which centres on the polarity between individual voluntarism and social determinism. Different theorists in the past have sacrificed one or the other, seeing humans as either isolated intelligences or manipulated herds. Pannenberg cannot afford to sacrifice either individual freedom and responsibility, or socially mediated meaning. His dilemma is that he must make use of aspects of social science formed under such a dichotomy without wanting to subscribe to it himself. Pannenberg's assumption of cultural unity and emphasis on system lead to a view of ideas, meaning and culture that is basically static and has limited possibilities for change. The priority that he gives to culturally shared meaning as ideas, and his stress on rationality as distinct from action, lead him to a basic individualism. His explanation of social phenomena is consequently not coherently developed, and he is unable to account for or tolerate cultural diversity. His account of the origin of social phenomena is fundamentally inconsistent and flawed.

Culture and meaning

There are four significant features of Pannenberg's view of culture. He claims culture must be internally unified; it must be collective but not a product of society; it must be an independently valid source of meaning; it can be fundamentally identified with myth. Pannenberg is clearly proposing the kind of cultural homogeneity, attacked by Archer under the term 'Myth of Cultural Integration'. I shall analyse Pannenberg's arguments about culture in detail, to show up the limitations of his position.

To begin, it is necessary to understand Pannenberg's view of the essential role of culture in human social relations; he argues that the specific feature of humanity is not the fact that the shared life of individuals has a 'social structure' but rather the cultural character of this life (1985:315). Pannenberg asserts that while culture may be expressed in many components – values, behaviours, traditions, buildings, art etc. – there must be a mechanism specifying and uniting the phenomenon as a whole. He is clear that a given cultural tradition must be defensible as unique, separate and internally unified. His dependence on Herder, seen earlier in his developmental understanding of the image of God, emerges again. Archer has demonstrated that this tradition of continental anthropology, conditioned as it came to be by the early studies of exotic and 'primitive' peoples, subscribed to this view of cultural unity and integration, which is empirically dubious (Archer, 1996:7-21). Pannenberg shows his affinity with the previous generation by continuing with it.

Pannenberg seeks to support the role of culture as the repository of shared meaning with appropriate social theory. He rejects the explanation of culture in terms of social institutions given by Malinowski, for what Pannenberg sees as its failure to address the question of cultural specificity. He prefers the explorations of culture which concentrate on the human capacity to symbolise, and cites Cassirer, Geertz and Levi Strauss as providing more fertile beginnings (1985:317). But Pannenberg asserts that culture cannot be simply identified with symbol creating, because that is initially the activity of individuals, and culture is a group phenomenon, requiring a connection with the life-world. On the other hand, social institutions are not an explanation in themselves, and so cannot account alone for culture. Pannenberg concludes that a satisfactory account of culture will encompass both aspects. He is concerned to protect what he terms the 'objectivity' of culture, against explanations which would reduce it to either the sum of symbol-making activity or to the 'false consciousness' produced by social institutions.

Pannenberg's argument is hard to follow because he does not separate out its various components; symbol-creating, for instance, cannot be the activity of individuals alone, because shared meaning is an essential component of symbolism. Pannenberg does not separate the ideas and meanings of a culture from the social interactions which transmit, modify and express it. He wants to preserve the independent truth status of the contents of culture. This leads him to criticise Durkheim's concept of society's precontractual foundations; Pannenberg inappropriately interprets this as Durkheim asserting the 'superiority of society over its individual members' (1985:318). What Pannenberg wishes to establish is the necessity and epistemological legitimacy of a background of meaning for society, which is not merely generated by it but is independently valid. He postulates unity not only for culture, but society as well.[4] He often conflates the two. Pannenberg does not say whether this is an ideal unity to be worked towards; or what kind of unity could exist in present societies, which exhibit so much empirical fragmentation. This is typical of his approach to this area, which is often confusing and sometimes self contradictory. He argues that if culture cannot be reduced to either individual activity (as he has characterised symbol creating) nor to the activity of what he calls society, then a third level, distinct from both, must be found. Pannenberg sees this level as being occupied by myth (1985:319). He uses myth only in terms of its ideational component; he does not consider the interaction of the ideas of myth with social behaviour. He is again concerned to protect it from misunderstanding as either reducible to individual activity or as reification of group projections. He takes issue with M Landmann's view of culture as human creation on these grounds, noting the sense of gift or endowment that accompanies ancient traditions. His metaphysical stance emerges clearly where he says:

> The treasure accumulated in the process of cultural transmission is made up of disclosures of reality ... In speaking of human creativity we must not lose sight of the fact that in human creative activity reality is in the process of manifesting itself. (1985:320)

Here, Pannenberg's concern for the independent or objective nature of culture obscures his characterisation of what actually constitutes human creativity; he could be construed as implying that humanity is merely the passive agent of an unfolding, Hegelian reality.[5] For Pannenberg, myth is the formulation of the reality that emerges in the unity of culture, but it is not the whole explanation of that unity. He concedes that myth alone is not sufficient; reality is disclosed, he says, by the interaction between the mythical-religious tradition and the experience of the social world in which it is manifested (1985:321). But he gives no mechanism anywhere to explain how this tension between myth and religion as ideas, on one hand, and the life experience of the community, on the other, can actually issue in cultural change or renewal. This is particularly important and I will return to it at the end of this chapter. However, at this point he is arguing for culture as originating in the meanings represented in myth and religion. Here, myth occupies Pannenberg's 'third level'; it is said to be neither social nor individual in its origin. But his account of psychology, in the previous chapter, suggested that meaning arises in the consciousness of the individual, as a consequence of the structure and function of

---

4 He says 'For, as I have pointed out, the unity of society needs for its establishment the foundational order of values that is supplied by the cultural system.' (1985:318)

5 For instance, Gillian Rose (1992:7) makes this accusation; it will be discussed further in the next chapter.

consciousness itself. Above all, in his certainty that culture is and must be unified, Pannenberg subscribes to Archer's 'Myth of Cultural Integration'. To use her metaphor of the library, in Pannenberg's view, all of the books contain the same ideas.

Play, meaning and culture

Pannenberg locates the interaction between myth and the social world in the area of play, following Huizinga.[6] Pannenberg argues that play is both socially and biologically directed, and that it connects the identity of the individual with the shared world beyond. He claims that it is therefore the appropriate phenomenon to analyse to find the link between the two, which must be the source of true social and cultural unity. But this is an inadequate argument, because other features of human behaviour are both biologically and socially constituted and contribute to identity – eating, for instance – so that a stronger case must be made for selecting play. Further, the association of a biological, a social and an intellectual component in one kind of behaviour is not sufficient in itself for arguing that such behaviour is the origin of the unity of social and intellectual entities in a group.

Pannenberg asserts that the significance of play is to be found in its freedom. It is behaviour which is neither goal-directed, nor 'appetitive', seeking some specific satisfaction. He thinks of behaviour in the categories of Lorenz, and quotes Lorenz in his description of play as exploratory, curious and open to the world. He cites the claim by Lorenz that while playfulness is present in young animals of other species, only in humans does it remain at the adult stage. Pannenberg accepts the explanation of this given by Lorenz, that adult humans remain at a delayed stage of development comparable to juveniles of other species, and identifies this as neoteny (1985:323). I have already criticised the misuse of the concept of neoteny in Chapter Three, and this represents another example of such misunderstandings. Firstly, Lorenz's suggestion that adults of other species do not play would be questioned by other zoologists. Secondly, humans have nervous systems which are just as developed as those of other species; there is no anatomical, physiological or biochemical hiatus in the development of humans compared to other animals. Pannenberg finds this (mis) use of neoteny important, as it give an opportunity for him to argue that humans are released from the 'ties of instinct' in that they are free to play, and not always compelled to behaviours controlled by drives (1985:324). This is essential for Pannenberg, since he has to find some space for human freedom in a theological sense, and he has made his task more difficult by espousing a determinist biological account of human behaviour.

---

6 Huizinga's work, *Homo Ludens: A Study of the Play Element in Culture* (1949), was influential in post-war Continental anthropology.

He cites Piaget in support of the thesis that play begins as imitative behaviour, but almost immediately this requires symbolism – the wooden broom handle becomes the nursery hobby horse. By school age, the symbolisation of reality has developed a special intensity; the child is 'seized' by the game. Pannenberg again cites Lorenz, this time to show that children's play exhibits this inspired transport in symbolic role playing. Pannenberg identifies this as the most important kind of play, which includes self discipline and a desire to succeed (1985:325). This is true as far as it goes, but it describes only one kind of children's play. Children play with other kinds of pretending, such as that there are fairies in the garden, and they make imaginative constructions like dams in streams, or sand castles. In concentrating on the socially utilitarian, Pannenberg may lose insight from other kinds of play. Certainly, play requires commitment, and once others join the game, its persistence depends on agreement as to the joint rules, insofar as there are any. Pannenberg argues that the representational element fades once other individuals are involved, and the crucial feature becomes the observation of the rules, which eventually develops into contest.

Huizinga's original argument was that all culture derives from either representational or competitive play. Pannenberg develops the argument from representational play, because of its symbolic content. He also wants to draw parallels between religious cult, artistic performance and symbolic play, in that all involve the 'exaltation ' of the player or performer, and all involve the symbolic re-presenting of an absent reality that thereby becomes present (1985:327). Interestingly, he does cite Gadamer's assertion that the involvement of the audience is necessary for the representation of reality in artistic performance to be completed. It is unusual for Pannenberg to promote such reciprocity in understanding. Pannenberg recalls traditional theological caveats about representation and image. He notes that the Christian tradition rightly contains warnings against confusing symbol and reality; the presence of God is to be found in the action of Christ in the community, not in the symbol which only points to it (1985:329).[7] Having acknowledged this caution in the matter of representation, Pannenberg develops his analysis of play to include competition. In games of contest, Pannenberg argues, the representational element is in the rules of play, which represent the order of the social world, so that the ritualisation of conflicts between the players represents the integration of such interactions into the shared beliefs and practices of the culture (1985:329). Pannenberg cites Huizinga's case that such ritualisation has clearly taken place in the development of institutions of justice, economics and the military sphere. He recognises some criticisms that have been made of this thesis, in particular, the point that Huizinga may be said to trivialise areas of human life that are regarded as serious by the majority. For

7 But he does not mention the attack on objectification in representation made by Ellul in *The Humiliation of the Word* (1985), which suggests that the symbol can be made to diminish the reality.

example, the social requirement for justice surely cannot be based on or reduced to the issue of fairness in school playtime. Pannenberg argues that such a critique (and he responds mainly to Buytendijk) neglects the element of commitment and inspiration in true play, and he stresses the need to avoid using a model of a debased form of play as pretence. Pannenberg is also aware of arguments suggesting that children's play is derived from former cults, but he asserts that the independence of children's thought in play makes this unlikely. Indeed, he argues that far from being cultic remnants, children's games have a dimension that point to the sacred (1985:332). As often, Pannenberg turns the argument on its head, and uses it to support his assertion that there is an inescapable religious dimension to human social interaction, which can be found in children's play, albeit unreflected on in that situation, and which he will demonstrate to be foundational for cultural value and meaning.

Pannenberg does not acknowledge that his argument, in parallel with Durkheim's views, depends on the assumption that the social order is somehow 'given' – for how else could the rules of play represent the social order? How can play both supply the shared meaning foundational for social order, and yet depend itself on social order for implementing the 'rules' of play? He does have to acknowledge that play does not occupy a large role in Western industrialised societies. He asserts that the representational element of play has atrophied, and that play is confined to leisure. Pannenberg attacks postmodern society for the lack of commitment to meaning and value which allows culture to become a matter of private choice, and which deprives play of its role in representing communal value. He says:

> ... play is limited to the area of leisure activities and as a result, like the entire content of a culture based on leisure (this includes art and religion), stands under the sign of arbitrariness and of the depletion of meaning to which arbitrariness leads ... Now the limitation of play to an arbitrarily ordered leisure time has largely reduced it to a matter of pretense. The heritage of one's own cultural tradition and the records of alien cultures have become interchangeable consumer goods. (1985:333)

The last sentence could be misread in a modern, multicultural society. He may simply be arguing that contemporary societies are losing all the cultural traditions extant in them. Or he may be adverting to the Western interest in exotic religions of the East. However, his use of the term 'alien' could also be read as a threat; does Pannenberg's regard for the unity of culture lead him to be suspicious of infiltration by different cultures? If so, one may ask how else a given culture is to develop and grow, if not by assimilation from others?

Pannenberg is clear about the political use of such a privatising and separating out of cultural meaning; he makes the parallel between modern society's leisure time and the Roman 'bread and circuses', and concedes the Marxist critique of it. He notes that modern Marxists (and he cites Moltmann in this context) have called for the reintegration of freedom and self realisation into the world of work, rather than seeking to protect and extend so called free time. He observes that the modern concepts of both work and play have become similarly alienating because of the evacuation of meaning from public life. Communal discourse is dominated by economic and bureaucratic rationality (1985:334). Pannenberg here offers a serious political critique of postmodern society, from a perspective that social theorists such as Bauman would recognise. Pannenberg effectively concedes the failure of Enlightenment rationality and describes the empirical effect of this on present society.[8] However Pannenberg is most unusual in locating the problem in the loss of play in modern society. He argues that this is serious because it is the place where commitment is learned, and, in the context of his biology of drive, the point at which sociality suppresses individual biology (1985:335). His argument is unclear, because he has provided no evidence that children play less, and the learning components of play he refers to must surely take place in childhood. It is adult play that he claims to be missing from contemporary society. Again, his adoption of the biology of Lorenz leads to a Hobbesian view of humans as innately antisocial animals that need domesticating. Pannenberg also claims that play, being meaningful in itself, is an end in itself, whereas work in modern society is experienced only as a means to an end. If work could become an end in itself similar to true play, then it would become a free activity as play is. Pannenberg does not venture any further in this idealistic direction, apart from observing that 'conflict and compulsion' are empirical aspects of human society and work must be organised to allow for that (1985:336). He cites the importance of cultic play, in the form of games and festivals, for societies down the ages. In an almost nostalgic strain, he claims that the meaning made present in religious feasts and sacred play has been evicted from the 'modern work world' (1985:337). However, it could be argued that the 'modern work world' is not so empty of meaning as Pannenberg claims. There are rituals and practices surrounding birth, marriage and death, for instance, which are not confined to churches and church-goers, but which mediate meaning in Pannenberg's sense of it. Pannenberg himself claims this full meaning in present times only for the Christian liturgy, as sacred play. He contends that human exocentricity issues in play, which originates with children's play and is completed in religious worship (1985:338). The problem with the astonishing sweep of this argument is that there is no logically compelling link between the development from child to adult and from ancient cult to present day religious practice. Pannenberg frequently mixes these analogies of child to adult development with development of human culture over time. Similarly, he assumes an identity between the observable outward orientation of children in play and the theologically defined exocentric destiny of humans as expressed in the Christian religion. But he has

8 One wonders if all his commentators in the USA (e.g. see Braaten & Clayton, 1988, Murphy, 1990, Shults, 1999) fully realise his position. However, it is clear that Pannenberg regards the situation as retrievable; value could be recovered. In this he differs from many postmodern social theorists.

presented no argument that could justify such an *identity*, although he has devoted much effort to showing that his chosen biological accounts are *compatible* with Christian anthropology. He very briefly acknowledges some of the negative possibilities of play, in terms mostly of the demonic in the context of religions. He does not talk at all about the negative possibilities of cults of nationality, which have been so significant in this century, or any other similar problems. He concludes that 'cultic play is the organizing center of the shared human world and of its unity' (1985:338), without any further discussion of alternative theses which might give value and meaning a primary role but locate them elsewhere. He seems unaware of evidence that the shared human world is not totally integrated and unified.

Interestingly, Pannenberg only uses a couple of footnotes (1985:327) to refer to Gadamer's extensive discussion of the role of play in *Truth and Method* (1979). Gadamer's analysis is significantly different from Pannenberg's. Gadamer does not regard children's play as the fundamental expression of play as such, but instead, looks at the relation between adult play and art, in terms of poetry, literature and theatre. He agrees with Pannenberg in viewing play as ecstatic, but does not agree with attempts to base it in biology. He does not regard play as a mere revealing of values, as Pannenberg seems to suggest, but as a performance, 'not merely repetition, but bringing forth' (1979:103) of truth. This cannot be objectively cut out of its context, but must remain incomplete, against a background of undecided possibilities. Actor and action cannot be considered apart from the spectator and reception, if the truth of the performance is to be understood. So there is an element of new creation in the re-presentation involved in play.[9] Pannenberg's perspective on this is different; he sees the values revealed in play as objective, extractable, and he sees no need for interaction between the player and the auditor, although the auditor must be present for the disclosure of reality. The implication of Pannenberg's account is that the social structure arising from play is one externally imposed on individuals, not one created by reciprocal experiences.

Language and culture

Pannenberg gives considerable importance to language in mediating the shared world of meaning and value that founds culture. He distinguishes between reason and language, making reason the prior apprehension of meaning, and language its secondary expression (1985:339). This is not the view of Gadamer, who sees language and meaning as intrinsically and reciprocally related. The question of whether reason precedes language is also controversial in science. For instance, there have been arguments that deaf children's ability to form concepts is seriously

9 There are interesting parallels between Gadamer's view of representation and those of Sölle as expressed in *Christ the Representative* (1967).

impaired if they primarily use sign language rather than written words. Pannenberg also attempts to provide support from ethology for the precedence of thought over language, although not wholly appropriately, as I discussed in Chapter Three.

To maintain the significance of language for the expression of meaning underlying culture, Pannenberg has to deal with various reductionist and relativist arguments which would limit the role of language and reduce culture to a specific, determinate world view. He gives a pointed survey of philosophical influences on the understanding of language. Cassirer's understanding of symbolism and Heidegger's analysis promoted the significance of language for thought; Chomsky suggested a mechanism for language which depended on prior mental processes, and Pannenberg recruits Wittgenstein to the ranks of those who assert that thought is not reducible to language. Pannenberg also presents speculative arguments from developmental child psychology, and from archaeology, in both cases arguing that concepts precede the appearance of language.[10] Even if it is conceded that thought preceded language, this is not sufficient to explain the complex relation between language and thought. In particular, it might be argued that language is the product of an individual's thought, and it would then be an action. Pannenberg is concerned to establish language as essential for the bearing of the meaning and value, i.e. knowledge, that is foundational for culture. As I have already shown in earlier chapters, he wishes to preserve the process of knowing from the contamination of action, since this would endanger its certainty. It is consequently extremely important for his enterprise that he eliminates explanations of language as action.

Pannenberg therefore revises the arguments of Austin and Searle, that some uses of language may be seen as actions, whether performative, as in promise, or illocutionary, as actions in themselves. Pannenberg asserts that action, as intentional, is goal oriented. Are speech and language fundamentally goal oriented? Pannenberg does not deny the existence of performative acts, but he does not accept that, for instance, statements of fact constitute actions. He argues that speech act theory is inadequate in that it reduces language to action and cannot account for the objective content of statements (1985:369). One might note that others disagree, interpreting Searle's speech act theory as including a satisfactory treatment of the propositional content of utterance.[11] However, Pannenberg cites Chomsky's critique of Searle, arguing that language can be essentially expressive of meaning, and any action is then subservient to this. Pannenberg focuses on the concept of conversation as being illuminating in this area. He follows Bühler in characterising speech as having elements of expression, representation, and communication, and suggests that conversation must have a large element of representation, since it mediates between expression and communication. This would suggest that such conversational speech is less of an action, since the role of

---

10 See Pannenberg (1985:340-360).

11 e.g. Chapter Eight of Thiselton (1992).

communication (for an end) is reduced. Pannenberg also uses the resources of sociology to support his argument. He cites Goffman's ethnomethodological studies on conversational interactions as showing the absence of goal directed action, and exemplifying the ecstatic nature of conversation (1985:371). Pannenberg makes the connection between such experience and those that in the past were spoken of as experiences of 'spirit', and cites such usage in the Old and New Testaments. But this again is an unsatisfactory argument, because Goffman is describing everyday, ordinary conversation whereas experiences of the spirit are unusual.

Following his theological commitment to providing a philosophical legitimation for experience that cannot be reduced to the mere sum of empirical facts, Pannenberg explores the possibilities of speaking of the 'spirit' of a conversation. He gives a brief discussion of the Old Testament *ruah* and the New Testament *pneuma* in terms of the wind that blows unseen and yet carries away those exposed to it. Similarly, he seems to argue, a conversation carries away its participants, and an explanation for this is required. A conversation is a freely created pattern of subjects, not determined in advance, and yet connected in some way. Pannenberg sees the openness of language as the basis of this. He argues that language continually produces new 'determinate meanings', which are at the same time in the context of a whole range of possible meaning (1985:374).[12] Further, the openness of language is complemented by the shared horizon of a totality in which speakers anticipate the complete setting of emerging meaning. The correction of anticipated meaning is the source, for Pannenberg, of the elements of direct action that may enter a conversation as specific communications or explanations. He identifies a religious element present in all language; he says 'In the "trance" into which the participants in a successful conversation fall, the spirit of life as a totality finds expression' (1985:376). Pannenberg is optimistic, I think; the key words there are 'successful conversation' and he does not consider the unsuccessful ones. How do we identify them and what are the consequences of failure? There may be a 'religious dimension' to all utterance of any kind whatever, but the basic religious question is the awareness of the good and the bad. If Pannenberg's religious dimension is diluted to a vague, unthematic totality, then it isn't any use. If it is an explicit thematic, then he is in danger of blessing whatever is the dominant discourse. This is made more difficult by the lack of reciprocity or exchange in his view of conversation. As described earlier, he argues that conversation must contain a large element of representation; it is a process of putting two points of view clearly, so that they may be rationally evaluated.

Pannenberg does allude to the problem of the distortion of language, and this is in the context of the role of imagination. He sees this as a source of inspiration, in terms of the anticipation of the horizon of meaning which is basic to Gadamer's view of understanding. Pannenberg gives a primacy to the inspirational component

---

12 On this point, Pannenberg claims to agree with Gadamer, who is referred to in a footnote (1985:374, note 161).

of imagination, and gives it a foundational role in the phenomenon of human freedom. He claims that imagination frees the individual from being determined by their context, but he acknowledges that imagination itself can be corrupted, and that this will consequently distort language (1985:381). Here he guards himself against the suggestion that he could be promoting any kind of theory of inspiration, where truth is located less in reason than in these transcendent experiences of seizure in play and language.[13] Pannenberg considers the status of explicit language about God in the light of all this, distinguishing between the mythical and the magical use of words, and pointing to the transmission of the transcendental as characteristic of myth, whereas magic is the exertion of control. He is again concerned to maintain the epistemological status of the content of the Gospel, and to prevent it being reduced to the sum of human activity.

Pannenberg's claims about human speaking can be summarised briefly in three points. Firstly, language is the medium by which culture is transmitted. It should be noted that arguments for such dependence of culture on language, as put forward by Bauman (1973) and Giddens (1976), have been extensively criticised by Archer (1996). Cultural codes, she argues, are not as tight as grammatical ones, and action is not so tightly integrated into cultural codes as into linguistic ones. These arguments apply just as well to Pannenberg's view of the role of language in disclosing the meaning foundational for culture. Secondly, in Pannenberg's view human speaking cannot be explained by completely reducing it to the sum of biological, psychological or semiotic components. Thirdly, human language has objective content which is not diminished by its also having an intrinsic openness to the transcendent, the possibility of which is independent of human activity. Pannenberg stresses the priority of reason and meaning; he strives to preserve 'objectivity' of content; he minimises any dimensions of language as action. Overall, his position represents a marked shift from Gadamer's creative view of language in the direction of a more fixed, unidirectional and content centred approach.

Culture and Social Institutions

In *Anthropology in Theological Perspective*, Pannenberg evaluates sociological explanations of social institutions as such. He again declares unacceptable arguments which reduce cultural phenomena to the products of human activity (1985:397). To this end, he reviews the issues raised by classic accounts of social institutions – Durkheim, Malinowski and Talcott Parsons – defining the particular areas that he sees as having implications for his theological agenda. He draws back

---

13 He suggests that such imaginative disorder in language could lead to neurosis, and that there could be a connection between the linguistic community, hermeneutics and therapy (1985:382, footnote 180).

from discussion of the role of institutions in the wider social system, but concentrates on the controversy about the relation of social institutions and individual behaviour. He says:

> Is the social system, together with its partial systems (institutions), to be understood ultimately in the light of the behaviour of individuals? Or, on the other hand, are individuals simply interchangeable as component parts whose individuality is irrelevant for an understanding of the social system ... Is not the asserted priority in principle of institutions, or, as the case may be, social systems over individual behaviour really a pseudo-theological assertion, inasmuch as this priority replaces the primacy of God (or, in the case of Durkheim, of universal human nature) over the concrete reality of individual and communal human life? (1985:399)

The problem with this is that here Pannenberg appears to put together Comte, who did appeal to the priority of a universal and collective human nature, and Durkheim, who did not, although the latter does give great significance to the social. This is typical of the confusing way in which Pannenberg approaches social theory. Pannenberg observes that the kingdom of God cannot be identified with the kingdom of the world, even if that is the social system. He alleges that Durkheim claimed the priority of the social over against the individual, and points out that this amounts to a kind of political theology (1985:400). This would be the case if Durkheim's position is as Pannenberg views it. But although Durkheim seeks to explain the totality of human behaviour in terms of the projection of shared value, the cultural system, he does not argue for the priority of the social order which originates meaning and value. For Durkheim, the precontractual foundations of society are simply given, even though society depends on the values they provide for the regulation of human conduct. Pannenberg notes that Malinowski's explanation roots social priority in the response to basic human needs such as nutrition, reproduction, shelter, etc. But not all institutions can be traced back to such needs, either primary or secondary.

Pannenberg seeks an alternative view in that of Talcott Parsons, who regarded social institutions as performing functions required for the integrity of the social system as a whole. He viewed the social system itself as built on the interactions between individuals reflecting patterns of cultural values. At this point, Pannenberg appears to be allying himself with a position that would parallel Archer's 'downward conflation'. Pannenberg agrees that social institutions can be thought to have arisen from value directed, role related behaviour, but in modern societies there is a discontinuity between the existing institutions and the roles or division of labour in society at large; the institutions now appear to operate with subsets of rules independently within society. Pannenberg wants explanations of the basis of social institutions which fit his theological agenda, and he turns to Gehlen in the tradition of German philosophical anthropology, for an account that will preserve the independence of the individual, and to Berger and Luckmann for a contemporary analysis.

Gehlen, like Huizinga, uses the concept of play in his explanation of institutions; although this is the game or contest understanding of play, not the symbolic-representational picture. Gehlen's metaphor of institutionalised play does not explain the general acceptability of social institutions, and Pannenberg looks to Berger and Luckmann (1966) for this. They also start their explanation of institutions in the observation of play-like behaviour, but this is ritual or customary behaviour, which is established before any division of labour (1985:404). Pannenberg points out the similarities between Gehlen and Berger, tracing the influence of philosophical anthropology via Luckmann into sociology.[14] As well as Gehlen's observation of stable customary behaviour as foundational for culture, Pannenberg adverts to the sense of obligation in the responses in such stereotyped behavioural exchanges, which is referred to by Gehlen. In the face of this, Pannenberg says that the main problem in explaining social institution is accounting for their independence (1985:404). Pannenberg analyses the different explanations for the independence of institutions; he claims that Durkheim's view of objectification or reification and Gehlen's view of institution as dependent on individual action are echoed in the work of Berger and Luckmann (1966). They regard social institutions as the result of the activity of humans, who are then in some sense separated or alienated from the results of their activity, and thus give it an independent reality. But Pannenberg claims that Berger and Luckmann do not agree with Durkheim as such, because they see a reality behind the independence of institutions. Their explanation depends on the importance of meaning to individuals in establishing and maintaining all the reciprocal behaviours that are foundational for social structures. Such meaning has to be socially shared to be effective, and is therefore constructed as an umbrella under which activity takes place. Pannenberg argues that such meaning has effectively to exist prior to activity, and that this explains the precedence of institutions over individuals (1985:406). It should be noted that there are alternative interpretations of the view of Berger and Luckmann, such as those of Wuthnow (1986), Gaeder (1986) and Mechling (1986). For example, Mechling characterises Berger's position as altogether more subtle; she says Berger asks:

> ... whether theological thinking is possible, *given* (in a sense) the sociological analysis of the social constructedness of religion ... Once every plausibility structure, including scientific sociology's, has been relativized, 'the question of truth reasserts itself in almost pristine simplicity' writes Berger ... (he) turns to philosophical anthropology to propose an empirical starting point for theology's asking questions of truth. 'I would suggest that theological thought seeks out what might be called *signals of transcendence* within the empirically given human situation'. Signals of transcendence are empirical phenomena we encounter in our natural attitude to the world 'but appear to point beyond that reality'

14 Berger has an explicit debt to the continental tradition, particularly to phenomenology – see Ainley, in Hunter & Ainley (1986:31-54) – and draws on Gehlen directly (see Hunter, in Hunter & Ainley, 1986:91-95).

> ... Berger then proceeds to offer his tentative list of five prototypical human gestures that signal a transcendent reality: ordering, play, hope, damnation and humor. (1986:212)

This differs from Pannenberg's position, in that he does not recognise the absolute relativisation or social dependence of any knowledge, let alone scientific knowledge.[15] However, Mechling also points out that Berger does not expect even this approach to yield absolute knowledge, and that truths can be forgotten as much as discovered (1986:213).

Pannenberg does not acknowledge that he is turning these authors on their heads, so to speak, in ignoring their demonstration of the social component in human knowledge. He argues that since the existence of social institutions depends on reciprocal human behaviours in an over arching context of meaning, it follows that as means of human coexistence, social institutions may indeed be seen as meeting and ordering basic human needs. This allows him to say that social institutions can have a legitimate priority over individuals, but not be ends in themselves. However, it does not allow him to distinguish between social institutions, with their associated context of meaning, and mere sociableness or herding together. He attempts this by referring back to the role of language in establishing the unity and reality of the social world and the world of objects. While language mediates the social world via shared meaning and value, it also communicates the social validation of the object world. This allows the individual an independent criterion against which a specific group can be evaluated (1985:408). This is Pannenberg's solution to the classic problem of how to distinguish between the concept of community in a group of monks and a gang of robbers. Pannenberg here asserts that, as he has already argued, behind the use of language lies a shared context of meaning, which is social but nevertheless rooted in the world of objects. This means that individuals always have access to that reality, and as I read him, deliberate collusion between members of a group would be required for promotion of sectarian readings of that context of meaning.

In order to secure social institutions even more, Pannenberg links them to the role they must play in supporting humans to their proper destiny. This cannot involve social institutions making claims that would supplant God as that final destiny. Pannenberg argues that the experience of reality and its meaning that is disclosed in social interactions, and that lies behind formalised social institutions, is in fact the awareness of the call to a common human destiny. In other words, the Kingdom of God, both now and yet to come (1985:409). Here Pannenberg achieves his theological object, which is subordinating the social to the individual in representing the function of society as allowing individuals to 'experience as present their common destiny'. Pannenberg explicitly refers to the problems of

15 The 'signals of transcendence' themselves reflect the interest in philosophical anthropology that is common to Pannenberg and Berger. This will be discussed later in this chapter.

identifying any existing phase in human society with the ultimate kingdom of God. He argued that the shared awareness of meaning that undergirds any given social institution makes it possible for there to be reasonable critique of social phenomena by individuals. But if that is so, he must explain the persistence of corrupt social systems, and he does so by appealing to Malinowski's view of institutions. Even defective institutions can still meet some basic human needs, and therefore continue even after a crisis in the relevance of their meaning. However, this is not a satisfactory total explanation, because many institutions meet multiple needs, and conversely, there are phases in human civilisation when needs are not met by such institutions.

Pannenberg prefers the explanation of Berger and Luckmann, that institutions regulate human social relationships, and meeting needs is a significant part of that regulation. He suggests that understanding of social institutions is to be properly found in the 'reciprocity of relations between individuals' (1985:411). But here Pannenberg is reducing the insight of Berger and Luckmann to a form of individualism akin to a rational choice theory, which is not what they intend. Pannenberg argues that his reading does not imply that shared values are irrelevant; on the contrary, they provide the impetus for the particular form of realisation of social reciprocity that arises in a given cultural context. He is aware of the diversity of cultural and religious values in human societies, which contrasts with the apparently limited range of social institutions which seem to be universally encountered. There must be some explanation of this constancy, and Pannenberg seeks for it in the background to the rules governing the regulation of human relations.

He defines reciprocity in human relations as founded upon mutuality, the adaptation to the other, between independent individuals. He then observes that all individuals are not equally independent, because the family, par excellence, is the institution in which dependent individuals are supported. He concludes that this leads to a division of all institutions into one of two kinds. There are those in which the community has priority over individual, of which the main pattern is the family. There are also those in which the individual has priority over the community, and the institutions of property and economy represent the typical form of these (1985:413). Again, Pannenberg casts his argument in the form of the discovery of some primordial process or structure, which is then assumed to have a continuing ontological function in a present situation. But no reasoning is offered to make the link from past to present. Pannenberg warns that despite the differing emphases in these two types of institutions, both depend on a combination of the same two elements of mutuality and particularity. The loss of the minor element will lead to the disintegration of the institution. All social institutions are variants on these two themes, according to Pannenberg. Variants on the family theme include all social associations, such as tribe, people, state, and Pannenberg specifies, religious communities. Variants on the property theme include all kinds of institution which can be seen as enabling relationships in which individual independence is prior (1985:413). He has to admit mixed forms of institutions, such as farms (agricultural property) run by families, and educational institutions, which seek to assist individuals who are moving to independence, and yet must learn the social skills of both mutuality and particularity. He notes the historical tendency to increasing differentiation and separation of institutions from each other and especially, from religion. But he asserts that the balance between mutuality and particularity is always the foundation of any social institution, and this is the key to an acceptable theological explanation of social institutions. He parallels the relation between mutuality and particularity in social structures with the tension between exocentricity and centrality in individual human behaviour that he has discussed previously. He argues that the social is in fact built on the individual.[16] After all his claims to leave room for the transcendent, it appears that Pannenberg is settling for a kind of reductionism; social life and integration is explained by the competing human drives of exocentricity and centrality. This is also a very cold view of humanity; there is nothing here about love or cathexis, and no sense of being called out of the self; exocentricity is driven from inside. Furthermore, he seems to have swung from a position in which the social component of culture was explained by the overarching power of systems of value and meaning, to an explanation of socially integrated cultural life as due to the behaviour of individuals. In Archer's terms, he has moved from a position of downward conflation to one of upward conflation.

However, this permits him to tie up his theological package. He argues that the description of the necessity of social institutions for the working out of the mutuality-particularism balance can be used instead of the old language of the theological doctrines of the orders of creation. He actually suggests the 'replacement' of the doctrine (1985:415). This move must be seen against the historical background of the struggles between the Confessing Church and German Christians over the role of the state; in his footnotes Pannenberg cites Althaus and Bonhoeffer, as well as post-war Brunner. Pannenberg refers to the discussions in Germany about the discrediting of the Lutheran theological concept of the orders of creation. He argues that previous theologians have not had a satisfactory foundation for any theology of institutions and he criticises the Commission on Institutions of the Evangelical Church of Germany for failing to produce such a systematic foundation. Barth had rejected the idea of orders of creation completely; here Pannenberg is trying to rehabilitate the underlying concepts. He asserts that a properly theologically grounded anthropology is the only reasonable starting point for a theology of institutions (1985:416). His appropriation of Gehlen is his own starting point, but as this chapter has shown, it is highly problematic.

16 He says 'Social anthropology is thus referred back to the foundations of anthropology as such.' (1985:415)

Property

Pannenberg asserts that he has located the origin and legitimation of social institutions in the balance between exocentricity and centredness, between mutuality and assertion of individuality. Pannenberg presents an analysis of institutions classified under the headings of property or family, defined above in terms of their alleged balance between mutuality and particularity. In doing so, he deals with subjects subsumed under the heading of political theology by other authors, but which are classified as anthropology by Pannenberg.

His account of institutions of property and economic life is provided from a perspective that might be more or less the opposite of that of 'liberation theology', for instance. Pannenberg is explicit that the concept of property involves an absolute right of disposal (1985:416). He argues that property is a consequence of work, asserting that this is fundamentally individual. He asserts that the definition of work excludes enjoyment, and uses the example of food provision to illustrate this. His understanding of work depends on delayed gratification; work is behaviour with a delayed benefit, which confers security for the future. Pannenberg sees this as the key to the negative effects of property; increase in property represents increase in security, and the desire for property-based security may compete with what Pannenberg terms 'the religious dimension' of life (1985:419). On a less individualistic reading of property, the problem is that if one takes more for the self, others get less and may be damaged. Pannenberg's fundamental view of human nature makes everything a reading of the self. Here the sin of greed appears to be primarily one of damaging one's own religious development, and only secondarily one of hurting anyone else. Pannenberg is clear that the human desire for security through property is dubious, and that it is illusory to suppose that it can bring ultimate freedom. But he also wishes to assert the necessity for property in the establishment of conditions of life which permit any exercise of freedom. He can acknowledge a communal dimension to work and property, but it is not in the necessity of co-operation for production, but in the market. Pannenberg cites Adam Smith's argument for the development of social structures and the division of labour from basic exchange of products (1985:421). Pannenberg presents an account of Durkheim's view of division of labour, as if it was an extension of this argument.[17] Pannenberg contrasts this explanation of the division of labour with a Marxist interpretation in terms of alienation. He notes that the formerly communist countries wanted to develop a sense of social participation in their workforce, which private ownership of the means of production was thought to militate against. Pannenberg suggests that property itself is not an actual barrier to social integration of work, since it is itself a social institution (1985:423). Pannenberg also sees a communal dimension to the phenomenon of owned property because of the social and subsequent legal recognition extended to it. He does allow that this shows some

17 In fact, Durkheim opposed Adam Smith's utilitarianism.

priority of the social over the individual in respect of property. He then has to admit that the empirical observation of recognition of property rights always includes the reservation of the power to take and use property from an individual if the community interest requires it.

Pannenberg's respect for the theological tradition requires him to harmonise this high view of property with the early church's suspicion of it. He adverts to the assumption under natural law that humans originally held all things in common, and seeks to explain this in terms of philosophical deficiencies in the concepts available to the Church fathers. He asserts that 'the metaphysics of antiquity was as yet unfamiliar with the concept of person' (1985:424) and that it prioritised the universal over the particular. Pannenberg acknowledges that the reason for the ancient church's acceptance of such positions might have been connected with the obvious tension between the love enjoined by the New Testament message and the concentration on self implied by property. But, he says, since John Locke and Kant, modern thought has made it clear that property is an essential dimension of personal freedom and expression. It is interesting to note that Pannenberg uses the same method of interpreting or correcting the theological tradition when he is dealing with the implications of evolutionary theory for the origin of humanity and the interpretation of Genesis, as when he is dealing with the teachings of Jesus on property. He gives the impression that he evaluates ideas for philosophical coherence, without using any significant New Testament criteria for acceptability.

Pannenberg is concerned to incorporate Hegel's contribution to the status of property into his argument. This is based on the understanding of the basic ethical community or state, which must enable and secure the freedom of all its citizens to be themselves as individuals. This freedom of self-expression and development actually implies property as a necessity, as an essential feature of becoming human, according to Hegel.[18] Pannenberg cites Hegel's deriving this view of property from the Christian understanding of personal freedom. The fact that the connection between freedom and property was only made in the beginning of the nineteenth century is taken as evidence for the 'length of time mind requires for progress in its self-consciousness' (1985:425). On the basis of this view of Hegel, Marx can be, and is, criticised by Pannenberg for not accepting the proper importance of individuality in social life. Pannenberg regards the limitations set on the use of property as resulting from its legal designation. He does not argue for any ethically based restrictions on arbitrary destruction of property in the light of communal needs.[19]

Pannenberg is aware that his position is not uncontroversial. He refers to the work of Stopp and of Breidenstein as presenting alternative arguments, but he does

18 Pannenberg quotes Hegel thus 'In fact, Hegel even says that it is a "duty to possess things as property, that is, to exist as a person".' (1985:425)

19 For instance, the felling of a forest owned by an individual which may affect local rivers and cause environmental damage.

not mention the arguments of Moltmann or the theologians of liberation. He acknowledges that in the modern state, other institutions have taken over much of the welfare provision that property is the means of achieving on his model. Nevertheless, he sees the persistence of property as essential for guaranteeing human freedom of development and expression (1985:427). Pannenberg's interpretation of property as a primarily individual issue, which gives rise secondarily to associated social structures, appears to be a position of upward conflation, in Archer's terms. The collective values of the culture here derive from the acts of individuals. This appears to conflict with his position in describing the origin of culture as described in the first part of this chapter. Further, Pannenberg devotes little space to the problem of the unequal distribution of property in limiting human freedom, which in empirical terms, is an overwhelming global problem. His discussion of work is equally disappointing; he gives no analysis of creativity, and no theology of power. He can be read as providing a very narrow defence of a politically right wing European *status quo*. This is a pity, as work and vocation are surely areas where Pannenberg's understanding of the ecstatic could have great relevance.

The Family

Pannenberg regards the family as the paradigm of social integration. He begins his presentation on the family in *Anthropology in Theological Perspective* with a typically ethological account of sexuality, which I have criticised in Chapter Three. Pannenberg's dependence on the ideas of drive is again inappropriate, and his presentation of sexuality would certainly incur feminist critique. He refers to the non-seasonal nature of human sexual activity and the role of culture in modifying human sexuality. (1985:427-429). The subtext seems to be again the old idea of humans as potentially dangerous collections of drives, here sexual, that must be controlled. Pannenberg does indeed talk explicitly about the importance of the cultural integration of sexuality. While he links this with the institutions of marriage and family, he asserts that 'neither family nor marriage has for its primary purpose to regulate sexual relations' (1985:429). This statement is in direct contradiction to the views of the ethologists he has just cited, but he does not refer to this. Pannenberg wishes to argue that relationships arise from the human orientation to exocentricity, and that sexual encounters take place in the context of the awareness of the life-world that this brings. That includes the awareness of time, which is the context for the permanent nature of human sexual partnerships. He argues from his earlier analysis of the human psyche that awareness of time is what permits individuals to relate to their own life as a totality, and he suggests that this 'becomes thematic' in social, and particularly sexual, relationships. Such relationships are monogamous as a consequence, and 'the intention of a lasting relationship' is implied. Most strikingly, Pannenberg says:

> Implications of this kind play a part in all human relations in which persons bind themselves to one another. Precisely for this reason they are especially characteristic of the relation of the sexes. (1985:430)

One is tempted to ask, if he means this, why on earth does he pay so little attention to relationships and their dynamics? The whole of his treatment of psychology simply ignores the relation with the other. Even here, he is making relations with others arise from the consequences of the ego's relation to the self in time. Is it really credible to suppose that humans engage in permanent sexual relationships as a means of relating to themselves? And how can this be consistent with the biology of exocentricity and drive that he claims for the origin of sexuality? 'Binding' to one another is different from being exocentrically driven to the opposite sex. Pannenberg could make so much more of his understanding of the 'seizure' of conversation and play if he applied it to cathexis and attachment in human relations, instead of being hamstrung by the pseudo-biology of drives.

Pannenberg argues that the family is based in a wider social and cultural context than the simple formation of partnerships. He notes the precedence of clan over nuclear family in older society, and refers to the use of marriage in the social organisation of property in ancient times. He argues that the legal regulation of such situations gave protection to women and children from the arbitrary exercise of clan power, and that this regulation had its origin in the religious values and norms of the community.[20] He asserts that whatever explanations are given for the details, the basic social legitimation of the family as an institution is religious in origin. This follows because, for Pannenberg, only a claim sanctioned by religion can give precedence for the communal over the individual (1985:436). Pannenberg makes the important point that the public commitment to marriage is made to society acting as witness, not as authority. He uses the same grounding of marriage and family in a communally accepted but transcendent value system to establish the parental 'spheres of authority' (1985:437). Pannenberg does acknowledge that the priority of community over self requires justification, but argues that this can only be found in religion. In this legitimation of the family as social institution, he is arguing in the opposite way, methodologically, from the approach he used for legitimating social institutions generally. The latter was an argument from individual behaviour balancing reciprocity and mutuality to the existence of perceived shared meaning and value. Now he is arguing from overarching meaning downwards to social behaviour, and inclining to Archer's downward conflation.

Pannenberg extends his analysis to include Christian accounts of family through the period of decline of patriarchy. He admits that the general tenor of Old Testament writing appears to condone or assume a patriarchal organisation of

20 He spends considerable time in a discussion of the conflicting approaches to totemism of Gehlen and Levi Strauss in their explanations of the emergence of family in human societies, and of related issues such as the prohibition of incest (1985:432-435).

family. However, he claims that even the Old Testament is subversive of any attempt to absolutise family, and that this is even more striking in the teachings of Jesus, especially in his relations with women (1985:438). And he argues that social changes which affect the family can be evaluated in the light of these radical Christian principles. The 'political and economic changes in modern society' (1985:439) represent a chance to reconstruct marriage and family along properly Christian lines. Pannenberg asserts that in the doing of this, marriage is not to be subsumed under the needs of the family, but *vice versa*.[21] This is in keeping with his individualism, which would put the needs of the partnership before those of the family group, but it is in contradiction to his general, downward conflationist, account of the religiously sanctioned priority of the communal. In a footnote, he draws on Rendtorff for support in this position, and notes that it is not the dominant view in traditional Christian teaching on marriage.

Marriage seen as primarily partnership fits Pannenberg's purposes, because it allows the balance of the claims of mutuality and particularity. The willingness to accept children into the marital community follows from mutuality, the priority of community over the individual. The cultural shaping of the roles of the sexes must allow for individuality, and will change with time, being socially conditioned. But Pannenberg wants to argue for the necessity of some specific social differentiation. He quotes Margaret Mead describing the roles of men as protectors and providers, and of women as bearers and nurturers of children, and says that these roles represent demands that must be faced by any society. It follows, he argues, that the complementary relationships in marriage fulfil human destiny as social, and that 'early Christianity could look upon marriage as representing the entire human community as renewed by Jesus Christ' (1985:441). If, as he argues, human destiny is to live exocentrically, and marriage is an earthly fulfilment of this destiny for community, what is the significance and implication of complementarity? Is Pannenberg giving marriage an eschatological pre-eminence in human relationships?

Pannenberg buttresses this early twentieth century view of marriage by removing monogamy from the category of a mere social custom. He asserts that it was the norm in Hellenistic and Roman culture before Christianity. The distinctive role of Christianity was to give meaning to monogamy, as a relation of mutual love, which was not necessarily present in preceding cultures. He addresses the problem of the contemporary questioning of monogamy. This is interesting, because he does not appear to raise the same kind of questions about contemporary subversions of the Christian basis to property that he outlined previously. Pannenberg is sure that

21 He says 'It is essential for any such reshaping that marriage be no longer viewed from the standpoint of the family, but rather, the family from the standpoint of marriage. This means that first of all, marriage, being a communion of love between the partners, is an end in itself, and does not need to be justified by any further purpose, not even the generation of new life.' (1985:439)

present problems about the stability of marriage are due to the loss of the religious dimension to marriage; the basis of any true community requires acceptance of the role of the divine in maintaining it. But, says Pannenberg, in modern marriage, God is excluded from a relation that is between the partners alone (1985:443). He contrasts this with Christian marriage, 'entered into before God', which can be permanent because:

> In a Christian marriage ... the love of the partners for each other must be constantly renewed from the forgiving love of Christ for them. (1985:443)

This is notable as one of the very few places in *Anthropology in Theological Perspective* where Pannenberg actually mentions the love of God. It is clear that Pannenberg regards it as self evident, but it has not been discussed at all in the context of modern psychology or sociology. The human need for forgiveness, the possibility of love, the construction of community, are all areas of human experience with which the great sciences have had difficulty, but which they do comment on. Yet Pannenberg concludes his section on marriage and family with no further comment or discussion on this; he simply breaks off as if that is all that needs to be said. More seriously, his argument that the family's claim to authority is based on its ability to be a meaningful community for the individual depends again on the essential uniformity and totality contained in his concept of meaning. Pannenberg's theory is not so useful in the face of families which contain competing value systems, whether wealthy dynasties or inner city kinships. And his elaboration of the grounding of marriage and the family appears to be primarily one of downward conflation in Archer's terms, although at certain points he gives quite inconsistent accounts.

The State

Pannenberg defends the inclusion of the state as a social institution in *Anthropology in Theological Perspective* with an argument from Aristotle. This claims that humans can only be properly fulfilled in an ethical, and therefore politically organised, life (1985:444). Pannenberg actually rejects the notion of any biological drive to political behaviour as such.[22] This is interesting, and inconsistent, in view of Pannenberg's generally uncritical use of drive in other parts of his work. Pannenberg contrasts Aristotle's and Plato's view of the origin of political organisation, in the need for co-operation between humans for their ultimate fulfillment, with the views of the Sophists who saw it as a matter merely of convention. The modern version of the latter results in a view of the state as a

---

22 In the footnotes, a German author of 1934, Heller, is specifically criticised (1985:444, footnote 113).

contract to limit the damaging excesses of individuals (1985:445). In this case, the theological setting of the state is in the context of a consequence of sin, whereas in the case of the Aristotelian view, it could be related to human vocation and destiny. Pannenberg cites Reinhold Niebuhr's (1944) working out of human destiny, in terms of the 'primordial character of human community'. Pannenberg claims that his own views on the development of human identity, which I have discussed in Chapter Four, take full account of Niebuhr's critique. But Niebuhr gives a higher place to positive cathexis, active love, than is given by the social conditioning described by Pannenberg.

In his account of the state as social institution, Pannenberg again argues for a balance between the individual and the community. He asserts that while there can be no individual without community, yet the community does not determine the individual, which is in accordance with his theological agenda. This time, he gives priority in the balance to the community via the cultural system. He argues that the components of community are founded on shared meaning and values which have a religious basis, and it is the content of this in itself that allows criticism by the individual, and thus some independence (1985:446). Pannenberg repeats his argument that Christianity first made this balance possible, because it guarantees the importance of the individual. This is a piece of special pleading for Christianity that would require a much more extensive defence for it to be taken seriously by non-Christians, who would presumably point to counter instances in the history of Christianity. Pannenberg argues that the New Testament message is addressed to individuals as such, thus giving them independence. But its consequence is to draw the individual into community with Christ and the coming Kingdom of God, thus prioritising community (1985:447). Pannenberg is concerned to show that Christianity completes and perfects, as it were, the deficiencies in Aristotle and the Stoics. They both tended to regard the political nature of humanity as properly expressed in only one form of political organisation, the city-state. They also tended to see it as an end in itself. Pannenberg argues for the liberating effect of Christianity on both issues, because it holds politics to be only a partial realisation of the human destiny with God that is actually beyond the world. He notes that Christian doctrine has sometimes confined its treatment of politics to the problem of limiting evil, but he wishes to correct this. He claims that human justice is related to divine justice; that the 'creator's will to order is imprinted in creation itself' (1985:449) and that such order emerges from human social life. This is consistent with Pannenberg's strong eschatological emphasis on the partially completed, still-to-come nature of reality. He rejects versions of 'neo-Lutheran theology of the nineteenth and twentieth centuries' which viewed 'orders of creation' as static, preceding history and unaffected by it (1985:449, footnote 132). He goes on to assert that the idea of natural law is in this sense appropriate, not in denying the perversion of affairs by sin and evil, but affirming a divine will to order which is part of human and creation's destiny. It is that destiny which provides legitimation for the present political order, albeit a provisional one. Pannenberg observes:

> The mark of a tyrannical state is that it fails to recognize the limits of its authority and instead lays claim to the lives of its citizens. It is the primary political function of the church, on the other hand, to keep the state conscious that it is not the kingdom of God. The church does this because, unlike the political order, it permits human beings to share even now, though only through faith and in symbolic form, in the future of God and his kingdom. The role of the political order is to point ahead to the kingdom of God as a reality distinct from itself. (1985:450)

Pannenberg here implies a very high ecclesiology, but in his discussion of human community, as far as it goes, there is no mention of how the ecclesial community could have this special function. His view of the symbolic as re-presenting the transcendent allows him to see the church as a present sharing in the Kingdom. But it may be questioned from an empirical point of view; how real is Pannenberg's realised eschatology? What difference does it make? This is a problem with Pannenberg's future-oriented vision; will it collapse into a 'pie in the sky' solution?

Pannenberg connects these ideas to Augustine's views on the political order; in particular, to his understanding of peace as a 'universal ontological category' (1985:451). Peace is not the absence of war, but a good to which humanity is destined, even if present achievements of it are only partial. Discipline and order are necessary for the common good, but are to be distinguished from domination or the exercise of power for its own sake.[23] Pannenberg acknowledges that Augustine does not connect the earthly goodness given by the political order with the goodness of the kingdom of God that is to come. He suggests that consequently Augustine's view of the political destiny of humans involves an unnecessary disconnection from the affairs of this world. This is interesting in view of the possibility that Pannenberg himself is sometimes at risk of the opposite, of blessing the established order by claiming a fundamentally religious legitimation of it. Pannenberg does point out that, although Augustine ascribed despotism and the abuse of power to the influence of sin, he held to the distinction between *imperium*, as power exercised for the common good, and *dominium*, as despotic. Pannenberg asserts that because rulers were held to be divinely appointed and sanctioned, the question of whether *imperium* could remain untouched by sin was not asked until the modern period.

This question about the possibility of the legitimation of political order takes up Pannenberg's attention in the context of the issue of power. He says that modern discussions of political order do not start with an analysis of the requirement for community in human life, but with a reduction of human behaviour to a struggle for self assertion and rule. Pannenberg argues that power is more than this; that it has a social character as well, in that it deals with the power of the social over the

23 Pannenberg is surprised at the degree to which Augustine accepts Aristotle's version of human nature as political. He regards it as the more significant that Augustine does offer a criticism of the claim of Cicero and Aristotle that true justice can be found in a secular political order (1985:452).

individual (1985:454).[24] He acknowledges Foucault in a footnote as supporting this view. Pannenberg proceeds to criticise Max Weber's definition of power as reductionist, because despite the recognition of a communal action in which and against which power may be exercised, Weber thought of it primarily as a function of the individual will.

Pannenberg characterises the relationship between power and social consensus as requiring as a minimum some mutual agreement as to the possibilities and consequences of the exercise of power. In another footnote, he disagrees with Arendt's separation of power, which transcends the social, from force, which depends on it. He makes constructive connections between power and property. Both can be means to an end. Property as means (to legitimate personal well being) affects others indirectly, whereas power (to benefit the community) affects others directly. Property, like many other social factors, can be subverted from its proper end and used as a means to power. Power can have its basis either in the ability to satisfy need, or in the prevention of such satisfaction (1985:455). On this reading, power depends on the possession of the goods that humans need, which are either then given or withheld. Pannenberg questions if this is a sufficiently wide view of power, because power can include the ability simply to do harm, irrespective of need. In this case, actual acts of harm are not necessary for power to be felt; the threat is sufficient (1985:455). It may then be argued, on one hand, that this state of affairs cannot persist unless power is occasionally exercised, that is, force is used. On the other hand, it can be claimed that once power is used to deny satisfaction of needs, it erodes its own authority as a potential satisfier of need. Pannenberg does not agree with this latter position. He argues that power cannot be defined as inevitably dependent on the imputation of authority. Only when power is exercised for the common good does it acquire authority.

However, Pannenberg does agree that some social definition of need is required to legitimise power. Pannenberg is quite clear about this, and attempts to adapt his understanding of human biological drives to cope with it. He suggests that human needs are the result of interpreted and directed drives (1985:457).[25] He asserts that this interpretation or modification of drive is controlled by the 'context of meaning', by which the individual ascribes value to different aspects of his or her situation.

24 He uses an unfortunate image to illustrate this in that he refers to modern physics as having divorced the concept of force from body, and as regarding force in terms of fields (1985:454). This is in fact extremely controversial (for a discussion, see Russell, 1988). This example illustrates the kind of detachment from the context of science that is often found in Pannenberg, even as he seeks to involve his theology in what he regards as an essential feature of the real world. Such a tendency can expose theologians, as well as philosophers, to critiques similar to that of Sokal & Bricmont (1998).

25 This is another confusing comment on drives; he cites a 1926 paper which criticises drive in support of this claim that needs are modified drives. But he then gives a typical ethologist's account of drives as biologically based, before restating that they can be modified or overridden by the individual!

Pannenberg recognises that needs can be created; he cites modern advertising as an example (1985:458). Having established the dependence of need on a framework of meaning and value, he argues that political power, as being connected with the ability to meet need, must also have a context of meaning and value, and hence, a fundamentally religious context. He says:

> ... since the interpretation of need depends on a comprehensive consciousness of meaning that has been articulated in the course of the race's development, the result is a connection between the economic accomplishments of political power and religion. (1985:458)

Pannenberg's language is not very precise; he may mean to indicate humanity in general by the term race, but it is confusing in a work dealing with the sciences.[26] However, here Pannenberg is seeking to reinforce the ancient connection between government and religion again, this time by the argument that social agreement as to need and its satisfaction depends on the shared world of meaning that is ultimately legitimated by religion.

In the modern period, the concept of state political power has been extensively investigated and Pannenberg adverts to Hobbes, Kant, who offered a master/servant/conquest model, and Marx, who saw it in terms of labour/slave/exploitation. Pannenberg argues that the possibility of such criticism only arose when political rulers dispensed with the religious legitimation for power and justice, and replaced it with a claim to absolute power by the rulers themselves. Under these circumstances, political rule can be criticised as the coercive exercise of the 'special interests of those in power' (1985:459). Pannenberg complains that this has impoverished recent discussion of the nature of political power. He notes that the 'conquest' model is not much used at present, but that Marx and Engels are still influential. He argues that Engels is incorrect in ascribing state power to the desire to control private dealings because, according to Pannenberg, there is no evidence for the latter in ancient states (1985:460). He is concerned to retain the significance of religion in providing the context of meaning which legitimated political rule in ancient civilisations, and although this is clearly a matter of controversy among scholars, Pannenberg is able to cite material in support of his contention.

What he does not do is discuss present situations; a proper analysis of the origin of political power is a helpful adjunct to a sociological and philosophical analysis of its necessity for human kind, but surely a theological anthropology becomes irrelevant if it cannot apply recovered insights to present day situations? Engels may be wrong as a historian, but the phenomenon he describes is rampant today

26 Certainly, the plural term is not useful; there is no satisfactory definition of the human 'races' in genetics that would in any way carry the meanings of distinctness and shared identity that are implied by 'culture', and geneticists avoid the term (see, for instance, Lewontin et al., 1984).

and requires theological comment, surely? In his comments on the legitimation of the state, Pannenberg again depends heavily on his assumption of the ultimate coherence and homogeneity of cultural meaning and value. His arguments would be hard to put in multicultural Britain today, because, ironically, they appeal so little to the enterprise of building human community for the future. Pannenberg has tried to cast his whole epistemology in an eschatologically oriented mode, but he repeatedly proves to be unable to express this in concrete terms.

Justice

Justice also requires legitimation as a social institution. Pannenberg observes that while Weber discusses three modes of legitimation for political rule, he never deals with the problem of illegitimate rule. That is to say, he does not distinguish between the socially accepted justification of a ruler and the actual truth of such justification (1985:462).[27] Hence the legitimation of a particular political order is separate from its definition, and Pannenberg uses an analysis of the concept of the state in order to examine the grounds for its legitimation. He uses a definition of state as 'an association under rule' and recalls his earlier discussion of rule for the benefit of the common good versus despotic rule. He asserts that rule as *imperium*, for the benefit of the community, is essential for legitimacy, and that this indicates that the goal of the state is the provision of justice (1985:464). And he observes that this also is the ultimate reason given to legitimate the modern state; it exists to ensure justice. There is a two way relation between the state and the institutions of justice. On the one hand, the state provides and enforces laws, but on the other, it is itself legitimated by a transcendent justice (1985:465). The problem is the issue of how the state can promote justice by laws it frames itself, if that same justice is what guarantees the state. Again, Pannenberg has recourse to the period of classical Greece, and the problems of the city-states for his solution. The Aristotelian criterion for the legitimacy of the state is based on whether or not power is being exercised for the common good, and the practical problem is to know what that good is. If it is to be found in a cosmic or divine order of how things should be, rulers have to represent that order, as they did in ancient times. In modern times, the will of the people has replaced the old cosmic order. Pannenberg argues that:

> Once the people had been put in the place of God, it was possible for the modern consciousness to forget in great measure the religious roots of political representation and the political order. (1985:468)

27 This is one of the rare occasions on which Pannenberg agrees with Habermas (1985:462, footnote 178).

He traces the development of this through the theories of Hobbes and Rousseau. The legitimacy of any given state came to rest on the principle of the consent of the popular will to be governed. This gave rise to an independence of society over against the state or political order, which is also a feature of modernity. The interdependent interests operating in society can compete with the political order, and Pannenberg acknowledges his debt to Hegel with his characterisation of 'bourgeois' society.

Pannenberg runs a parallel argument for the reasons for this history. He cites the claim that the wars of religion in Europe in the sixteenth and seventeenth centuries led to the privatisation of religion, and its discrediting as a basis for public life, whilst promoting the concept of individual freedom. This reinforced the tendency to oppose the economic life of the individual to the constraining power of the state. Pannenberg argues that, with the wider constraint of religious value removed, the state became a means of social regulation (1985:471). Pannenberg accepts the critique from Hegel and Marx that such a state will not be able to resolve the tensions between opposing interests. He notes that the social revolution predicted by Marx has not manifested itself, and argues that Hegel's ethical state is a more functional model (1985:471). This is the nearest that Pannenberg gets to treating the problem of the just distribution of property and wealth.[28] Pannenberg sees Hegel's view as deficient, in that he does not express strongly enough the need for a metaphysical legitimation of the state. Going further, the principle of popular sovereignty is even more inadequate, and Pannenberg will not allow the concept of the welfare state to be any improvement. One may ask here if, as Pannenberg says, the provisional order on earth bears some relation to God's ultimate intention, surely a welfare state would be nearer to God's intentions than tyranny or indifference, and therefore more legitimate. Is it claimed for the welfare state that it can satisfy all needs and guarantee happiness? It might simply be argued that the welfare state is the best form in which political order can carry 'out the limited function that is assigned to it'.

Pannenberg concludes that the secular state is experiencing a crisis of legitimation, and that this is due to the loss of the religious grounding of the meaning and value which support it. He argues that such a crisis does not lead into political upheaval and disintegration, because with the loss of clear moral value the possibility of seeing an alternative is also lost (1985:473). Alternative contentions, that moral value is not quite so absent, are not considered, and their conclusions would not be in keeping with Pannenberg's aim of showing that human affairs cannot be successfully managed without reference to God. Throughout his discussion of justice, Pannenberg is clearly committed to a form of downward

---

28 Pannenberg cites Habermas as expressing the problem of legitimating political rule as the issues of 'distributing the surplus social product unequally yet legitimately', which seems to be the obverse of Pannenberg's statements of the problem (1985:471, footnote 216).

conflation, in which the transcendent values grounding justice issue in its proper social manifestation.

Religion

From Pannenberg's perspective, religion must be the great social institution, and he certainly has views on the role of religion in modern societies. He begins by claiming a foundational role for religion in society, citing approvingly the contemporary and sophisticated approach of Berger and Luckmann in sociology. It is possible that he misreads them at this point, in that in his footnote (1985:473, footnote 222) he seems to assume that the capacity of humans for constructing meaning is taken by Berger and Luckmann to preclude the possibility of such meaning being true. This is not the case, as demonstrated by Berger (1980, 1990); the issue is that the fact of the construction of perceived reality is neutral in respect of the ultimate truth of that reality, which must be established by means not invalidated by social processes. This has already been mentioned in the context of Pannenberg's general approach to sociological method.[29] Pannenberg and Berger do have an interest in philosophical anthropology in common. But, whereas Pannenberg seeks to use it to buttress a contention that the religious thematic is a rationally demonstrable and inescapable aspect of human nature, Berger sees it as providing only a pointer, a 'rumour' of transcendence. In the second edition of *A Rumor of Angels* (1990), he lets stand a comment on Pannenberg's *Revelation as History*; he says:

> I strongly endorse (his) approach, but I would prefer an emphasis on 'discovery' as against 'revelation'. To be sure, if one has already achieved faith, one will see any manifestation of transcendence as a revelation, or as Mircea Eliade puts it, a 'theophany'. But it is precisely this 'already achieved' status that I would like to get away from in terms of theological method, at least in its starting point. To speak of 'revelation' before one is just sure where one may speak of 'discovery' is putting the cart before the horse. (1990:94)

And Berger has made his position clearer in *The Heretical Imperative* (1980) in which he argues for a tentativeness and an openness to non-Christian traditions that would be unacceptable to Pannenberg.

Pannenberg locates the role of religion in bringing into focus a view of reality as encompassing past, present and future in its fulfilment in God (1985:473). He is then quite explicit about his view of the necessity of religion. Only religion grasps the world as meaningful in a way that can be made concrete in human social life (1985:474). Pannenberg has begun, via Berger, with a bottom-up explanation of religious meaning and value as located intrinsically in the nature of the human

---

29 For a useful discussion of Berger on this, see Gaede (1986).

individual. He has then moved to a top-down assertion that religion, as bearer of meaning and value, is the only valid legitimation for the political order. While legitimacy may be a problem for the modern state, and religion may provide such legitimacy, Pannenberg wishes to be clear that this is not the primary or essential function of religion. Religion which actually depends on baptising a given political order is, in Pannenberg's words, 'hopelessly corrupt' (1985:474). On the other hand, he reasons, the political need for legitimation, and the fact that both political order and religion are concerned with the overall framework of meaning of people's lives, lead to inevitable tension between religion and the political order. In keeping with his linking of order as provisional in the concrete now and yet part of the divinely-willed destiny of the world, Pannenberg treads a narrow path. He says that political power can be a manifestation of the divine order, or it can claim identity with that order, and supplant God as the fulfilment of human destiny (1985:475). This results in tyranny. Further, Pannenberg's analysis of the human situation demonstrates that no conceivable political order can satisfy all interests. He concludes that human destiny can never be definitively realised except in the kingdom of God. Under these circumstances, it is difficult to understand to what extent the political order can, in fact, manifest or present the divine order. Given the partial and provisional nature of political order, Pannenberg sees religion as a court of appeal against political claims to absolutism. This gives it an ambiguous role, since, for Pannenberg, religion is also the only true legitimator of political order. Pannenberg concludes that the modern state will decline because it does not acknowledge this need for religion, and has instead substituted ideologies of various sorts (1985:478). He repeats his assertion that religion transcends the political and the whole social order. Pannenberg again contends, *contra* the Enlightenment, that religion has actually guaranteed human freedom (1985:479).

As usual, although he speaks of religions in the plural, his explanation and examples are invariably from Western Christianity. He repeats the conclusion of his considerations of human identity, that:

> The norms that spring from social relations are never able fully to guarantee the integrity and identity of the individual. Identity and integrity that are whole and entire is the salvation that religion alone bestows and that human beings can acquire in it despite all the damage and failures that earthly life inflicts on them ... If individuals seek to achieve their identity directly through their social life, they will consistently overtax the capacities of the institutions of communal life. (1985:480)

His view of social institutions such as marriage, family, property and the state is governed by the need for acknowledgement of human destiny to a fellowship with God 'beyond the world'; all such institutions will be fully functional only if they make manifest that destiny (1985:481).

Having devoted several pages of *Anthropology in Theological Perspective* to the problems of these institutions in terms only of their lack of basis in meaning, and therefore religion, Pannenberg acknowledges the institutional nature of religion in three paragraphs! He admits that religious institutions too can be diverted from their true function of pointing beyond themselves, and misused for the special interests of individuals. He observes that the history of religions is always mixed, and contains elevating as well as disappointing instances. And without any further discussion, he presents a summary of his position which is part argument and part polemic. He warns of the demise of modern society in a collapse of social cohesion and an excess of individual antagonism (1985:482). Pannenberg looks to the ecumenical movement as the bearer of religious meaning and value that must contribute to a new culture. He says:

> The coming of such a culture will be aided by the fact that in this ecumenical age of Christianity the churches in their consciousness of faith have to a large extent risen above the dogmatism that, together with clerical claims to ascendancy, was chiefly responsible for the division of past centuries. This development is not a matter simply of outward accommodation but has originated in a deeper and more nuanced understanding of Christian revelation and the Christian faith. As a result, the basic modern idea of tolerance is today deeply rooted in the Christian consciousness of faith itself and has even altered Christian attitudes to the non-Christian religions. A revitalization ... of the Christian foundations ... should not cause a relapse into the intolerance of the religious wars from which the modern state emerged. (1985:483)

In the afterglow of Vatican II, such optimism could be understood, but in present times, it seems hopelessly misplaced. The question would be better served if Pannenberg had included consideration of what sociology can tell us about religious differences. Berger, in particular, has opposed a dissolution of Christian identity into secularism that he thinks may sometimes accompany the ecumenical process.[30] Pannenberg is careful to say that he does not look to any renewal of the fusion of church and state, but he hopes for the recovery of a religious context for the arts as well as the inclusion of the economy in the new culture.

Pannenberg's approach to the social and political sciences is consistent with his approach to biology and psychology. He seeks coherence, but is not always sensitive to the context from which he is taking material. Pannenberg is inconsistent in his arguments about culture, society and the individual. Sometimes he assumes a cultural uniformity into which interactions between complexes of ideas and the groups holding them are subsumed. This actually flies in the face of the empirical variability of cultural ideas and social groupings in the society he writes about. At other times he projects a world of ideas and meaning as arising from the nature of human individuals making up society. Pannenberg does not give any mechanisms for the development of culture; he presents culture as that meaning which has been present from the beginning, and which slowly reveals itself, via myth and sacred play, independently of the social groups involved. Pannenberg's universe is a

30 See his comments on the Hartford Declaration in the introduction to the second edition of *A Rumor of Angels* (1990).

supremely rational world, in which taste, preference or prejudice are dissolved and reasoned away, and in which agency and interest groups have a subordinate or non-existent role.

In terms of Archer's analysis, Pannenberg is inconsistent. Pannenberg certainly subscribes to a concept of cultural homogeneity. He does not account for the difference between an actual commitment to intellectual ideas and the acceptance of them on a social basis, usually because they are peripheral to the current interests of the individual. Pannenberg operates with a view of culture that assumes rational commitment to all ideas to the same degree, and without any social modification of those ideas. In his account of the origins of culture in myth, the family and the state as representing some transcendent order of meaning, he is clearly a downward conflationist, subsuming social interactions into the ideational component of the cultural system. But in his account of the origin of social institutions and property, he tends to a position of upward conflation, where social interactions give rise to cultural phenomena. Pannenberg veers between these positions, although more often he tends to being a 'downward conflationist' in Archer's terms. He appears always to describe culture as uniform and social cohesion as tight. Consequently, his picture of society is always in Archer's state of Concomitant Complementarity, in which there is cultural stasis.

It is clear that, whatever evaluative social theory is chosen, Pannenberg's views on social interactions and social institutions are internally inconsistent and inadequate to the facts. He appears to be more intent on fitting sociology to his theological presuppositions than on allowing the social sciences to illuminate his theology. He acknowledges the empirical failure of the Enlightenment to bring about social relations ordered by rationality. But his solution seems almost a repeat of the failed prescription. He does not engage with any form of postmodern social theory. One would expect him to reject Baudrillard's (1983) assertions of the end of modernity, but the re-evaluations of modernity by Bauman (1991, 1992) or Giddens (1990, 1991) are exceedingly relevant. Pannenberg's extreme rationalism makes an encounter with postmodern developments such as the reconstruction of the role of the body in sociality of Mellor & Shilling (1997) both necessary and unlikely.

Chapter Six

Rationality and Transformation

I have so far presented a detailed evaluation of Pannenberg's approach to the sciences, for the most part in terms of those sciences themselves. In this final chapter, I shall consider the broader question of the theological status of Pannenberg's enterprise in the light of this evaluation.

In the introduction, I suggested that there were two important components of postmodern debate that are of special relevance to Pannenberg's work. One, the problem of providing a secure basis for knowledge in the face of critiques of the Enlightenment, is part of Pannenberg's overt concern. He acknowledges the historically conditioned nature of knowledge and yet seeks to retain the ultimate coherence of all knowledge and objectivity in language. He seeks to deal with the potential for relativism by eliminating action or *phronesis* and conversational reciprocity from his account of knowledge.

The other significant postmodern concern is the disclosure of hidden value and ideology, expressed as the 'hermeneutic of suspicion'. In the preceding chapters, I have demonstrated that Pannenberg's own work invites the application of such suspicion. In the area of the natural sciences, there are serious flaws in Pannenberg's work. How has Pannenberg come to make so many mistakes, inappropriate judgements, omissions and misunderstandings in his treatment of the sciences? I do not think that Pannenberg's problems are fortuitous. There is a clear pattern in his approach to the sciences, and I claim that it follows primarily from his basic epistemology. His view of humanity certainly determines the content of the science he uses, but the problem is less such content and more the process by which his use of science is determined.

I believe that his views on the unity and coherence of truth, the objectivity of knowledge, the nature of conversation and understanding and the priority of rational thought in culture lead to positions lending themselves to the misuse of science. His insistence on the ultimate coherence of all reality gives rise to a deterministic tendency. His exclusion of action from understanding leads to a suppression of the social and a fundamental individualism. His univocal account of conversation leads to a neglect of reciprocity and the possibilities of change. These are the areas that I highlighted as problematic in Chapter One. Pannenberg's attempt to engage postmodernity is itself very vulnerable to a postmodern critique. This must begin with an assessment of how successful Pannenberg has been in his attempt to secure the status of knowledge, both theological and scientific, from relativist critique.

The role of hermeneutics

It was made clear in Chapter Two that Pannenberg's epistemology rests on an interpretation and development of Gadamer's hermeneutics, in which knowledge is viewed as understanding. This takes place with the recognition that the distance between past and present can only be perceived in the light of the future. That is, knowledge at any one time may be incomplete, but will prove to be coherent with the total reality that is revealed at the end of time. This insight, which admits the time-conditioned nature of knowledge without making knowledge merely relative to time, is a major contribution to theological epistemology after modernity. In a definitive survey of theology and hermeneutics Anthony Thiselton presents the introduction of the dimension of the future as the one of the most significant of Pannenberg's achievements.[1] Pannenberg also highlights the importance of time in his analysis of the human psyche. He accepts Heidegger's criticism of the idealist concept of the timeless self, and incorporates the temporality of development into the process of human reflection on itself that gives identity.

The problem of developing a theologically adequate philosophical hermeneutics centres on the compass of positions available. They range from a relativist-subjectivist stance where understanding is expressed simply in terms of local effects on the reader through to a metacritical stance where factors transcending all context are used to evaluate interpretations.[2] Against this background, Pannenberg is important for developing the non-relativist end of this spectrum, and he merits Thiselton's positive evaluation:

> Pannenberg has developed a foundational metacritical theory that modifies and corrects Gadamer's hermeneutics while taking seriously the problem of historical finitude, historical understanding and the contextual nature of hermeneutics within traditions and communities. (1992:337)

For Thiselton, the significant theological issue is that the relativist-subjectivist stance that he characterises as 'socio-pragmatic hermeneutics' is innately

---

1 'If we move to the world of the New Testament, we find strong justification for identifying metacritical or foundational realities with futurity ... It is precisely "hope" that is said to constitute a foundational or fixed "anchor" (Heb 6:19) ... as a principle of hermeneutical theory, Pannenberg has shown that it is not only coherent and intelligible, but deserves to be taken seriously in the widest possible context. It contributes to a theological understanding of the foundations of knowledge.' (1992:338)

2 Thus Thiselton 'At one end of a spectrum stands contextual-relative socio-*pragmatic* hermeneutics: "This is the effect of the text on me and my community". It runs through pietism, radical reader-response theory, pragmatic forms of narrative theology, and post modern elements of literary theory. At the other end of the spectrum stands *metacritical* and *socio-critical hermeneutics.* Some trans-contextual basis is sought for the comparative evaluation of contextual criteria of interpretation and indeed for the purposes in relation to which each set of criteria gains its currency.' (1992:6)

conservative and eschatology-denying. He argues that if it cannot provide criteria for its own self criticism, then it cannot be satisfactory theologically, because 'it can leave no room for a theology of the cross' (1992:7). Pannenberg's metacritical approach should in principle be able to do this; whether or not it succeeds will be discussed in the last section of this chapter.[3]

Pannenberg's postmodern credentials are also evident in his rejection of positivism and the critical rationalism of Albert and Popper. It must be noted that there have been claims that Pannenberg's basic epistemology resembles that of Imre Lakatos, who offered a modification of Popper's position. In *Theology in the Age of Scientific Reasoning*, Nancy Murphy (1990) argued that Lakatos' account of scientific knowledge was applicable to theology as a discipline. This is very problematic. The examples of 'testing' of theological knowledge that she gives are actually of religious experience. Further, theology does not allow for the rejection of God as a failed hypothesis, whereas science must always include the potential for abandoning a research programme. On Lakatos' view, a failing programme is simply discarded. Nevertheless, in her book Murphy attempts to describe Pannenberg's approach as one of testing his central core of suppositions about God by recruiting evidence from the various biological and human sciences. In fact, Pannenberg would not consider that the Christian understanding of the centrality and reality of God is negotiable, and I do not think that he has any sense of 'testing' this. Rather, he demonstrates the congruence of theology and science which he is sure, on theological grounds, of being able to expose. Murphy does not offer any evaluation of Pannenberg's hermeneutic epistemology; indeed, Gadamer is not mentioned in her book. This lack of context is fairly characteristic for the discussion as it has proceeded in the USA. In a collection of symposium papers on his work in science (Albright & Haugen, 1997), Pannenberg has responded to the suggestion that his work could be described as a Lakatos-style research programme:

> I have no problems with that description. I could have used that notion myself in describing the theoretical form of theological explanation if the work of Lakatos had been available to me when I wrote my book *Theology and the Philosophy of Science*. But at that time, around 1970, the latest phase of the discussion was represented by Thomas Kuhn. (1997:430)

3 It may be noted that a recent study in the USA has claimed Pannenberg as a 'postfoundationalist' on the basis of his theological anthropology; the author does not discuss Pannenberg's dependence on Gadamer. Indeed, he says 'Pannenberg himself has never been fond of postmodern hermeneutics, usually dismissing it as a fad' (Shults, 1999:81). It appears that there are semantic differences here between the USA and the UK. In the discussion of Shults, foundationalist seems roughly equivalent to modernist as used in this book, antifoundationalist to relativist, and postfoundationalist to positions such as Thiselton's metacritical approach.

This would appear to involve Pannenberg in a change of direction, because the theories of Lakatos do not marry well with an understanding of knowledge from the hermeneutic perspective; they are a modification and extension of Popper's falsification-oriented methodology. And Lakatos was a major opponent to Kuhn throughout the sixties and seventies.[4] But Pannenberg proceeds in the next sentence:

> I perceived Kuhn's ideas on revolutionary science and paradigm shift not as proposing a relativistic outlook on science as some of his critics did, nor did I take his opposition to Karl Popper as complete rejection of his ideas, but rather as a refinement of Popper's approach. To me the most important point was a less restricted recognition of the role of rival metaphysical visions in the history of science and the description of scientific theories as interpretations of empirical evidence, more comparable to hermeneutics than Popper would admit. Thus, use of Kuhn's ideas was not very far from the strategy of Lakatos in defending and developing Popper's description of scientific explanation. (1997:430)

I think this reveals the source of the confusion; to some degree, Pannenberg and his American dialogue partners are talking at cross purposes. From Pannenberg's perspective, Popper contributed a robust rejection of positivism and gave a place, however limited, to the metaphysical in scientific theory formation. From the perspective of Anglo-Saxon philosophy of science, Popper tried to secure the status of experiment and is often a starting point for those who wish to hold onto 'objective' truth and reject significant social dimensions to the foundation of scientific knowledge. Pannenberg's comments above make it clear that he is not familiar with the demarcations of territory in the English speaking parts of the world of philosophy of science. However, Pannenberg does express some reservations about the appropriation of the theories of Lakatos; he agrees that Murphy's characterisation of what he calls his theological system is acceptable, but he does not think that his method could be described in the terms used by Lakatos. He says:

> In terms of *systematic structure* the framework of theological explanation as I envision it may be adequately described in Lakatosian terms. The question of *method* is somewhat different ... my method in dealing with the secular sciences has been to take 'secular descriptions as provisional versions of reality' which imply a further dimension, the dimension of reality as constituted by the presence of God. It is the task of theology to make that dimension explicit. (1997:431)

Pannenberg goes on to argue that such 'transformation' of secular descriptions might be considered as auxiliary hypotheses in the terms of Lakatos. But such a procedure was certainly not envisaged by Lakatos and could hardly be acceptable

4 e.g. his contribution to *Criticism and the Growth of Knowledge* (Lakatos & Musgrave, 1970).

to him. Overall, the discussion does little to illuminate Pannenberg's position; it reinforces those concerns which were already apparent in *Revelation as History* and *Theology and the Philosophy of Science.* Attempts at dialogue between science and theology such as these are surely a positive sign. However, a much greater awareness of current positions in philosophy of science as well as in theology would promote greater understanding, and in the case of Pannenberg, some explication of his place in the contemporary German philosophical context would be useful for English speaking readers.

In the same symposium, Philip Clayton argues for the necessity of meta-criteria for the evaluation (he uses the term 'control' for this, which could be confusing) of the fields of theology and science. He observes that philosophy of science cannot itself provide Pannenberg with the criteria necessary to regulate a dialogue between science and theology.[5] In relation to the human sciences, Clayton acknowledges Pannenberg's use of Dilthey, Heidegger and philosophical anthropology, but he does not appear to recognise the influence of these traditions on social theory.[6] However, Clayton is here concerned to ask again what criteria could be used to evaluate theology's interaction with the social sciences, and he settles for theology's ability to give coherence to the total context of the believer's world, from whatever sources that world is constructed (Clayton, 1997:403). This is a long way from Thiselton's metacriterion of the cross. Clayton seems to me to be mistaken, both because he appears to regard meaning as mere coherence of knowledge, and because the priority of the non-theological beliefs of the individual means that 'the world' will define 'the word'. Barth warned theology of the dangers of that position; it should be the other way round. Clayton notes that Pannenberg's choice of criteria for evaluating the relation between science and theology is not concerned with the formal structure of knowledge-claims, but is more concerned with 'exploring the relative merits of various systematic positions'.[7] Clayton does not refer to the importance of the philosophy of hermeneutic and the work of Gadamer for Pannenberg. He does refer to the inescapable necessity of some kind of meta-criteria for the science-religion debate, and suggests that this requires some movement among those involved in the USA toward an engagement with wider philosophical traditions.[8] But Clayton does not seem to recognise that Pannenberg's

---

5 '... Popper's strict programme has failed, and its failure has fuelled the fires of Kuhnian incommensurability and subjectivist construals of science. If Pannenberg makes the philosophy of science his foundational discipline, he is liable to end up with ... inconsistencies ...' (1997:399).

6 e.g. his comments on p 402 (1997). But see, for example, Bauman (1978), Hunter & Ainley (1986).

7 He rejects van Huysteen's suggestion that Pannenberg is heavily influenced by Albert and Kuhn – indeed, that would be difficult given their radically opposed positions (1997:398).

8 He says 'And the contemporary thinkers whom we heed will include, in addition to scientists, philosophers of science, and theologians, also speculative and systematic

pursuit of coherence is always within the context of the totality of truth that will be revealed at the *eschaton* and that has been anticipated in Jesus Christ.

There can be no doubt that Pannenberg's incorporation of the dimensions of historicity and the future into epistemology represents a highly successful adaptation of postmodern insights in respect of both theology and science. Following from this, we may enquire into the requirement he makes for the ultimate coherence of all knowledge.

The unity and coherence of knowledge

For Pannenberg, the process of understanding is based on human reason, not human action, and takes place in the context of awareness of the infinity of all that is. All true knowledge is coherent with this unity, which arises from the reality of God. This position has been criticised, and an especially detailed critique has been offered by Paul Molnar (1995). He acknowledges the importance of Pannenberg's project, but takes issue with it, arguing that Pannenberg's adaptation of the concept of anticipation results in subjectivism.[9] The starting point for this is Pannenberg's assertion that speaking about the whole of reality and speaking of God have to be mutually related, and the consequence that God's action is 'in' history; for Pannenberg, God does not 'come from outside' in any sense. Molnar argues that this has the effect of grounding theology in philosophy, since 'history' is a result of human experience and reflection. However, following Pannenberg's presentation in Volume One of the *Systematic Theology*, he concentrates on the question of how Pannenberg sees the unity of all truth that is ultimate in God. He cites Pannenberg's use of Augustine's argument that the claim that God is truth is founded on the observation of the unity and relatedness of all things. Molnar says that Pannenberg substitutes the observation of unity for the unity itself.[10] He puts his finger on a set

---

philosophers. All this would be a radical shift – and, in the United States at least, not an overly popular one – for the science-religion debate. But I believe it represents the essence of Pannenberg's programme in science-theology as he has developed it since ... the early 1950s ... he has now convinced me that such a treatment is unavoidable. When we begin to talk of provisional versions and objective reality, it is time to turn from methodology to metaphysics.' (1997:407)

9 He says 'Among recent reconstructions, Wolfhart Pannenberg's systematic theology is one of the most influential attempts to overcome authoritarianism and subjectivism ... I argue that by grounding theological knowledge in a version of Heidegger's concept of anticipation, Pannenberg has not escaped his own religious subjectivism. Thus theological meaning inevitably results from a philosophy of existence grounded in an anticipatory grasp (*Vorgriff*) of the totality of reality which is presumed to refer to the reality of God.' (1995:315)

10 He says 'Here a subtle shift in logic has taken place. Instead of saying that the thought that God is truth is and remains grounded in *God alone*, Pannenberg argues that this

of relationships that lie at the back of all Pannenberg's arguments; the priority he gives to the *perception* of unity in history. In the case of theological anthropology and the natural sciences, Pannenberg seeks to construct an integrated account involving zoology, ethology, phylogenetics, psychology, sociology and so on. His assumption is that not only must there be a fundamental unity between these disciplines, but that it must be demonstrable. But Pannenberg's desire to perceive unity may lead to an assumption of coherence between theories when there is, in fact, none. It certainly leads him to false interpretations of biology by its own internal standards. Pannenberg's approach to ecology, ethology and genetics and his mishandling of the concept of neoteny exemplifies this.

A further issue arises about the status of human experience in Pannenberg's epistemology. His anthropology is directed to establishing the primacy and necessity of an essential religious dimension to human nature. Molnar points out that Pannenberg gives, in Volume One of the *Systematic Theology*, the theological deduction from this, that such experience becomes a criterion of theological truth.[11] Molnar accepts that Pannenberg's own account rejects such natural theology, but argues that his philosophical presuppositions imply it. He argues that Pannenberg resembles Rahner in locating the 'meaning of the word God' in the 'totality of reality and of our existence' (1995:329) rather than in the revelation of God in Christ. According to Molnar, then, Pannenberg's characterisation of his primary agenda as theological is not secure; it is, in reality, primarily philosophical. This contention is supported by the very rational and philosophical nature of Pannenberg's theological account of anthropology. The explanation of the theological issues in *Anthropology in Theological Perspective* confines itself to an account of the image of God theology without reference to the New Testament. His major exploration of Christology, *Jesus – God and Man*, deals with the history and the theological and philosophical consequences of the death and resurrection of Jesus, but spends little or no time on the humanity of Jesus as lived out, for instance, in his relations of love and reconciliation with marginalised people. In the section on anthropology in Volume Two of *Systematic Theology*, Pannenberg expands the biblical and early church background to the theology of the image of God, and then recapitulates the account in *Anthropology in Theological Perspective*, from the medieval period, via the Enlightenment, to a specific tradition of philosophical anthropology in the

---

truth is grounded in the *perception* of the coherence and unity of all that is true. Theology shifts away from God (and the need for faith) to our perceptions and then discovers God as the locus of this presupposed unity.' (1995:322)

11 Pannenberg presents this on pp 48 and 157 (1991). Molnar says 'Thus unless Christianity makes the world's questioning of the reality of God its own question, Christian doctrine itself will not be true. But it is just here that from within Barth's theology, Pannenberg compromises Christian faith by starting on common ground with atheism's questioning of God's reality and then by grounding human knowledge in religious experience rather than in God's Word and Spirit.' (1995:327)

present. The overall philosophical framework and rationally centred method remain consistent throughout Pannenberg's work.

This philosophically based coherence also results in a requirement for truth as unity. In Chapter Five I discussed the problems raised for social theory by assumptions of intellectual homogeneity in culture, such as those criticised by Archer, and I argued that Pannenberg's understanding of culture was subject to a similar objection. Interestingly, Warnke observes that Gadamer's view of the appropriation of a tradition by its members conflates the committed acceptance of ideas and the rather different acknowledgement of their existence in an intellectual framework. The consequence of such conflation is that it can be mistakenly assumed that members of a tradition are 'also its ideological supporters' (1987:106). Warnke offers a defence of Gadamer's intentions which I shall discuss further under the heading of objectivity and authority. But here what is important is the observation that Gadamer does not deal with the patent heterogeneity of cultural ideas, and Pannenberg follows him in this.

The difficulty that this presents is that consistency, coherence and unity are key features of rational knowledge in Pannenberg's view. He therefore judges the claims of any given aspect of science in terms of its potential coherence with his own philosophical position. His method does not allow for conflict or incommensurability. Hence science that does not obviously fit with his intellectual objectives is ignored, as in the case of humanistic psychology and psychiatry, or contested, as in the case of sociology.

Objectivity and authority

Pannenberg argues that language is the expression of understanding, and the content of language is isolatable – that is, objective knowledge is possible. He argues for the conservation of the epistemological content of the statement as such. The issue is that although there can be no description or meaning without a context, the contextualised description or meaning is expressed in a way which permits comparison with other contexts; texts can be tested against traditions and histories, and the question of truth is not avoidable. Thiselton notes Pannenberg's difference from Gadamer on this point.[12] But as I claimed in Chapter Two, for Gadamer the truth is integrally dependent on context, including what is not said. So Pannenberg's view that the isolated statement can be given objectivity because it has abstractable content comparable with other texts seems to me deficient. Thiselton sees it more

12 He says 'Like Gadamer, then, Pannenberg stresses human historical finitude, and the hermeneutical dimensions of understanding which lie behind or within any claim to knowledge. But unlike Gadamer, Pannenberg assigns a more fundamental status to testable propositions or assertions, and argues for the scientific status of theology.' (1992:335)

positively because it is in opposition to relativist modifications of Gadamer, such as Rorty's.[13] I will argue that although this is prompted by a desire to secure certainty, this retrieval of objectivity, by reinstating assertion, is a crucial undermining of Gadamer's achievement. It contributes to Pannenberg's over-valuing of science and to an ultimate authoritarianism. In his use of science, it allows him to extract aspects which fit his argument. For instance, in Chapter Three I dealt with his use of the alleged effect of domestication on the inhibition of instinctive behaviour, which was abstracted from the context in which the argument was put – in this case, a speculative claim that humans could be characterised as belonging to so-called degenerate or non-degenerate races.

It might be argued that the problem goes further back than Pannenberg, and that he is merely reflecting a conservative authoritarianism alleged to be found in Gadamer. But Gadamer can be defended on this account, because he certainly would not agree with Pannenberg's account of the objectifiable content of statements, and his view of the role of pre-understanding and tradition can also be supported. Warnke reviews such attacks on Gadamer by Habermas and argues that several features of Gadamer's approach serve to guard against authoritarianism. One is the way in which understanding implies application, or moral knowledge. Warnke gives the example of a present day understanding of *Huckleberry Finn*. The question of racism is a contemporary one, but it is itself part of the horizon of understanding that is to be brought into play with the text from the past, so that in the conversation that constitutes understanding the text itself is challenged as well as being challenging (1987:96). Sullivan (1989) also defends the basic concern with the ethical in Gadamer's view of knowledge and understanding, in the context of his attitude to the political. It is noticeable that this concept of application (*phronesis*), the moral component of knowledge, is not stressed in Pannenberg, and indeed, in his desire to evacuate all traces of action from reason, Pannenberg excludes it at a theoretical level. As well as asserting this in his explicit discussion of Gadamer's epistemology, Pannenberg also eliminates action from his account of personal identity and psychology. In Volume Two of the *Systematic Theology* he makes this quite clear.[14] The theological consequences of this suppression of action and agency have been noted by Schwöbel when he comments on Pannenberg's attempt to separate ethics and theology. He finds Pannenberg's attempt to have a

13 He says 'Pannenberg fundamentally supports Betti in his criticism of Gadamer's "loss of objectivity". This loss arises, he asserts, because Gadamer has followed Heidegger in the "existentialist devaluation of the statement". Pannenberg does not deny Heidegger's point that propositions are embedded in wider frames of a "totality of involvements", just as he endorses Gadamer's language about an "unexpressed horizon of meaning". But there remains a conceivable and abstractable propositional content which can be "objectified" in the process of interpretation. Here Pannenberg reinforces the ground marked out in his earlier essay "Hermeneutic and Universal History". Interpretation transposes his horizon "into an explicit statement".' (1992:335)

14 See p 202, footnote 85 (1994).

knowledge of God which excludes the question of human agency and action questionable. He argues that it does indeed have the consequence that Pannenberg claims for it, of excluding ethics from theology. But such a diminished theology is at risk of giving an inadequate account of God, since the relation between God and humanity is actually inescapable. Schwöbel sees the relation between ethics and theology as one of mutual reciprocity, which 'enables dogmatics to be more than theory and protects its theory from becoming speculative' (1996:527). Certainly, in this study of his use of science, Pannenberg proves to be less sensitive to ethical issues than one would wish.

Warnke and Sullivan have shown that Gadamer can be defended against the charge of authoritarianism by virtue of his inclusion of *phronesis* as application. The problem of the question of the ultimate legitimacy of authority remains, and this has also been considered by Warnke (1987:136). Some independent knowledge is required to either legitimate or criticise authority, and if knowledge cannot be in some sense objectified, how can it be independent? If reflection can neither overthrow nor legitimate authority, then what rational foundation can be given to authority? Warnke argues that the implication of Gadamer's argument is the conservative position that actual overthrow of tradition cannot be rationalised. But this does not exclude the possibility that reflection will indeed modify tradition or critique authority. She asserts that Gadamer gives a conservative tone to his hermeneutics that is not actually implied by it. The fusion of horizons which is part of understanding 'includes disagreement and distantiation' and the authority of a tradition is always changing as new knowledge is brought into its context (1987:138). Gadamer's position is best seen in the light of possible alternatives, and Warnke compares the relativism of Rorty with Gadamer's quite different situation. She concludes that while Rorty abandons the attempt at cross-cultural rationality, Gadamer demonstrates the rootedness of rationality in time-conditioned human interaction and conversation.[15] Pannenberg's approach to the critique of theological tradition is the opposite of Rorty's. It involves less 'disagreement and distantiation' and more optimistic harmonisation. He will invariably demonstrate, often by reference to a minor figure, that the tradition as such has been right all along, despite the indisputable error of the majority involved. For example, his tracing of a developmental explanation of the image of God theology, from Irenaeus via Pico della Mirandola and Herder, is a masterpiece of scholarly excavation, but he does not engage with the consequences of the widespread occurrence and long term persistence of substantialist ideas of the image of God in Christianity. Yet these ideas, that the image of God lay in human attributes of reason or intelligence, fed into the stream of thinking that those apparently lacking reason or intelligence were

15 She says '... far from giving up on the notion of a reason that can transcend conventional bounds, as Rorty does, Gadamer tries to preserve it while recognizing the demands of history ... we form ourselves historically and reason emerges through a dialogue with others in which we become *gebildet*'. (1987:166)

less than fully human. This eventually contributed to the racism in the twentieth century that Lorenz and von Uexküll endorsed and that Pannenberg does not discuss. Pannenberg's overvaluing of objectivity leads, in my view, to an authoritarianism that is not warranted by his use of Gadamer and which seriously limits his engagement with science.

The exclusion of conversation, and reciprocity from understanding

I have argued that Pannenberg rarely actually engages with science; on only one occasion does he regard science as providing a novel insight superior to part of the theological tradition. I think that it is highly significant that the science in question is one of the few pieces of modern science to constitute a historical claim. The issue is the theory of evolution and the traditional story of the Fall, where Pannenberg says explicitly that theological understanding of original sin must be recast in the light of the evolution of mankind from prehuman ancestors.[16] But this example proves the rule, because Pannenberg regards historical knowledge as foundational, and the theory of evolution may be seen as historical assertion. Pannenberg does not generally accept any new insights from science, and this is especially noticeable in the area of psychology. His practical use of the relation between science and theology is unidirectional; theology dictates the status of the human as internally driven to an exocentric orientation, aware of the religious question of God by virtue of human psychic structure and so on. Science is allowed to provide pieces of corroborative detail.

This absence of real dialogue fits, I think, with Pannenberg's own characterisation of conversation. In Chapter Two, I detailed some of Pannenberg's differences with Gadamer on this point. Gadamer views conversation as a significant part of all understanding, as a reciprocal exchange, requiring an empathetic connection to the other's horizons of understanding. Pannenberg requires the unadulterated statement of each individual's position, lest truth and objectivity be compromised. Thiselton points out that in considering the understanding of a text, the model of conversation is limited.[17] The question here being, how can the text *speak* and yet avoid both a fixed preservation of a given meaning from the past and the ascription of the preoccupations of the present interpreter? Warnke makes Gadamer's position clear in that he looks for a transformation of the positions of both the interpreter and the interpreted. This

16 See *Anthropology in Theological Perspective* (1985:57), *Systematic Theology Vol 2* (1994: 118-136).

17 He says 'Pannenberg also offers a cautiously positive evaluation of Gadamer's use of the notion of dialogue and conversation as *that out of which* some new or third thing arises above and beyond what each partner already brings. This model, however, has limitations as a model of *textual* interpretation.' (192:333)

prevents overvaluing of either the interpreter, resulting in subjectivism, or of the interpreted, resulting in the domination of the status quo.[18] The problem is that Pannenberg appears to accept a minimal transformative component of hermeneutics in principle, and in practice he does not appear to be much transformed by his experience of science. It is significant that in his selective appropriation of psychology, he includes no material at all dealing with reciprocal and conversational relationships. This is interesting in that he is not prepared to modify his theological view of humanity to include positive capacities for cathexis and love. This is generally regarded as a key feature of Christianity; that love has transforming power. For instance, Thiselton explains the possibility of understanding as described in the philosophy of hermeneutic as fundamentally dependent on love as the power by which horizons of understanding can be ultimately transcended. He says (his italics):

> *In theological terms, however, love represents the major transforming force of all systems and criteria of relevance. Interests which have hitherto gathered round the self as a system of self-centred relevance begin to be re-grouped and re-ranked around the self of another, or even the Other.* (1992:609)

Love and transformation are completely absent from Pannenberg's discussions of understanding and communication. There is no doubt that Pannenberg's thought remains supremely rational; he sees understanding as a rational process, and conversation as a reciprocal stating of points of view, to establish the logical truth of one or other by an intellectual process. This position is very problematic for theology, which must admit communication between God and humanity to be more than a matter of logical rationality. Since present day accounts of the philosophy of science have also moved beyond such an uncomplicated perspective, it is not surprising that there are deficiencies in Pannenberg's grasp of the structure and processes of science.

---

18 She says 'The successful conclusion of a dialogue thus reflects a shared understanding and one that, moreover, reflects a transformation of the initial positions of all the discussion partners. Gadamer argues that the same kind of shared understanding and transformation also marks the successful conclusion of the hermeneutical dialogue with aspects of one's own or another tradition. His analysis here is helpful in countering both the conservative thrust of the anticipation of completeness and the subjectivist implications of the account of application. Genuine understanding, on his view, derives not from an imposition of one's own prejudices or needs on the object to be understood, ... neither does it result in the abject acceptance of the views of that object.' (1987:101)

Determinism

I have argued in this book that Pannenberg's use of philosophical anthropology and biology both tend to a determinism which is reinforced by his interpretation of Freudian theory. Other authors have claimed that Pannenberg's work has determinist consequences.[19] Drees, a physicist-philosopher, is clear about the incompatibility of time as Pannenberg conceives it with its presentation in scientific theory. He argues that Pannenberg moves from consideration of the totality of time to the primacy of the future as making the whole complete. This is in conflict with a physical understanding of time in which completeness would not derive from moving to the future but from a situation in which all times were present.[20] Drees is further concerned with the implication of Pannenberg's understanding of the relation between God and the created world. If God is the all-determining reality, how can an optimistic determinism driven from the future be avoided?[21] Sponheim reaches a similar conclusion to that of Drees, from a more theological analysis of Pannenberg's work. He suggests that Pannenberg's account of the relationship between God and humanity is directed from the future, in such a way as to put into question the possibility of human responsibility for history.[22] Sponheim argues that trust can properly exist only between freely independent entities, and that God can only be trusted in this context, not as sole determiner of history. He is sure that Pannenberg's objectives would be better served by a theology which gives a more

19 Apart from discussions in the context of science, this charge has been made from theological perspectives e.g. Polk (1989). For another viewpoint, see Hardy (1996:108-110).

20 Drees says 'He seems to argue from the primacy of eternity, of the whole of time, or the infinite, to the primacy of the future. The argument needs for its cogency the idea that it is the future which makes the whole complete; past and present are already available ... This seems unclear and deviating from the physical understanding of time. If one focuses on the evolutionary picture, one has a past and a future with respect to any assumed presence. However, past and future are equally "not-present". Completeness is not achieved by moving towards the future, as with each change in present there is also a change in the "not-present". Completeness is only achieved, within the context of physical understanding, by moving to the other level of description, in which all times are equally present at once. However, this level of description is atemporal; it is meaningless to consider such wholes as future wholes; they are just the entities of the theory, and hence of reality as described by that theory.' (1997: 241)

21 He says 'Is he ... opting for an understanding of God as a complement to and present in, our reality? This seems to fit with his description of God as the "all-determining reality" and with the (apparent?) determinism from the future, hence the determinism towards a "happy ending" ... But how does Pannenberg avoid the theological dangers of such an approach: the danger to the sharpness of evil, injustice and imperfection ... that we fail ... doing whatever we can do against injustice and evil?' (1997:242)

22 See his discussion (1997:390-394).

developed account of the relation between God and humans, acknowledging its inequality, but defending the mutual freedom of the partners.

More critical is Rose in *The Broken Middle* (1992), where she cites Pannenberg as one of those who attempts to escape from the omnipresence and determinism of the Hegelian system.[23] Unlike Thiselton, she regards this attempt as unsuccessful. In his desire to locate the possibility of the truly novel in God as 'ground of the unity of contingency and continuity', she says that Pannenberg postulates an unfolding of history and truth in which everything becomes congruent. The ground of this congruence is also the source of all action, so that no real contradiction can ever occur – 'development does not presuppose aporia but excludes it' (1992:7). So, she argues, whereas a truly open philosophy cannot begin by either denying system or presupposing experience, for Pannenberg the end is already contained in the beginning.

Pannenberg's choice of apparently deterministic biology and psychology is more understandable in the light of such philosophical critiques; his underlying theological agenda has a powerful effect on his interpretation of the scientific story.

Community and sociality

In Chapter Five I showed that Pannenberg effects a dissolution of the social. He reduces social institutions and processes of social cohesion to the level of the rational individual. A theological critique of Pannenberg's undervaluing of the social is implied by relational understandings of God – for example, Hardy's social trinitarianism. Here, relationality is seen as an essential aspect of humanity because it is an essential aspect of God.[24] On this view, human social structures cannot be properly explained if the explanations depend on factors extrinsic to humans rather than their intrinsic sociality. Hardy asserts that plurality and diversity are essential for the self-criticism and questioning that gives rise to sociality in Christian terms. If he is right, Pannenberg's asocial, rationalist individuals are deprived of the means of participating in the 'redeemed sociality' which is given by God in creation.[25] Pannenberg's focus on individual human experience as the horizon against which awareness of God is possible is criticised by Hardy. He claims that it leads to the

---

23 Rose writes in the context of a critique of the politico-ethical failures of modernity. It should be noted that Gadamer, on the basis of Pannenberg's early essay on 'Hermeneutics and Universal History' (Pannenberg, 1983a), concluded that Pannenberg definitely does 'not propose to renew Hegel's claim'. (Gadamer, 1977:36-37)

24 He says 'There is an inevitable interaction between conceptions of social structure and those of God. ... A more satisfactory reconception of social structures therefore requires a recovery of their relativity to a God who is seen himself to be relative to the world he has created and redeemed.' (1996:174)

25 Hardy says 'the social transcendental ... which underlies all society ... should be traced to the *Logos* of God operative in creation'. (1996:202)

loss of God as the 'other'. The historicity of revelation and the personhood of God are diminished.[26] Here theological as well as ethical consequences are imputed to an individualist anthropological stance.

Pannenberg has also eliminated any social component of knowledge insofar as that may be associated with action or conversation. In his account of culture as shared meaning in human society, Pannenberg stakes all on the ideational content of culture. In the dichotomy of 'life world' and 'system', he regards the 'life world' as subsidiary. The dichotomy between life world and system has been very important in the development of hermeneutics in relation to the social sciences. Thiselton recognises the importance of this for philosophical and theological hermeneutics. He cites the argument from Bauman's *Hermeneutics and the Social Sciences*, in which Bauman asserts that humans cannot be understood by splitting objectifiable, measurable aspects of human community, the 'system', from an understanding of individuals as particular, contingent agents in their own 'life-world'. Thiselton sees epistemological consequences resulting from particular balances between life-world and system. He argues that a preference for life world over system leads to relativisation and pragmatism, while excessive prioritising of system results in a positivist formalism.[27] Pannenberg strikes a balance that avoids relativism. But Thiselton acknowledges that in comparison with Habermas, Pannenberg stresses system rather than life world.[28] Further, he admits that Pannenberg's work lacks a 'vigorous dynamics of social critique' (1992:391). Thiselton situates Pannenberg in company with Habermas in seeing the need for 'system' to provide a metacritical standpoint, but further along that path at the expense of social awareness. This is of course to be expected if Pannenberg's understanding of the life world is only in terms of rational individuals. We see here the same process as that mentioned above which Schwöbel noted in terms of Pannenberg's understanding of God in

---

26 Hardy (1996:107-109).

27 He says 'Ever since the work of Dilthey it has been recognised that hermeneutics arises from the interaction or dialectic between the general and the particular, the universal and the contingent, the critical and shifting horizons of life worlds. Objectivism and a pre-occupation with wholly "scientific" deductive and inductive generalizations about texts collapses the tension into a scientific, positivist, or formalist-doctrinal, system. Contextual relativization, social pragmatism and deconstructionism, collapses the tension into a socio-contingent, fluid, life-world, in which horizons constantly shift simply in accordance with the flow of life as it is.' (1992:611)

28 He says 'Habermas examines the relation between knowledge and human "interests". In his later work, he argues convincingly that the questions raised by hermeneutics at a metacritical and social level necessitate exploration of both the historically finite contingencies of the hermeneutical *life-world* and a broader trans-contextual critique involving in some sense, *system*. Pannenberg's volume *Theology and the Philosophy of Science* reflects a similar dual concern, but with perhaps a more controlling interest in system.' (1992:12)

relation to humanity. Pannenberg's elimination of the social leads to a loss of an ethical perspective.

This is reinforced by a consideration of Archer's critique (1996), initially referred to in Chapter Five. She claims that there are other flaws in the positions occupied by Habermas, Bauman, and by implication, Gadamer and Pannenberg. Archer claims that the distinction between life-world and system is inadequate, because the assumption of homogeneity is made in the intellectual content of system, and interactions between social groups and system are assimilated into it. Archer's view of culture as containing a library of beliefs and ideas allows for those ideas not necessarily being held by everyone at any one time. Different social groups choose what they will promote or expand in the library, and what they will ignore or suppress. The ease with which this happens is affected by the tightness or looseness of the social groups, and the degree of coherence and integration of the ideas. Archer claims that Habermas sees the ideas in the library as acting only to constrain choice, and the social groupings as only to enable it, because he sees the system as only containing certain of the ideas in the library. Bauman, on the other hand, does not distinguish between variation in the social groups and variation in the ideas, but conflates the two, and Pannenberg does not see any variation in the ideas; everyone reads the same thing.[29]

Archer can account for the dynamics of cultural change in a way that these other theorists do not. In Archer's view, combinations of highly coherent ideas and tightly linked groups interacting with those ideas leads to protection and consolidation of culture because such social dynamics do not favour change (Archer's 'Concomitant Complementarity' between a highly coherent 'Cultural System' and tight 'Socio-cultural Integration').[30] This corresponds to the state of affairs that I claim Pannenberg assumes for all kinds of knowledge at all times. But if ideas are, at the time, not closely coherent, and social groupings are only loosely linked, then different ideas are promoted by different groups until some eclipse the others, because competition between groups and ideas is generated by these social conditions. The result is cultural change (Archer's 'Competitive Contradictions' between a 'Cultural system' of low coherence and a low level of 'Socio-cultural Integration'). It describes radical cultural change, which Pannenberg does not consider, and for which he offers no mechanism in his account of culture. Archer describes other results for other combinations of circumstances, and her theory is complex and difficult to follow. Her significance, however, is that she gives an explanation with predictive power for the effects of social interactions on the accumulation of knowledge, without adopting a relativist stance. Indeed, she

29 This represents an extremely simplified account of the discussion in the second edition of *Culture and Agency* (1996:301-315).

30 As sketched in Chapter Five of this book. See Chapters Seven and Eight of *Culture and Agency* (1996).

specifically rejects Bloor's version of the 'strong programme' in the philosophy of science (1996:112 & ff.).

Archer's explanation fits the empirical study of science better than the alternatives. It is clear that social groupings do influence the outcome in competitions between theories or interpretations. 'Fashion' or socially influenced promotion or selective forgetfulness of material is recognisable in science. This is not to say that rational criteria do not play a role; rational, critical evaluation is an indispensable part of science.[31] But at any one time, an individual or group can be actively concerned with only a small part of the scientific horizon, and a judgement or choice must be made as to what will be relegated to background information. This is precisely the situation referred to by Warnke cited above. The study of science has increasingly taken these kinds of factors into consideration in the last fifty years, as I pointed out in the introduction, citing the work of Price (1963), Ravetz (1971), and above all, T.S. Kuhn (1970). An example of an overview of the issues can be found in Ziman (1987). Archer's account of cultural stability appears to have parallels with Kuhn's description of normal science, and her description of the conditions for cultural elaboration may correspond to his characterisation of revolutionary science. In any case, the view of science presented by Pannenberg, and discussed in Chapter One, dealt purely with the rational, intellectual or ideational component of science. His only concession is a brief reference to Kuhn, and this is in the context of the compatibility of Kuhn's historical view of science to Pannenberg's interpretation of hermeneutics. Pannenberg seems indifferent to the problems raised by the internal evaluations, judgements, preferences and choices made within all scientific communities as an essential part of the process of science. He passes by the critiques made of Lorenz, Eibl-Eibesfeldt, and Freud with hardly a mention. Yet attention to them might have prevented Pannenberg from at least some gross errors.

By ignoring the social dimension of culture, Pannenberg leaves himself in a position from which he is unable to evaluate these social dimensions of knowledge in science. His political insensitivity springs from this, as does his indifference to social questions in relation to feminism or racism. It should be noted that Pannenberg's difficulties cannot be ascribed to his appropriation of Gadamer. His understanding of application in the context of hermeneutics permits Gadamer to entertain suspicions about science; the essays in *Reason in the Age of Science* provide ample evidence of this as I discussed in Chapter One.

Transformation, novelty and God's action in the world

An essential feature of Thiselton's approach to theological hermeneutics is the necessity of change. Thiselton asserts that the world should not be used to change

31 See Stenmark (1995).

the word, but that the word does change the world (1992:604 & ff.). The crucial feature for this is the need for a hermeneutic which can allow for novelty, which permits enlargement, but does so critically. Pannenberg's approach to the growth of horizons which is postulated by Gadamer as part of understanding has already been criticised for its unidirectionality. Growth involves transformation, as opposed to mere assimilation. Thiselton follows Bauman's discussion in *Hermeneutics and Social Science* in seeing understanding as the transcending of a horizon, not its incorporation into an existing one.[32] But in Pannenberg's hands, aspects of science are simply recruited to the theological view of humanity he is already committed to. There is no transformation of his vision, and no development of it. Despite his admiration of Gadamer's insight, Pannenberg's practical approach to the 'fusion of horizons' is not identical with its originator's. Nothing actually new appears. But if God really acts in the world, then there must be genuine novelty in it. Thiselton notes, over against a positivist position, that a temporal dimension is required for such novelty to emerge, and he approves of Pannenberg's introduction of the context of the future (1992:336). But this approval is qualified by recognition that whereas Moltmann uses this eschatological orientation to develop a theology of practical change, Pannenberg uses it for an epistemological investigation.[33]

This philosophical critique is paralleled by a social one which I draw from the implications of Archer (1996). She is clear that culture cannot change, that is, new meanings be developed and accepted, without prior heterogeneity in cultural ideas, and similar variation in the way different groups take up and act on those ideas. Pannenberg does not recognise cultural heterogeneity, and denies the link between knowledge and action. He certainly gives no recognisable mechanism from social theory for the advent of the radically new.

Thiselton is clear that for Christian theology, the cross and resurrection are key horizons of interpretation. He is also clear that Christian theology is:

---

32 He says 'Bauman's main points are that (a) understandings of "present situations" are always interactive understandings, *always on the move*; and (b) that *in principle* the present is to be understood as a sub-form of life to be contextualised within the *larger or "higher"* frame or form of life, shared by the interpreter, that transcends *both* horizons of particularity ... We do not understand the present by *incorporating it within some larger frame;* we do not "understand" simply by making the "present situation" equivalent to the horizon of understanding.' (1992:608)

33 He says 'Both Moltmann and Pannenberg stress the importance of eschatology and promise, and the possibility of creative novelty in history. But Moltmann draws from this eschatology a hermeneutical *praxis* of liberation and social change, whereas Pannenberg directs the main focus of his attention of {on?} epistemological questions ... Moltmann sees eschatology in the context of social change and socio-critical hermeneutics; Pannenberg develops the concept to raise questions about the foundations of knowledge.' (1992:336)

> That which offers a *critique* of life and *not merely a descriptive reflection of it as it is.* (1992:611)

I claim that Pannenberg's theological anthropology reads, not as a critique of life, but as a reflection, not of what it is, but of what Pannenberg thinks it is. There seems to be no room for the new creation or new transformation of the real world in Pannenberg. His view of humanity has determinist undertones in biology, and his accounts of society are static, as either a collection of individuals or a cultural monolith. But if God acts in the world at all, this must surely be in those undetermined social spaces where love, reconciliation and forgiveness are located. Thiselton sees the source of creative transformation in the biblical tradition as the Cross. It is universally transforming because it acts itself as meta-critique.[34] It is undetermined, free and relational. This meta-critique of transformed power subsumes the various theologies about the Cross which are contained in the New Testament. I feel that Pannenberg does not see the message of the New Testament as containing plural valid readings, but as contaminated with contemporary errors, such as the Hellenistic ideas he often criticises. Further, the universality of the cross and resurrection is bound to its nature as promise for the future. Thiselton agrees with Pannenberg that the resurrection is the focus of a transcendent horizon encompassing all reality, but he argues that this still leaves Christian interpretation vulnerable to error.[35] It is precisely this fallibility of Christian interpretation that the cross illuminates because it relativises all claims of self interest, whether of male or female, Jew or Gentile.[36] Pannenberg shows great unease with such accommodation of cultural variation. His aversion to conversation, his monolithic view of culture and his tendency to see the fusion of horizons as assimilation all militate against this. The difficulty this creates for a theological position can be further illustrated

---

34 He says that the cross is 'not only a critique of human self-affirmation and power, but also as a *meta-critique which assesses other criteria, and which transforms the very concept of power.* It is *power-in-weakness* (I Cor. 1:23-25) ... *It revaluates self-affirming, manipulative, dominating power as self-destructive*'. (1992:615)

35 He says 'On the one hand, as Pannenberg rightly insists, the resurrection and Christology provide a "centre" for a universal horizon which transcends this or that context-relative life-world. On the other hand, it does not deliver Christian interpretation from fallibility, and from the need to revise understanding as horizons temporally expand.' (1992:618)

36 Thiselton says the cross 'relativizes and calls into question the respective corporate claims and corporate self-interests of Jews and Gentiles, male and female, slave and free. As Paul argues throughout Romans, it places Jewish Christian and Gentile Christian, Jew and Gentile, precisely on the same footing as debtors to divine grace. On such a basis different cultural traditions are to "accept one another" (Rom. 15:7). The decisive factor in determining the hermeneutical significance of this universal eschatological horizon is the dimension of promise and of the unrevisable divine evaluation which is expressed in language about the last judgement'. (1992:617)

by comparison with Thiselton. He finishes *New Horizons in Hermeneutics* (1992) with a quotation from Bonhoeffer:

> God is not necessarily 'a God who in some way corresponds to me, is agreeable to me, fits in with my nature'. (1992:619)

It seems in keeping with the spirit of this that Thiselton has devoted serious thought and analysis to the hermeneutics associated with feminism, and to that of liberation theology. Problematically, such signs of cultural variation cannot be found in Pannenberg. His reaction to any intellectual tradition other than his own is usually hostile, and this must be fundamentally connected with the lack of an emphasis on the relational aspects of the cross in his theology. Pannenberg is concentrating on system at the expense of the life world, but in theology, the cross holds the two together and neither is dispensable.

Science, theology and postmodernity

In this book, I have examined Pannenberg's use of biology, psychology and sociology as he relates it to his understanding of theological anthropology, in the light of his hermeneutic epistemology. I have claimed that much of his understanding of the science he cites is inadequate and mistaken. I suggest that this arises from his attempt to make knowledge in both science and theology a matter solely of logical rationality, excluding the element of human action and judgement that gives a moral dimension to knowledge. This leads him to underestimate the significance of the social aspect of knowledge. I also suggest that his well known eschatological perspective is diminished by a tendency to determinism and a lack of explanations for the transformative processes which can 'make all things new'. I have argued that Pannenberg's construction of the natural world does not actually leave room for God's innovative or transforming action. This is regrettable in the light of his great achievement in introducing both hermeneutical epistemology and an orientation to the future into the dialogue between science and theology.

I have cited the account of hermeneutics by Thiselton as an example of an alternative theological approach to that of Pannenberg. Thiselton makes clear that Christian interpretation takes place always with the dimension of promise, openness and newness. New interpretations are not always comfortable, and may be challenging to our social interests. The epistemology of Gadamer, which makes understanding central to knowledge, gives a role to humans as creators of meaning in a process which retains significantly undetermined elements. Thiselton rightly points out that this position can be developed either to a radical relativism, with as many meanings as there are interpreters, or to an objectification in which there is only one possible system. The criterion which defends knowledge from either fate is, for Thiselton, the ethical evaluation of the Cross. Bauman also considers that hermeneutic cannot avoid coming under ethical judgement (1978, 1989). A response to the ethical question is unavoidable in postmodernity. Pannenberg has depressed the significance of *phronesis* in his modification of Gadamer, and has sought to separate knowledge from action. In doing so, he has lost the ability to evaluate the values behind the knowledge systems and communities of expertise that he seeks to use, and he has lost the source of the undetermined and therefore open possibilities in human understanding and knowledge. His view of psychology provides evidence to reinforce this conclusion; he does not mention the psychology of relationship, of forgiveness, reconciliation, conversion and transformation. To the extent that he is caught in a rationalist and determinist net, he remains a modernist.

Further progress in the dialogue between science and theology will require a respect for and greater understanding of the social processes of science, as much as it requires a respect for the social processes of religion, that is, the interaction of the practice of the believing community with its traditions of knowledge which gives rise to theology. Acknowledgement and explanation of the interactions between community and knowledge is a central feature of postmodern responses to the critique of Enlightenment rationalism. Some adequate epistemology, whether the hermeneutics of Gadamer or Habermas, or the knowledge-bearing tradition of MacIntyre, will be required. It will also require openness to the reciprocally transformative possibilities of true conversation; both science and theology are part of an intersecting network of subcultures which change and develop as they interact. It must be possible to look for mutually positive results in such interactions. And above all, such dialogue must be sensitive to the issues of value and ethics which bedevil both science and religion in contemporary societies. If the ethical question is not the one which defines postmodernity, as Bauman claims, it is nevertheless one of the most significant to be raised. Pannenberg's monumental contributions to the discussion of science and theology point us in these directions.

Bibliography

Note: In the case of material first published in a language other than English, I have given a full reference to the edition of the English translation to which I had access, with the date and language of first publication given in square brackets at the end of the reference.

Adorno, T. (1986), *The Jargon of Authenticity*, London: Routledge & Kegan Paul. [German ed. 1964]

Albright, C.R. & Haugen, J. (eds) (1997), *Beginning with the End: God, Science and Wolfhart Pannenberg*, Chicago & Illinois: Open Court.

Appleyard, B. (1992), *Understanding the Present*, London: Pan Books.

Archer, M.S. (1996), *Culture and Agency: The Place of Culture in Social Theory* (2nd ed.), Cambridge: Cambridge University Press.

Bandura, A. (1977), *Social Learning Theory*, New Jersey: Prentice-Hall.

Barbour, I. (1990), *Religion in an Age of Science*, London: SCM Press.

Barnett, S.A. (1973), 'On the Hazards of Analogies', in Montague, A. (ed.), *Man and Aggression* (2nd ed.), Oxford: Oxford University Press.

Bartley, W.W. (1962), *The Retreat to Commitment*, New York: Alfred A. Knopf.

Baudrillard, J. (1983), *Simulations*, New York: Semiotext(e).

Bauman, Z. (1973), *Culture as Praxis*, London: Routledge & Kegan Paul.

Bauman, Z. (1978), *Hermeneutics and Social Science; Approaches to Understanding*, London: Hutchinson.

Bauman, Z. (1989), *Modernity and the Holocaust*, Cambridge & Oxford: Polity Press and Basil Blackwell.

Bauman, Z. (1991), *Modernity and Ambivalence*, Cambridge: Polity Press.

Bauman, Z. (1992), *Intimations of Postmodernity*, London: Routledge.

Bauman, Z. (1993), *Postmodern Ethics*, Oxford: Blackwell.

Berger, P. (1980), *The Heretical Imperative*, London: Collins.

Berger, P. (1990), *A Rumor of Angels* (2nd ed.), New York: Anchor.

Berger, P. & Luckmann, T. (1966), *The Social Construction of Reality*, New York: Doubleday.

Berger, P., Berger, B. & Kellner, H. (1973), *The Homeless Mind*, New York: Random House.

Berkowitz, L. (1969), 'Simple Views of Aggression', *American Scientist*, 57: 372-383.

Berry, P. & Wernick, A. (1992), *Shadow of Spirit*, London: Routledge.

Bird Stewart, J.A. (1987), 'Genetics in Relation to Biology', *School Science Review*, June issue: 645-653.

Bleicher, J. (1980), *Contemporary Hermeneutics*, London: Routledge & Kegan Paul.

Boulding, K. (1973), 'Am I a Man or a Mouse – or Both?', in Montague, A. (ed.), *Man and Aggression*, Oxford: Oxford University Press.

Braaten, C.E. & Clayton, P. (eds) (1988), *The Theology of Wolfhart Pannenberg; Twelve American Critiques with an Autobiographical Essay and Response*, Minneapolis: Augsburg.

Brooke, J.H. (1991), *Science and Religion: Some Historical Perspectives*, Cambridge: Cambridge University Press.

Bubner, R. (1981), *Modern German Philosophy*, Cambridge, New York, Melbourne: Cambridge University Press.

Caputo, J.D. & Scanlon, M.J. (1999), *God, the Gift and Postmodernism*, Bloomington: Indiana University Press.

Clayton, P. (1997), 'From Methodology to Metaphysics', in Albright, C.R. & Haugen, J. (eds), *Beginning with the End: God, Science and Wolfhart Pannenberg*, Chicago & Illinois: Open Court.

Crook, J.H. (ed.) (1970), *Social Behaviour in Birds and Mammals*, London & New York: Academic Press.

Crook, J.H. (1973), in Montague, A. (ed.), *Man and Aggression*, Oxford: Oxford University Press.

Curd, M. & Cover, J.A. (eds) (1998), *Philosophy of Science; The Central Issues*, New York & London: W.W. Norton & Co.

Dawkins, M.S. (1986), *Unravelling Animal Behaviour*, London: Longman.

Dewsbury, D.A. (1978), *Comparative Animal Behaviour*, New York: McGraw Hill.

Dobzhansky, Th., Ayala, F.J., Stebbins, G.L. & Valentine, J.W. (1977), *Evolution*, San Francisco: Freeman.

Drees, W. (1996), *Religion, Science and Naturalism*, Cambridge: Cambridge University Press.

Drees, W. (1997), 'Contingency, Time and the Theological Ambiguity of Science', in Albright, C.R. & Haugen, J. (eds), *Beginning with the End: God, Science and Wolfhart Pannenberg*, Chicago & Illinois: Open Court.

Eibl-Eibesfeldt, I. (1974), *Love and Hate*, New York: Holt, Rinehart & Winston.

Eisenberg, L. (1972), 'The *Human* Nature of Human Nature', *Science*, 176: 123-128.

Ellul, J. (1964), *The Technological Society*, New York: Vintage. [French ed. 1954]

Ellul, J. (1985), *The Humiliation of the Word*, Grand Rapids: W.B. Eerdmans.

Ellul, J. (1989), *The Presence of the Kingdom*, Colorado Springs: Helmers & Howard. [French ed. 1948]

Ford, D. (1997), *The Modern Theologians*, Oxford: Blackwell.

Ford, D. (1999), *Self and Salvation*, Cambridge: Cambridge University Press.

Frankl, V. (1987), *Man's Search for Meaning*, London: Hodder & Stoughton. [German ed. 1946]

Futuyma, F. (1986), *Evolutionary Biology* (2nd ed.), Sunderland, Massachusetts: Sinauer.

Gadamer, H.G. (1977), *Philosophical Hermeneutics* (ed. D. Linge), Berkeley, Los Angeles & London: University of California Press. [German ed. 1967]

Gadamer, H.G. (1979), *Truth and Method*, London: Sheed and Ward. [German ed. 1960]

Gadamer, H.G. (1996), *Reason in the Age of Science*, Cambridge, Mass. & London: The MIT Press. [German ed. 1976]

Gaede, S. (1986), 'The Problem of Truth', in Hunter, J.D. & Ainlay, S.C. (eds), *Making Sense of Modern Times*, London: Routledge & Kegan Paul.

Galloway, A.D. (1973), *Wolfhart Pannenberg*, London: George Allen & Unwin.

Geertz, C. (1962), in Scher, J. (ed.), *Theories of the Mind*, New York: Free Press.

Gehlen, A. (1956), *Urmensch und Spatkultur*, Bonn: Athenum.

Giddens, A. (1976), *New Rules of Sociological Method*, London: Hutchinson.

Giddens, A. (1990), *The Consequences of Modernity*, Cambridge: Polity Press.

Giddens, A. (1991), *Modernity and Self-Identity*, Cambridge: Polity Press.

Gilligan, C. (1982), *In a Different Voice*, Cambridge, Mass: Harvard University Press.

Gould, S.J. (1980), *Ever Since Darwin*, London: Penguin.

Grenz, S.J. (1990), *Reason for Hope*, New York & Oxford: Oxford University Press.

Grenz, S.J. & Olson, R.E. (1992), *20th Century Theology; God and the World in a Transitional Age*, Carlisle: Paternoster Press.

Habermas, J. (1972), *Knowledge and Human Interests*, London: Heinemann.

Hall, D.J. (1986), *Imaging God*, Grand Rapids: W.B. Eerdmans.

Hartley, O. & Willmer, H. (1990), *Church and Politics*, London: British Council of Churches.

Hearnshaw, L.S. (1989), *The Shaping of Modern Psychology*, London: Routledge & Kegan Paul.

Heelas, P. (1998), *Religion, Modernity and Postmodernity*, Oxford: Blackwell.

Helmuth, H. (1973), 'Human Behaviour: Aggression', in Montague, A. (ed.), *Man and Aggression*, Oxford: Oxford University Press. [In German 1967]

Hinde, R.A. (1974), *Biological Bases of Human Social Behaviour*, New York: McGraw Hill.

Holton, G. (1973), *Thematic Origins of Modern Thought*, Cambridge, Mass: Harvard University Press.

Hubner, K. (1983), *Critique of Scientific Reason*, Chicago: Chicago University Press. [German ed. 1979]

Huizinga, J. (1949), *Homo Ludens: A Study of the Play-Element in Culture*, London: Routledge.

Hull, D. (1974), *Philosophy of Biological Science*, New Jersey: Prentice-Hall, Inc.

Kalikow, T.J. (1976), 'Konrad Lorenz's Ethological Theory 1939-1943', *Philosophy of the Social Sciences*, 6: 15-34.

Kalikow, T.J. (1978), 'Konrad Lorenz's "Brown Past" ', *Journal of the History of the Behavioural Sciences*, 14: 173-180.

Kalikow, T.J. (1983), 'Konrad Lorenz's Ethological Theory: Explanation and Ideology', *Journal of the History of Biology*, 16: 39-73.

Kevles, D.J. (1986), *In the Name of Eugenics*, Harmondsworth: Penguin.

Kuhn, T.S. (1970), *The Structure of Scientific Revolutions* (2nd ed.), Chicago & London: University of Chicago Press.

Küng, H. & Tracy, D. (1989), *Paradigm Change in Theology*, Edinburgh: T. & T. Clark.

Laing, R.D. (1960), *The Divided Self*, London: Tavistock.

Lakatos, I. & Musgrave, A. (1970), *Criticism and the Growth of Knowledge*, Cambridge: Cambridge University Press.

Latour, B. & Woolgar, S. (1979), *Laboratory Life*, Beverley Hills & London: Sage.

Laudan, L. (1977), *Progress and its Problems*, London: Routledge & Kegan Paul.

Lehrman, D.S. (1953), 'A Critique of Konrad Lorenz's Theory of Instinctive Behaviour', *Quarterly Review of Biology*, 28: 337-363.

Levinas, E. (1979), *Totality and Infinity*, The Hague: Nijhoff. [French ed. 1961]

Levinas, E. (1989), 'Ethics as First Philosophy', in Hand, S. (ed.), *The Levinas Reader*, Oxford: Blackwell.

Lewontin, R.C., Rose, S. & Kamin, L.J. (1984), *Not in Our Genes*, New York: Pantheon.

Lorenz, K. (1940), *Z. Angew. Psychol. u. Charakterkunde*, 59 (2): 56-75.

Lorenz, K. (1967), *On Aggression*, London: Methuen.

Lorenz, K. (1977), *Behind the Mirror*, New York: Harcourt Brace Jovanovich.

Losee, J. (1993), *A Historical Introduction to the Philosophy of Science* (3rd ed.), Oxford: Oxford University Press.

Luckmann, T. (1979), 'Personal Identity as an Evolutionary and Historical Problem', in von Cranach, M. et al. (eds), *Human Ethology*, Cambridge and Paris: Cambridge University Press and Editions de la Maison des Sciences de l'Homme.

Lundin, R. (1993), *The Culture of Interpretation*, Grand Rapids: W.B. Eerdmans.

Lundin, R., Walhout, C. & Thiselton, A.C. (1999), *The Promise of Hermeneutics*, Grand Rapids: W.B. Eerdmans.

McFadyen, A.I. (1990), *The Call to Personhood*, Cambridge, New York, Melbourne: Cambridge University Press.

McGrath, A. (1998), *The Foundations of Dialogue in Science and Religion*, Oxford: Blackwell.

MacIntyre, A. (1988), *Whose Justice? Which Rationality?*, Notre Dame: Notre Dame University Press.

Mackenzie, D.J. & Wajcman, J. (1985), *The Social Shaping of Technology*, Milton Keynes: Open University Press.

May, R. (1969), *Existential Psychology*, New York: Random House.

Mechling, J. (1986), 'The Jamesian Berger', in Hunter, J.D. & Ainlay, S.C. (eds), *Making Sense of Modern Times*, London: Routledge & Kegan Paul.

Mellor, P. & Shilling, C. (1997), *Re-forming the Body*, London: Sage.

Merton, R.K. (1973), *The Sociology of Science*, Chicago: University of Chicago Press.

Molnar, P. (1995), 'Some Problems with Pannenberg's Solution to Barth's "Faith Subjectivism"', *Scottish Journal of Theology*, 48: 315-339.

Moltmann. J. (1974), *Man*, London & Philadelphia: SPCK and Fortress Press. [German ed. 1971]

Montague, A. (1973), *Man and Aggression* (2nd ed.), Oxford: Oxford University Press.

Mulkay, M. (1979), *Science and the Sociology of Knowledge*, London: George Allen & Unwin.

Müller-Hill, B. (1988), *Murderous Science*, Oxford: Oxford University Press.

Murphy, N. (1990), *Theology in the Age of Scientific Reasoning*, Ithaca & London: Cornell University Press.

Niebuhr, R. (1944), *The Children of Light and the Children of Darkness*, New York: Charles Scribner's Sons.

Olby, R.C., Cantor, G.N., Christie, J.R.R. and Hodge, M.J.S. (eds) (1990), *Companion to the History of Modern Science*, London & New York: Routledge.

Pannenberg, W. (1968), *Jesus – God and Man*, London: SCM Press. [German ed. 1964]

Pannenberg, W. (1976), *Theology and the Philosophy of Science*, Philadelphia: Westminster Press. [German ed. 1973]

Pannenberg, W. (1979), *Revelation as History*, London: Sheed and Ward. [German ed. 1961]

Pannenberg, W. (1981), *Ethics*, London and Philadelphia: Search Press and Westminster Press. [German ed. 1977]

Pannenberg, W. (1983a), *Basic Questions in Theology*, Vol. 1, Philadelphia: Westminster Press. [German ed. 1967]

Pannenberg, W. (1983b), *Basic Questions in Theology*, Vol. 2, Philadelphia: Westminster Press. [German ed. 1967]

Pannenberg, W. (1985), *Anthropology in Theological Perspective*, Edinburgh: T. & T. Clark Ltd. [German ed. 1983]

Pannenberg, W. (1988), *Christianity in a Secularized World*, London: SCM Press. [German ed. 1988]

Pannenberg, W. (1991), *Systematic Theology*, Vol. 1, Edinburgh: T. & T. Clark Ltd. [German ed. 1988]

Pannenberg, W. (1993), *Toward a Theology of Nature: Essays on Science and Faith* (ed. T. Peters), Louisville, Kentucky: Westminster/John Knox Press.

Pannenberg, W. (1994), *Systematic Theology*, Vol. 2, Edinburgh: T. & T. Clark Ltd. [German ed. 1991]

Pannenberg, W. (1997), 'Theological Appropriation of Scientific Understandings', in Albright, C.R. & Haugen, J. (eds), *Beginning with the End: God, Science and Wolfhart Pannenberg*, Chicago & Illinois: Open Court.

Pannenberg, W. (1998), *Systematic Theology*, Vol. 3, Edinburgh & Grand Rapids, Michigan: T. & T. Clark Ltd and W.B. Eerdmans. [German ed. 1993]

Peacocke, A. (1993), *Theology for a Scientific Age* (2nd ed.), London: SCM.

Polk, D. (1989), *On the Way to God*, Lanham: University Press of America.

Polkinghorne, J. (1998), *Science and Theology*, London: SPCK.

Popper, K. (1972), *The Logic of Scientific Discovery*, Hutchinson: London.

Popper, K. (1972), *Conjectures and Refutations* (4th ed.), London: Routledge & Kegan Paul.

Price, D.J. de S. (1963), *Little Science, Big Science*, New York: Columbia University Press.

Proctor, R. (1988), *Racial Hygiene*, Cambridge, Mass: Harvard University Press.

Ravetz, J.R. (1971), *Scientific Knowledge and its Social Problems*, Oxford: Oxford University Press.

Ricoeur, P. (1995), *Figuring the Sacred*, Minneapolis: Fortress.

Rogers, C. (1942), *Counseling and Psychotherapy*, Boston: Houghton Miflin.

Rohls, J. & Wenz, G. (1988), *Vernunft des Glaubens*, Göttingen: Vandenhoeck & Ruprecht.

Rose, G. (1992), *The Broken Middle: Out of Our Ancient Society*, Oxford, UK & Cambridge, USA: Basil Blackwell.

Russell R.J. (1988), 'Contingency in Physics and Cosmology: A critique of the theology of W. Pannenberg', *Zygon*, 23: 23-43.

Russell, R.J., Stoeger, W.R. & Coyne, G.V. (1988), *Physics, Philosophy and Theology: A Common Quest for Understanding*, Vatican State: Vatican Observatory Publication, Notre Dame Press.

Ryle, G. (1963), *The Concept of Mind*, Harmondsworth: Penguin.

Sahlins, M. (1977), *The Use and Abuse of Biology*, London: Tavistock.

Scheler, M. (1961), *Man's Place in Nature*, Boston: Beacon Press.

Schillebeeckx, E. (1980), *Christ*, London: SCM. [Dutch ed. 1977]

Schwöbel, C. (1996), 'Rational Theology in Trinitarian Perspective: Wolfhart Pannenberg's Systematic Theology', *The Journal of Theological Studies*, 47 (2): 498-527.

Schwöbel, C. (1997), 'Wolfhart Pannenberg', in Ford, D. (ed.), *The Modern Theologians* (2nd ed.), Oxford: Blackwell.

Shults, F.L. (1999), *The Postfoundationalist Task of Theology*, Grand Rapids: W.B. Eerdmans.

Silverman H.J. (ed.) (1991), *Gadamer and Hermeneutics*, New York & London: Routledge.

Smith, R. (1997), *The Fontana History of the Human Sciences*, London: Fontana.

Sokal, A. & Bricmont, J. (1998), *Intellctual Impostures*, London: Profile Books. [French ed. 1997]

Sölle, D. (1967), *Christ the Representative*, Philadelphia.

Sponheim, P. (1997), 'To Expand and Deepen the Provisional', in Albright, C.R. & Haugen, J. (eds), *Beginning with the End: God, Science and Wolfhart Pannenberg*, Chicago & Illinois: Open Court.

Steiner, G. (1978), *Heidegger*, London: Fontana Collins.

Stenmark, M. (1995), *Rationality in Science, Religion and Everyday Life*, Notre Dame, Indiana: University of Notre Dame Press.

Sullivan, R. (1989), *Political Hermeneutics: The Early Thinking of Hans George Gadamer*, University Park: Pennsylvania State University Press.

Thiselton, A.C. (1992), *New Horizons in Hermeneutics*, London: Harper Collins.

Thiselton, A.C. (1995), *Interpreting God and the Postmodern Self*, Grand Rapids: W.B. Eerdmans.

Thoday, J.M. (1965), 'Geneticism and Environmentalism', in Meade, J.E. & Parkes, A.S. (eds), *Biological Aspects of Social Problems*, London: Oliver & Boyd.

Thompson, R. (ed.) (1968), *The Pelican History of Psychology*, Harmondsworth: Penguin.

Tillich, P. (1952), *The Courage to Be*, Welwyn Garden City: Nisbet.

Tillich, P. (1978), *Systematic Theology*, Volume 2, London: SCM Press. [1st ed. 1957]

Toulmin, S. (1972), *Human Understanding*, Oxford: Clarendon Press.

Tupper, E.F. (1974), *The Theology of Wolfhart Pannenberg*, London: SCM Press.

Von Uexküll, J. (1921), *Umwelt und Innenwelt der Tiere* (2nd ed.), Berlin: J. Springer.

Von Uexküll, J. (1933), *Staatsbiologie* (2nd ed.), Hamburg: Hanseatische Verlagsanstalt.

Warnke, G. (1987), *Gadamer: Hermeneutics, Tradition and Reason*, Cambridge & Oxford: Polity Press and Basil Blackwell.

Webster, J. (1998), *Barth's Moral Theology*, Edinburgh: T. & T. Clark.

Weinsheimer, J. (1985), *Gadamer's Hermeneutics*, New Haven & London: Yale University Press.

Wittgenstein, L. (1972), *Philosophical Investigations*, Oxford: Basil Blackwell.

Wuthnow, R. (1986), 'Religion as a Sacred Canopy', in Hunter, J.D. & Ainlay, S.C. (eds), *Making Sense of Modern Times*, London: Routledge & Kegan Paul.

Ziman, J. (1987), *An Introduction to Science Studies* (2nd ed.), Cambridge: Cambridge University Press.

Index